TRANSFORMERS PRIME

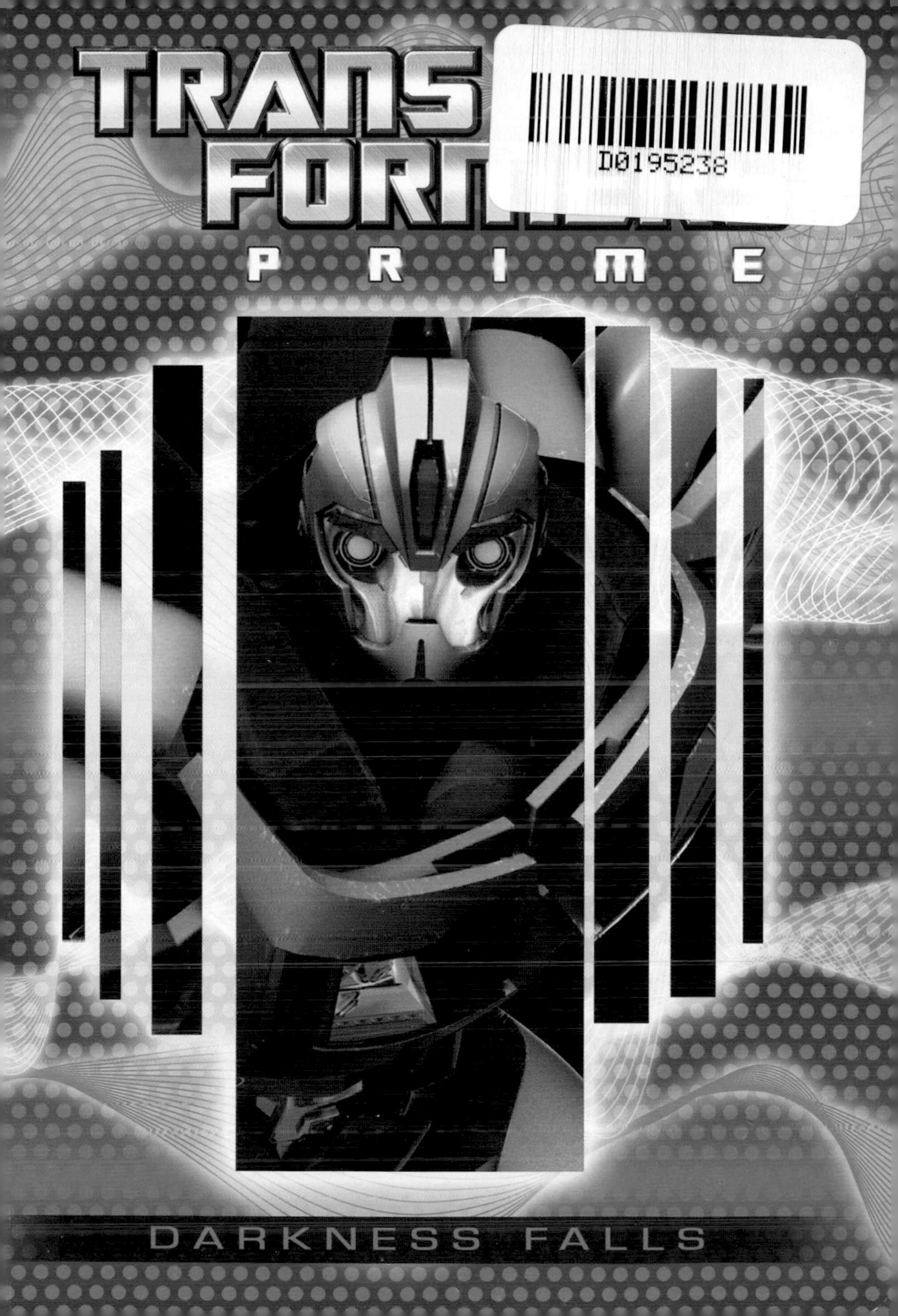

DARKNESS FALLS

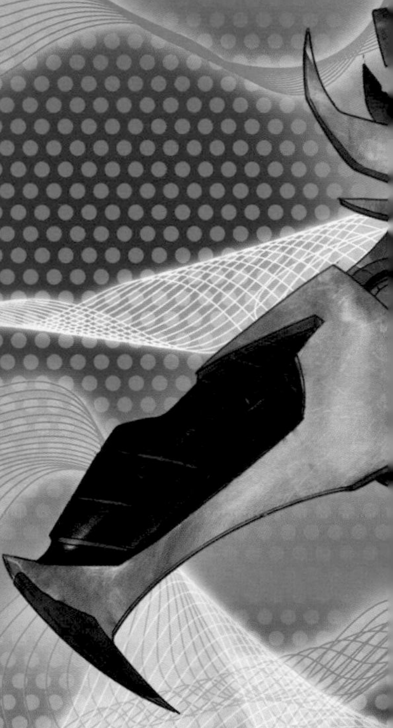

TRANSFORMERS PRIME: DARKNESS FALLS

DARKNESS RISING PART 3
WRITTEN BY: MARSHA GRIFFIN

DARKNESS RISING PART 4
WRITTEN BY: STEVEN MELCHING

DARKNESS RISING PART 5
WRITTEN BY: JOSEPH KUHR

ADAPTATION BY:
ZACHARY RAU

EDITS BY:
JUSTIN EISINGER

LETTERS AND DESIGN BY:
TOM B. LONG

Special thanks to Hasbro's Aaron Archer, Michael Kelly, Amie Lozanski, Ed Lane, Michael Provost, Val Roca, Erin Hillman, Jos Huxley, Samantha Lomow, and Michael Verrecchia for their invaluable assistance.

ISBN: 978-1-60010-910-2 14 13 12 11 1 2 3 4

IDW®

Licensed By: Hasbro

Ted Adams, CEO & Publisher
Greg Goldstein, Chief Operating Officer
Robbie Robbins, EVP/Sr. Graphic Artist
Chris Ryall, Chief Creative Officer/Editor-in-Chief
Matthew Ruzicka, CPA, Chief Financial Officer
Alan Payne, VP of Sales

TRANSFORMERS PRIME: DARKNESS FALLS. JULY 2011. FIRST PRINTING. HASBRO and its logo, TRANSFORMERS, and all related characters are trademarks of Hasbro and are used with permission. IDW Publishing, a division of Idea and Design Works, LLC. Editorial offices: 5080 Santa Fe St., San Diego, CA 92109. Printed in Korea.

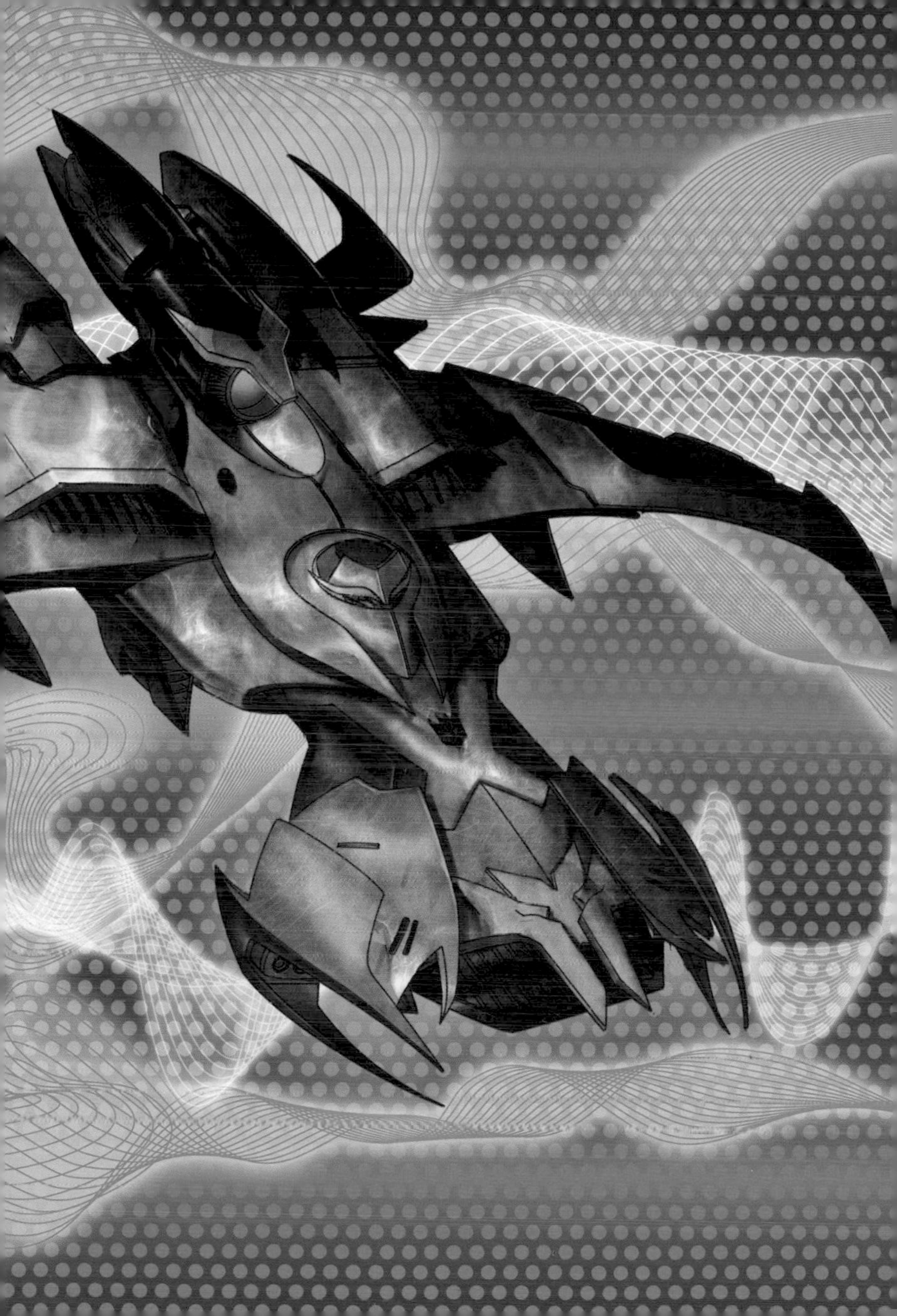

DUTY ROSTER

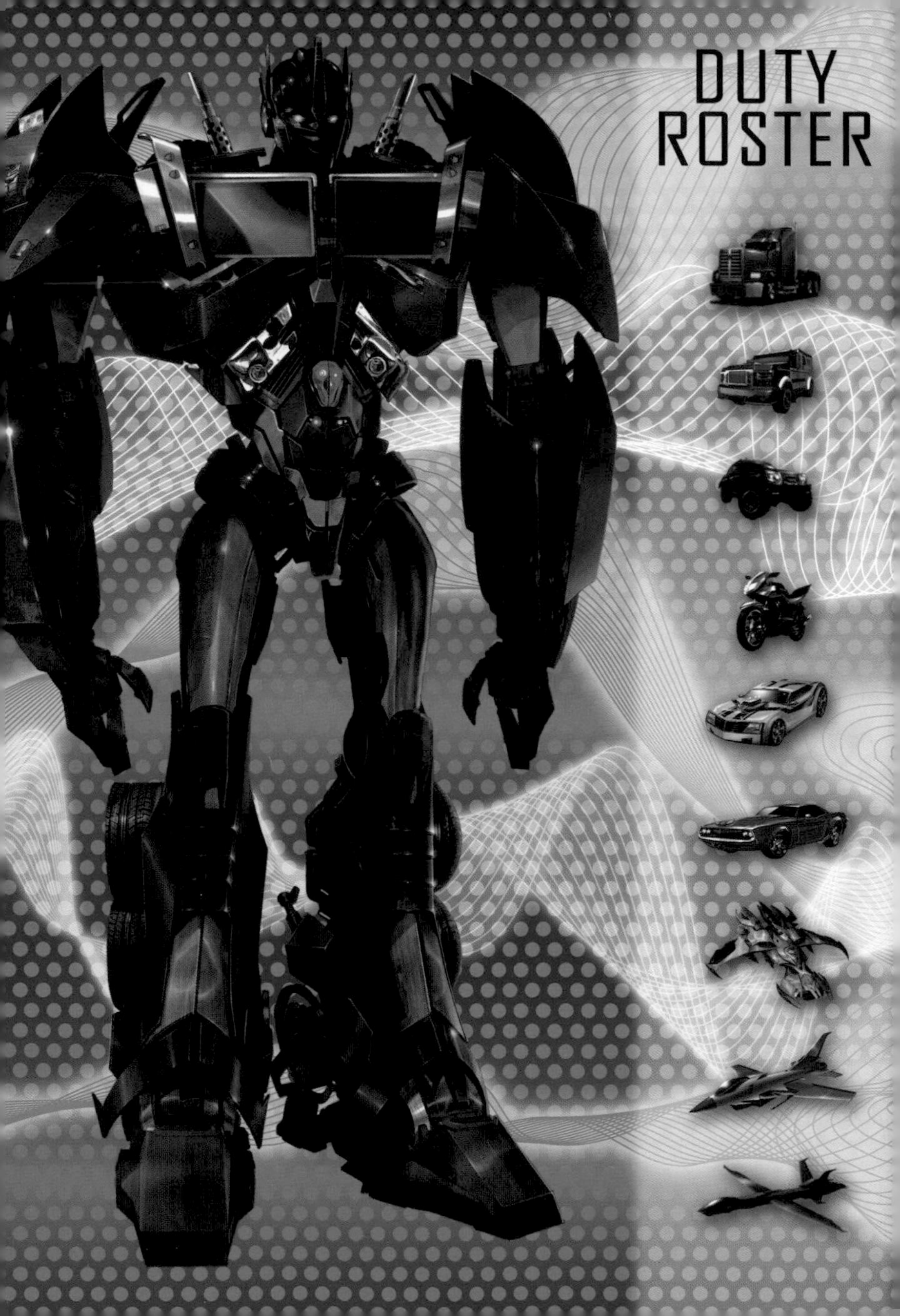

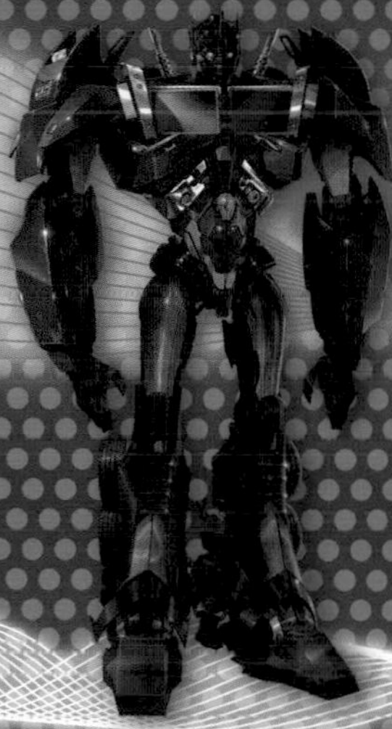

OPTIMUS PRIME

The Autobots' leader is the biggest, strongest, and smartest. OPTIMUS PRIME makes the plans and protects the humans during the war with the Decepticons.

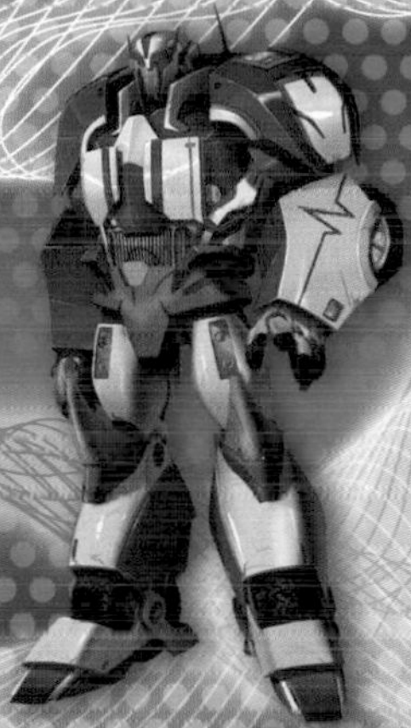

RATCHET

This emergency medical truck is the Autobots' medic. RATCHET fixes limbs and gears, and he works to make do with less and less Energon. He knows OPTIMUS PRIME best.

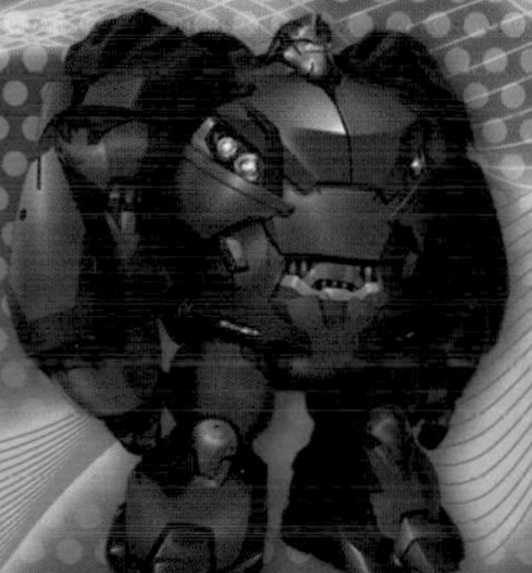

BULKHEAD

This giant is the muscle of the Autobots, but BULKHEAD's actually kind of sensitive.

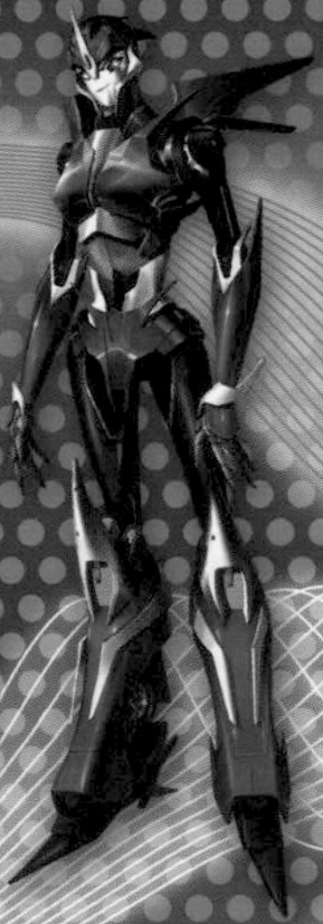

ARCEE

ARCEE is the Autobots' best soldier. She has a special bond with OPTIMUS PRIME and is his "go-to" bot.

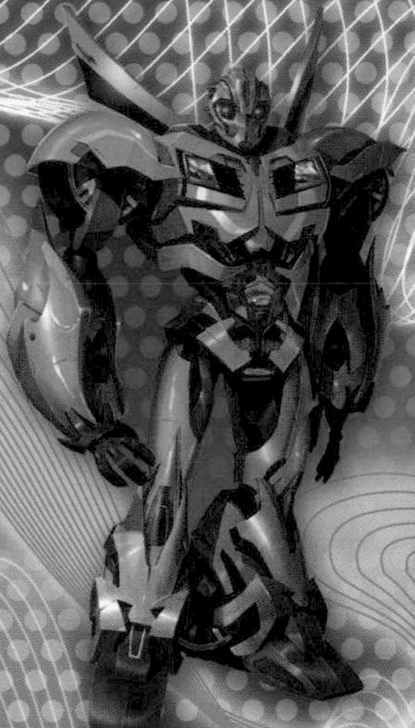

BUMBLEBEE

BUMBLEBEE is a yellow muscle car and the Autobot who's been on Earth the longest. So he knows humans best.

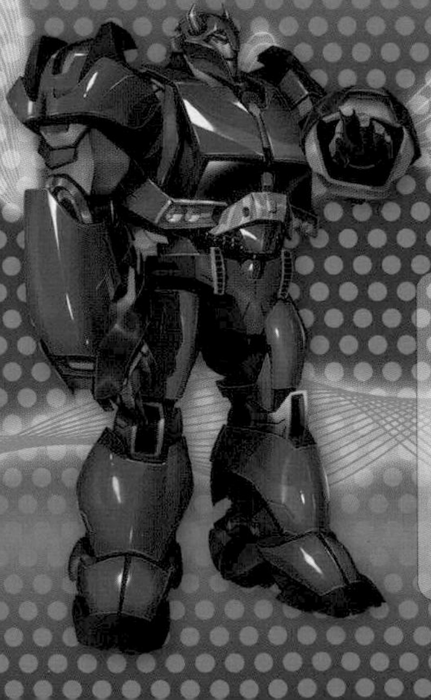

CLIFFJUMPER

CLIFFJUMPER is a red muscle car. He doesn't take too kindly to Earth's laws and he likes to scare its police officers whenever he can. He is very close with ARCEE.

MEGATRON

The head of the Decepticons is just as bad as the Autobot leader is good. Whether in alien fighter jet form or robot mode, MEGATRON's the most deadly of all the Transformers. He hates how much OPTIMUS PRIME cares about Earth, and won't stop until he defeats the Autobots and makes this planet his own.

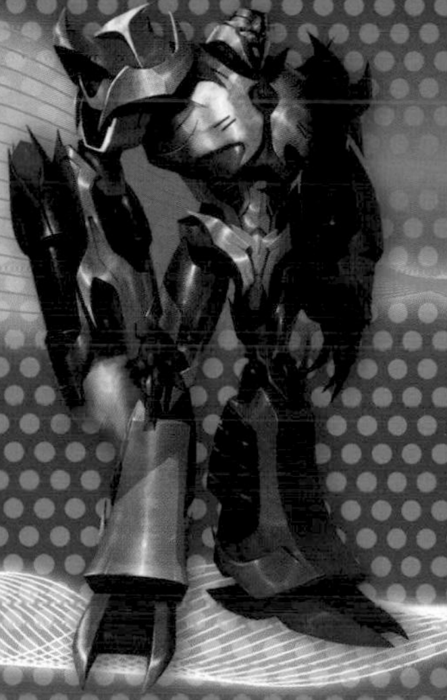

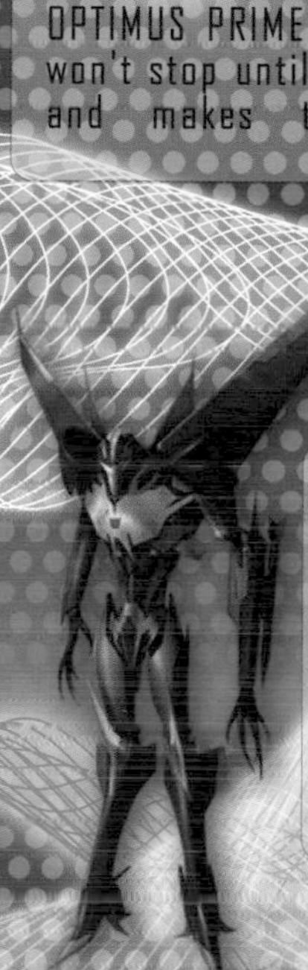

STARSCREAM

This military fighter jet is MEGATRON's right-hand man. STARSCREAM would rather sneak up on his victims than face them head-on, which makes him extra-dangerous. He's an expert planner, and that's one reason MEGATRON keeps him around. STARSCREAM always shows respect to his general, but he's really just waiting for a chance to take command of the Decepticons himself.

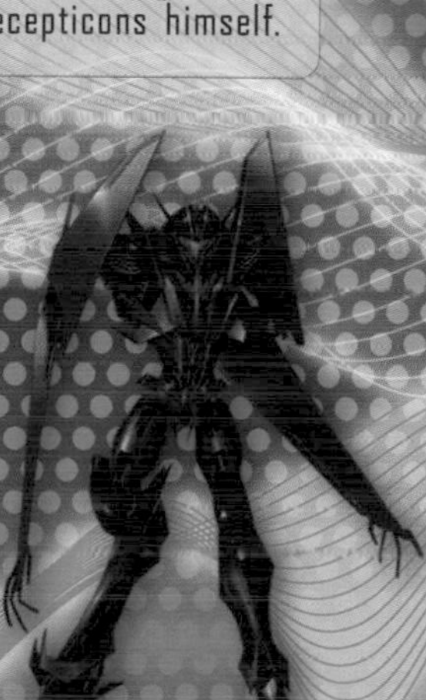

SOUNDWAVE

A stealth drone and the Decepticons' spy master, SOUNDWAVE has no face and doesn't say much. He just quietly finds information to use against the Autobots. He can tap into any transmission anywhere, except at the secret Autobot base. SOUNDWAVE's far-reaching tentacles can snap through concrete, but his main tools are the tiny Deployers in his chest.

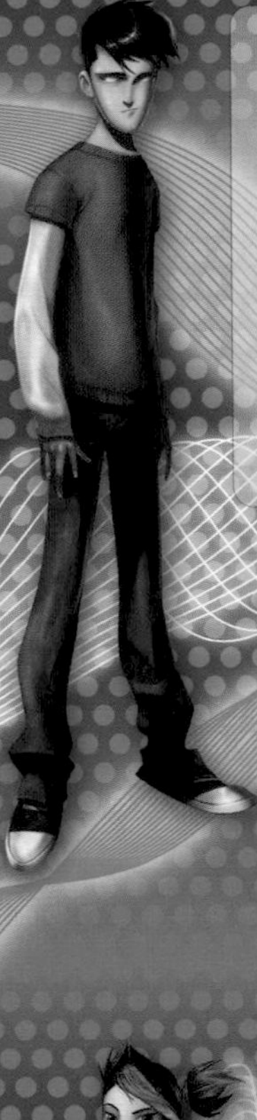

JACKSON DARBY

At 16, he was just a hard-working kid slinging burgers to save up for his first motorcycle. Then Jackson "Jack" Darby met ARCEE, his guardian Autobot, and scored a killer bike AND a big sister all in one. With pals Miko and Raf, he helps the Autobots fight the Decepticons. Jack's usually a smart guy and responsible leader... except when he wants to impress a girl.

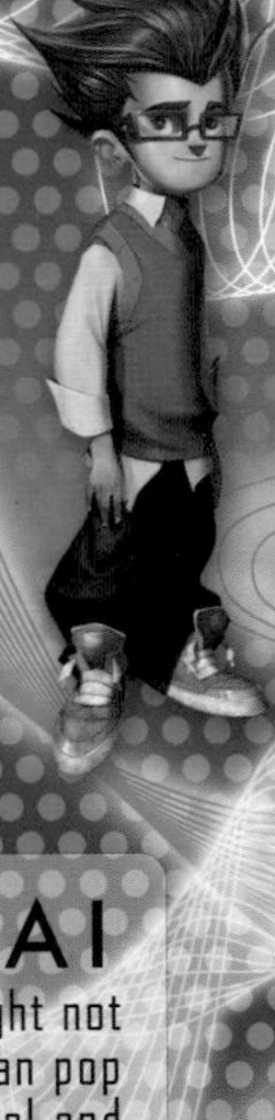

RAF

He's quiet, shy, and usually the teen most freaked by danger. But when Rafael "Raf" Esquivel sees any kind of software-based tech, he goes right into "the zone." That's handy at Autobot Central Command, since RATCHET doesn't know much about human tech. Raf's knowhow has saved both humans and Autobots.

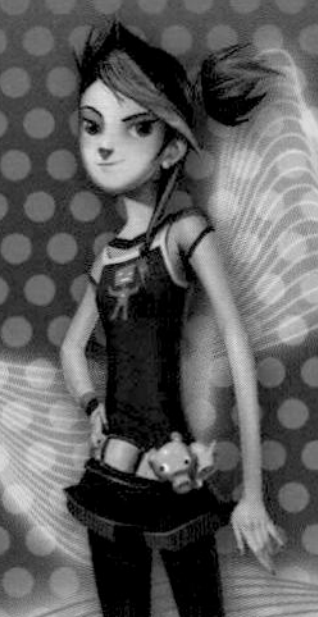

MIKO NAKADAI

She's 15 and from Japan—but you might not guess that, since she's so into American pop culture. Miko Nakadai loves speed metal and wild punk outfits, and her fearlessness makes her the perfect match for the massive BULKHEAD. Her thing for thrills can cause trouble for fellow teens Jack and Raf. But Miko means well, and she always looks out for her pals.

TRANSFORMERS PRIME

DARKNESS FALLS

PREVIOUSLY:

MEGATRON has returned to Earth and he has brought Dark Energon from across the galaxy. Dark Energon is much more powerful than common Energon. It can bring a bot back to life... back to life as a zombie that does MEGATRON's bidding. The Autobot CLIFFJUMPER, who was captured and killed by the Decepticons, was the first to be turned into a zombie.

With the safety of the whole planet hanging in the balance, the Autobots have taken in Jackson, Raf and Miko, three humans who have gotten caught in the crossfire of their war with the Decepticons. But time is running out! The Decepticon's numbers are growing and there are only five Autobots left on the entire planet.

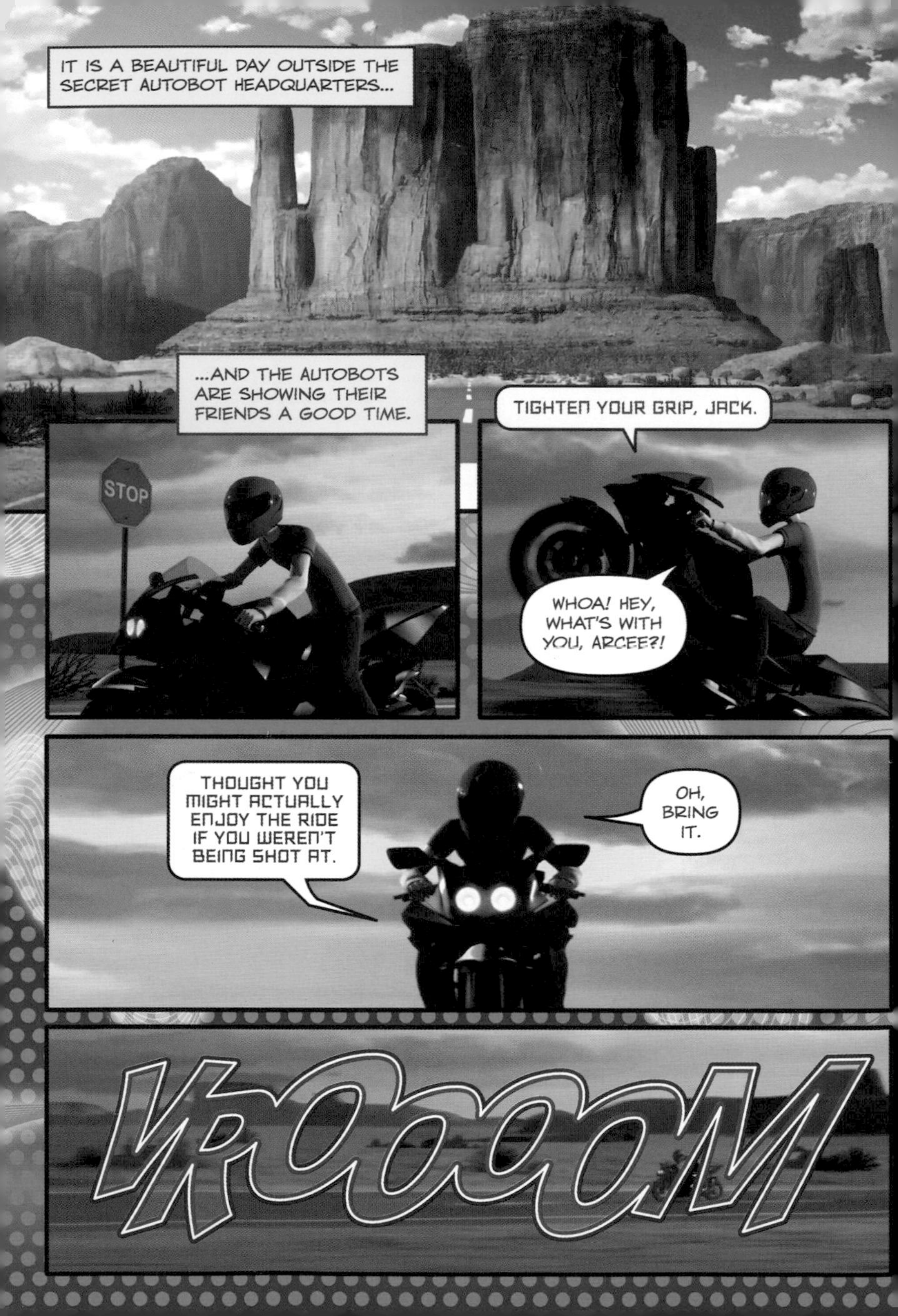
IT IS A BEAUTIFUL DAY OUTSIDE THE SECRET AUTOBOT HEADQUARTERS...
...AND THE AUTOBOTS ARE SHOWING THEIR FRIENDS A GOOD TIME.
STOP
TIGHTEN YOUR GRIP, JACK.
WHOA! HEY, WHAT'S WITH YOU, ARCEE?!
THOUGHT YOU MIGHT ACTUALLY ENJOY THE RIDE IF YOU WEREN'T BEING SHOT AT.
OH, BRING IT.
VROOOOM

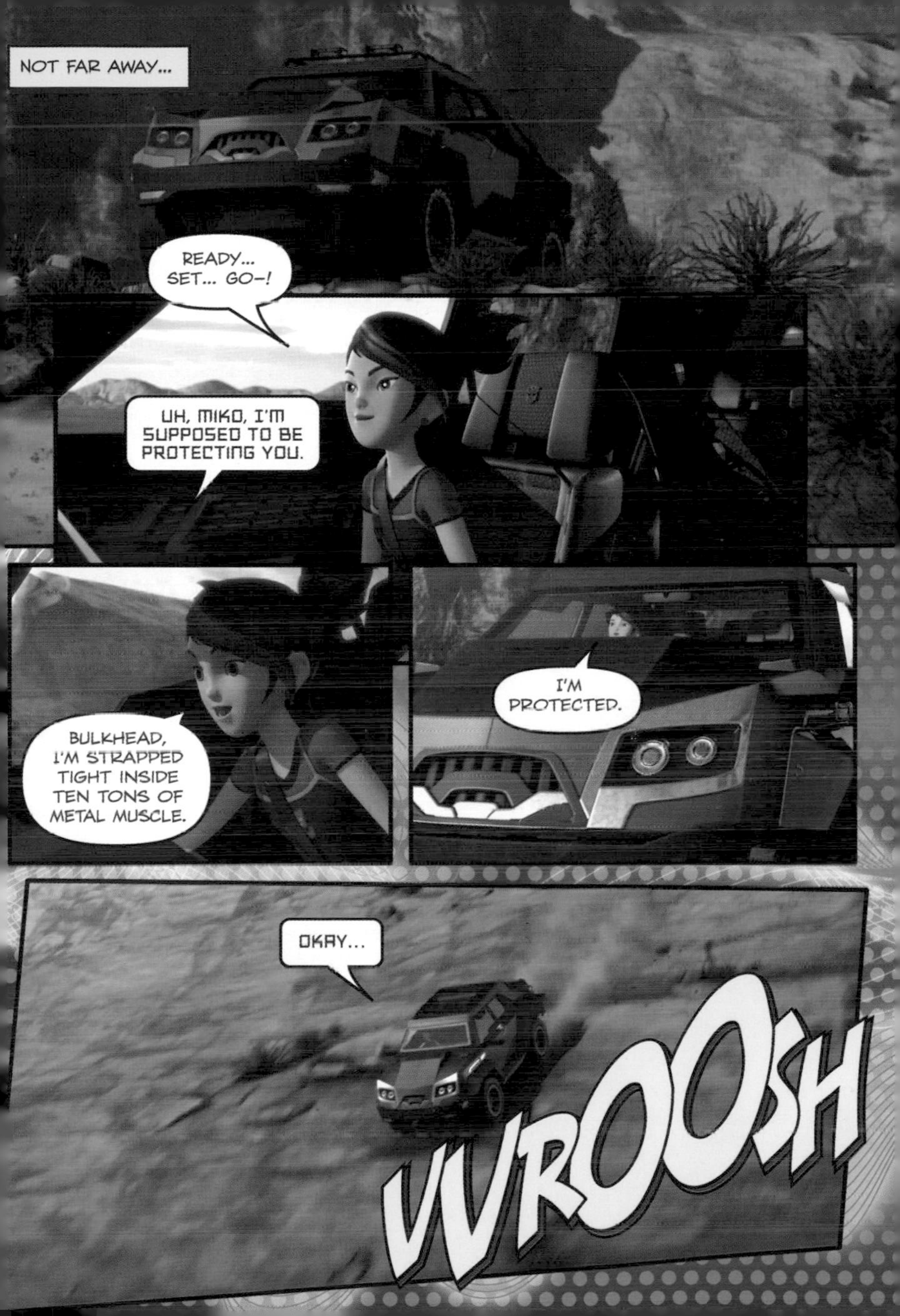
NOT FAR AWAY...
READY... SET... GO-!
UH, MIKO, I'M SUPPOSED TO BE PROTECTING YOU.
BULKHEAD, I'M STRAPPED TIGHT INSIDE TEN TONS OF METAL MUSCLE.
I'M PROTECTED.
OKAY...
VVROOOSH

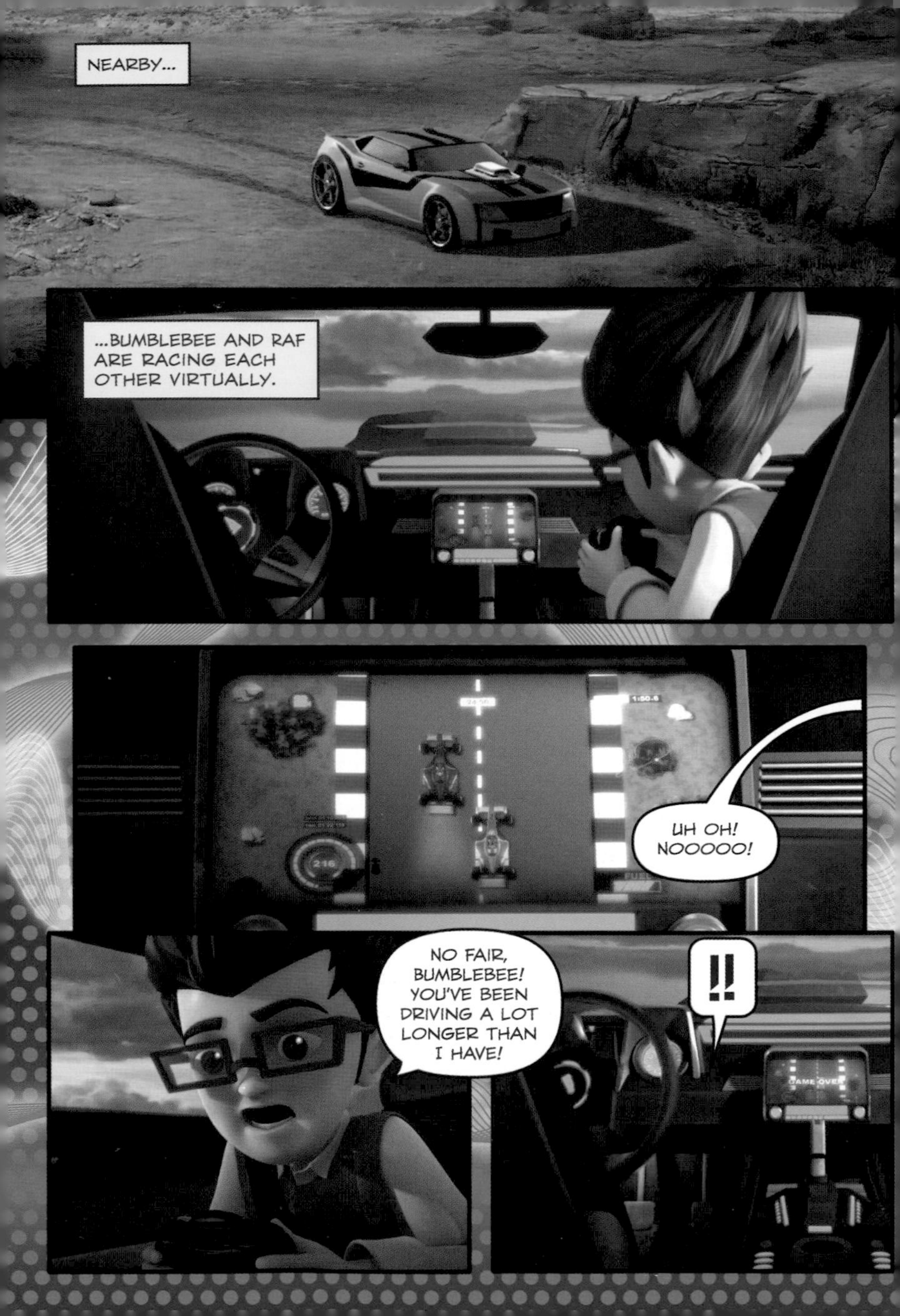
NEARBY...
...BUMBLEBEE AND RAF ARE RACING EACH OTHER VIRTUALLY.
UH OH! NOOOOO!
NO FAIR, BUMBLEBEE! YOU'VE BEEN DRIVING A LOT LONGER THAN I HAVE!
!!
GAME OVER

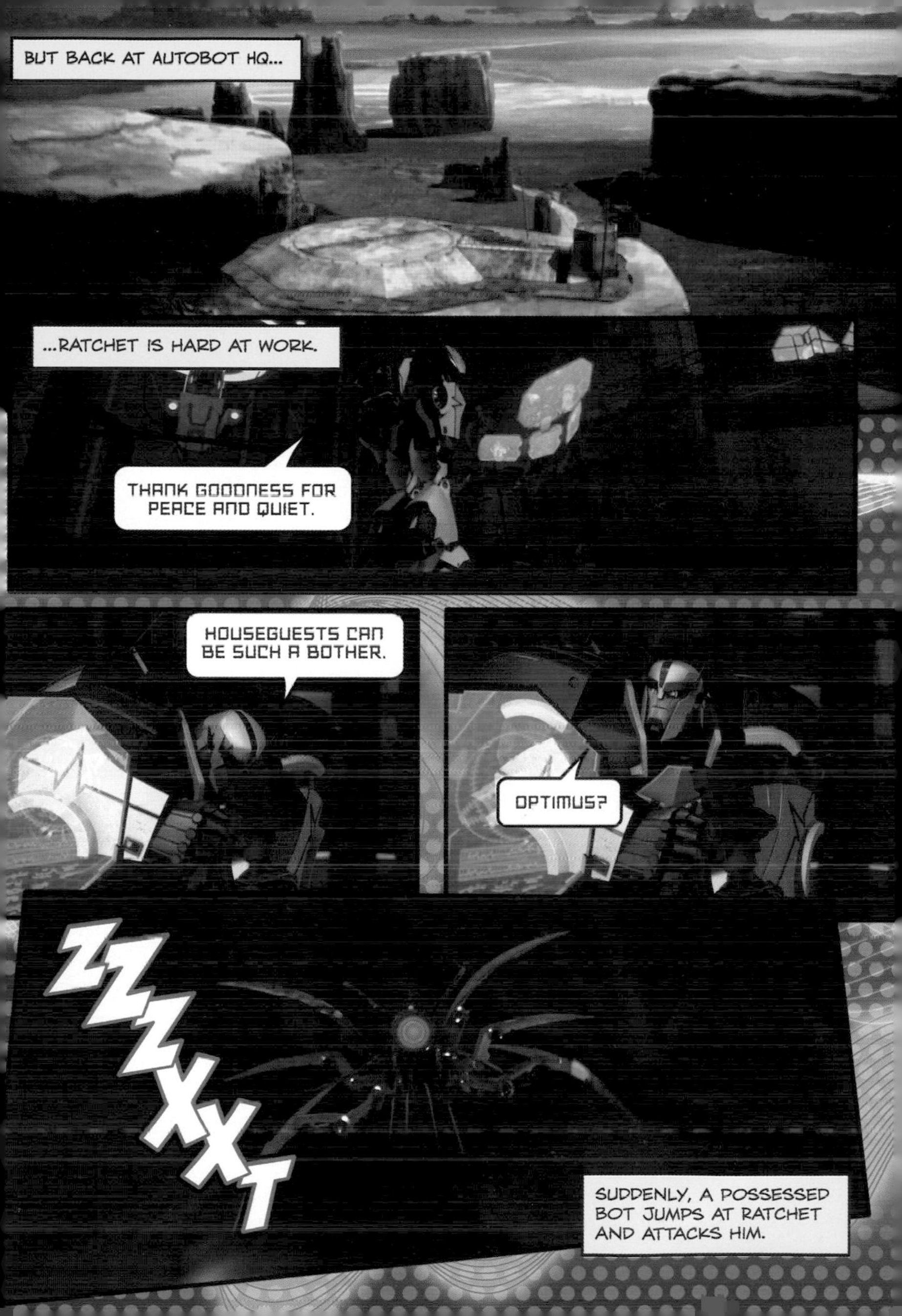
BUT BACK AT AUTOBOT HQ...
...RATCHET IS HARD AT WORK.
THANK GOODNESS FOR PEACE AND QUIET.
HOUSEGUESTS CAN BE SUCH A BOTHER.
OPTIMUS?
ZZZZXXT
SUDDENLY, A POSSESSED BOT JUMPS AT RATCHET AND ATTACKS HIM.

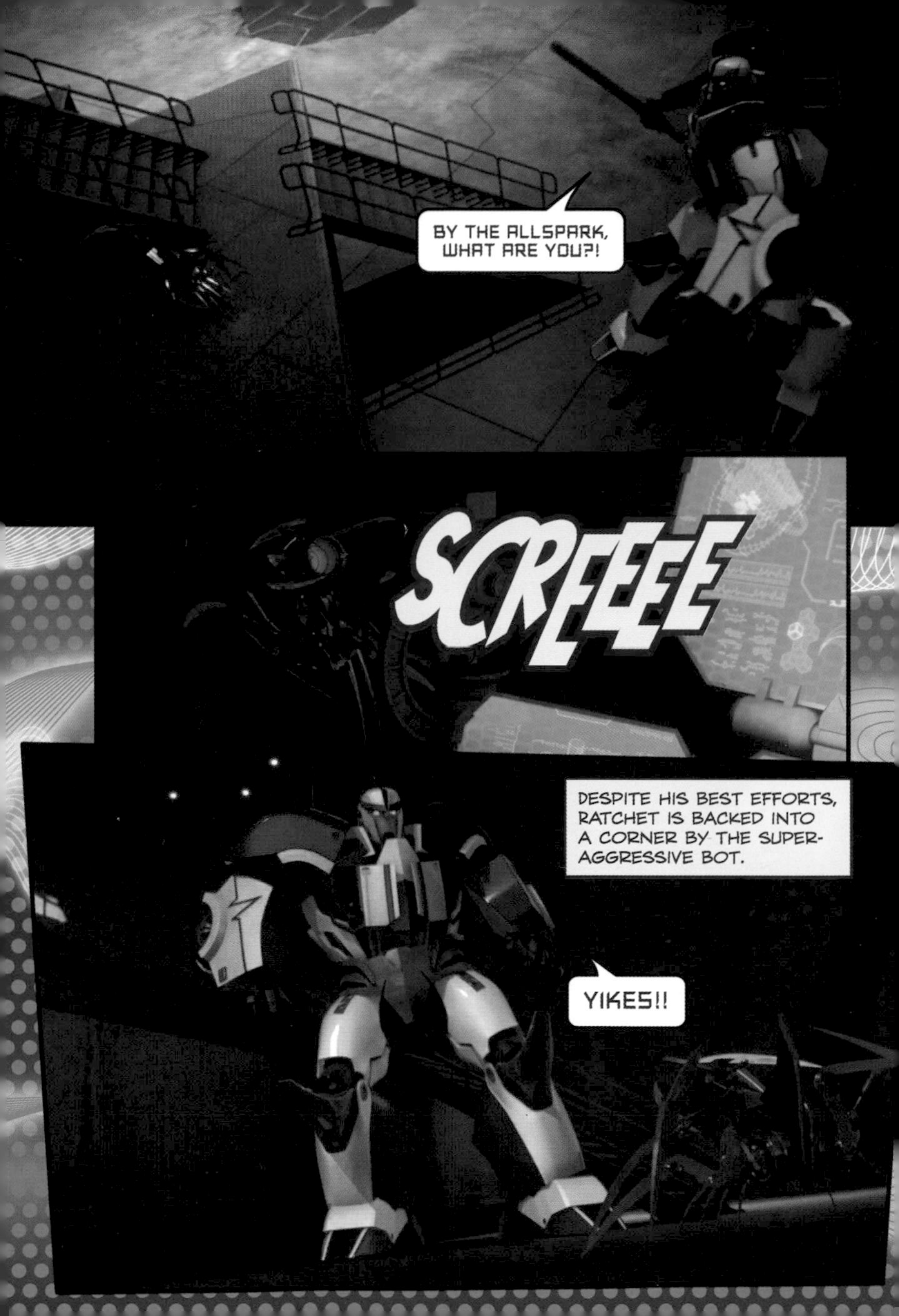
BY THE ALLSPARK, WHAT ARE YOU?!
SCREEEE
DESPITE HIS BEST EFFORTS, RATCHET IS BACKED INTO A CORNER BY THE SUPER-AGGRESSIVE BOT.
YIKES!!

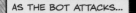

AS THE BOT ATTACKS...

...OPTIMUS SHOWS UP AND BLASTS IT INTO NEXT WEEK.

BOOM

AND STAY BROKEN!

KRAK

NOW WHAT COULD HAVE CAUSED THAT?!

I HAVE A GRAVE SUSPICION, RATCHET, THAT IT IS DARK ENERGON.

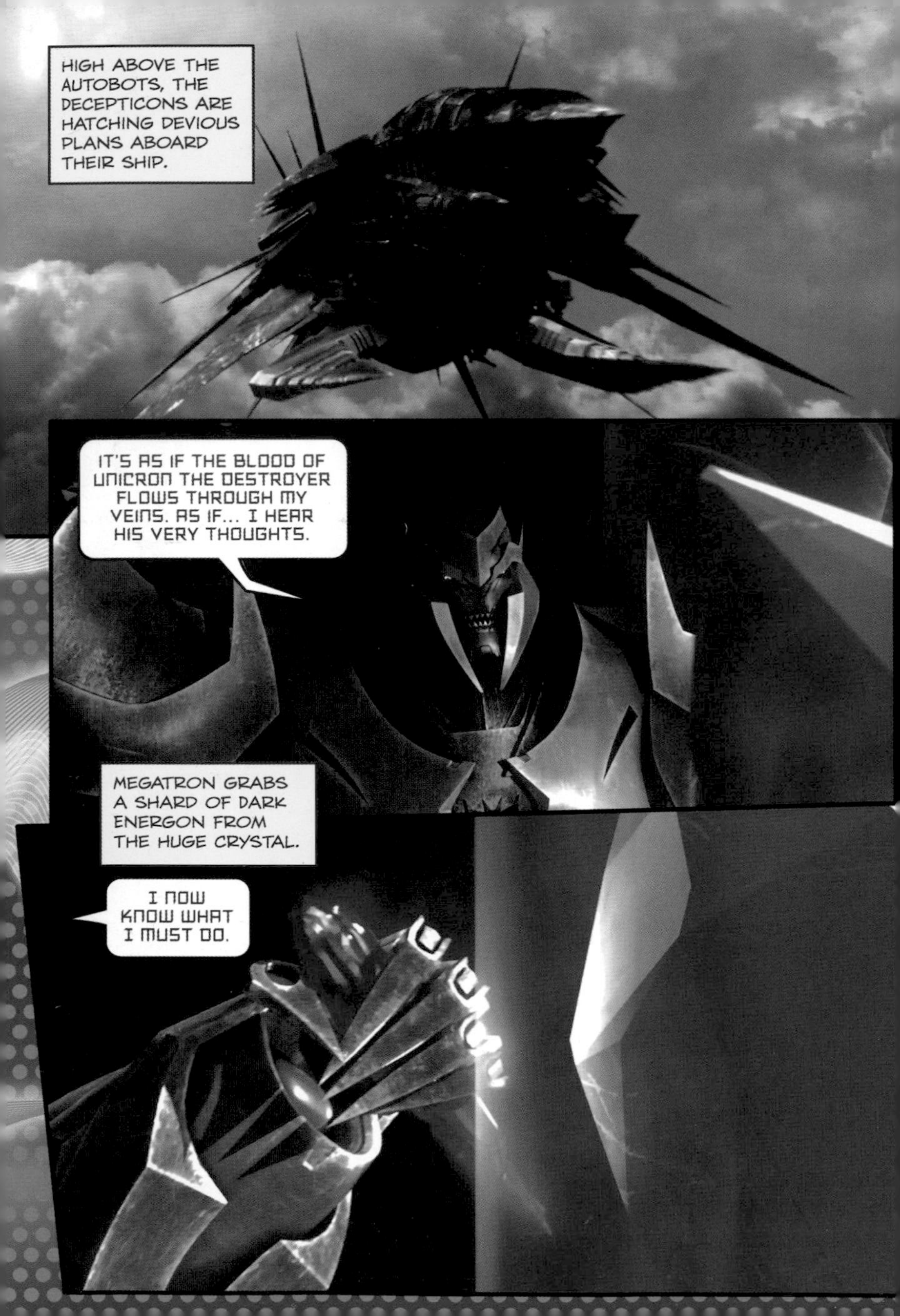
HIGH ABOVE THE AUTOBOTS, THE DECEPTICONS ARE HATCHING DEVIOUS PLANS ABOARD THEIR SHIP.
IT'S AS IF THE BLOOD OF UNICRON THE DESTROYER FLOWS THROUGH MY VEINS. AS IF... I HEAR HIS VERY THOUGHTS.
MEGATRON GRABS A SHARD OF DARK ENERGON FROM THE HUGE CRYSTAL.
I NOW KNOW WHAT I MUST DO.

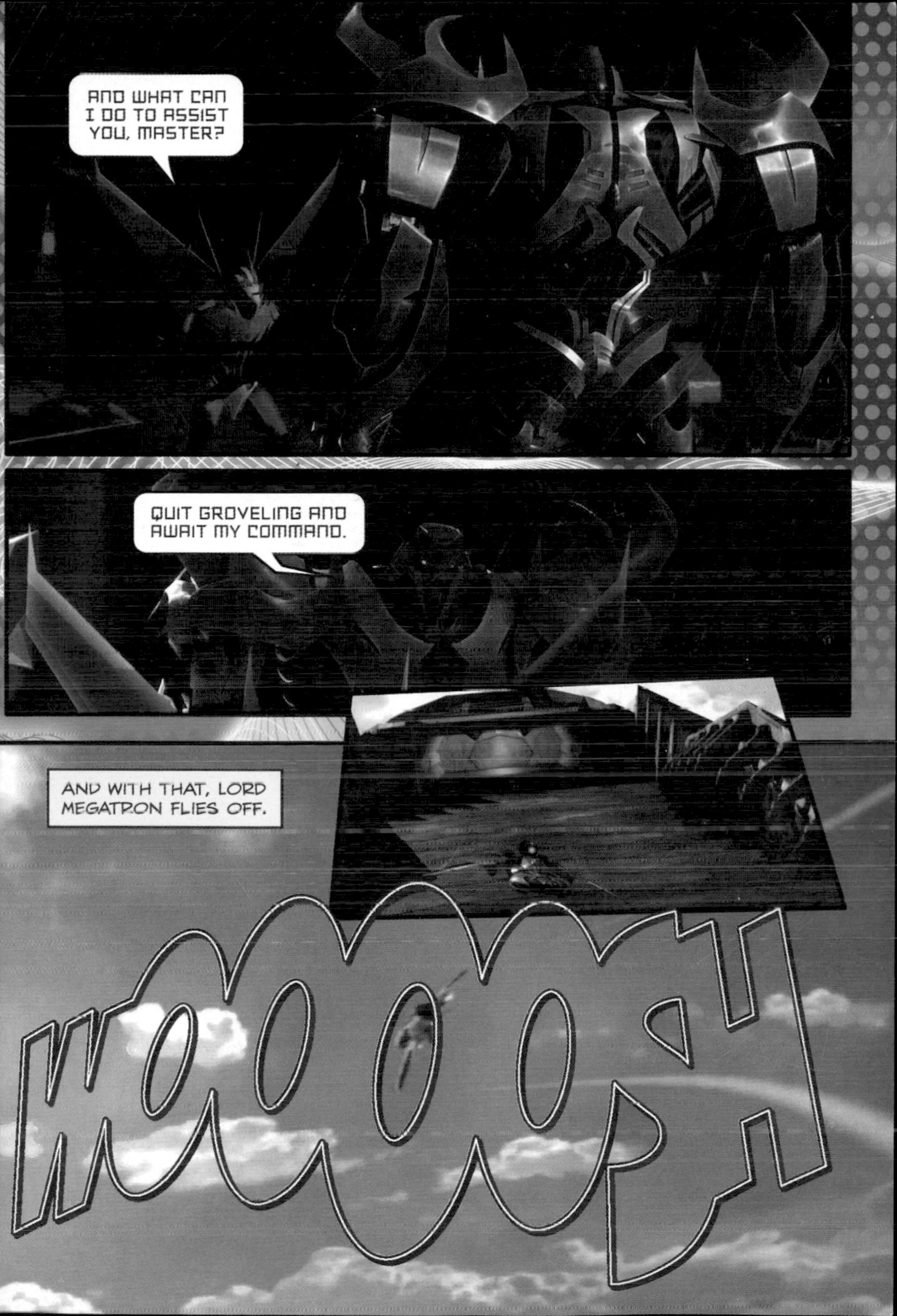
AND WHAT CAN I DO TO ASSIST YOU, MASTER?
QUIT GROVELING AND AWAIT MY COMMAND.
AND WITH THAT, LORD MEGATRON FLIES OFF.
WOOOOSH

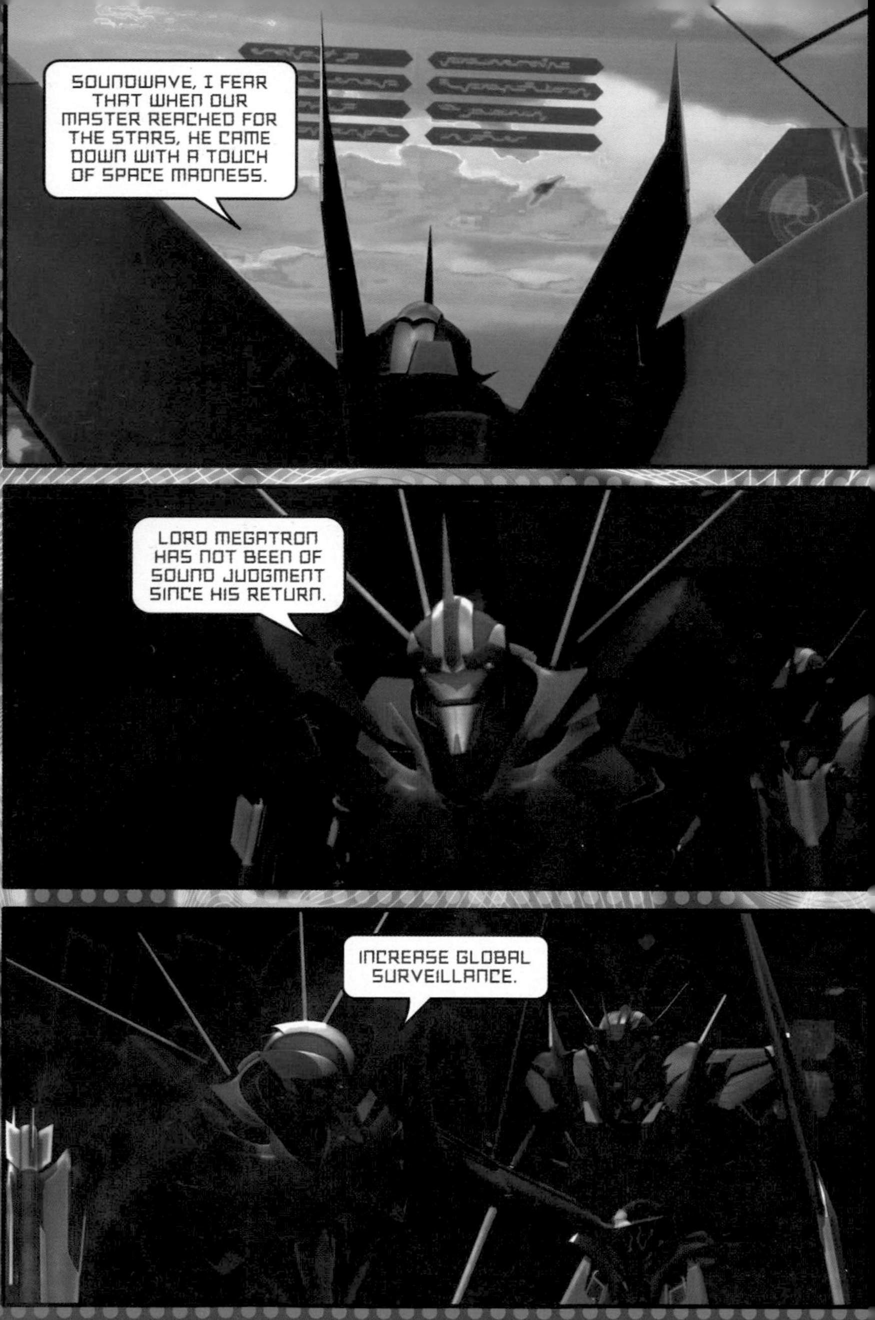
SOUNDWAVE, I FEAR THAT WHEN OUR MASTER REACHED FOR THE STARS, HE CAME DOWN WITH A TOUCH OF SPACE MADNESS.
LORD MEGATRON HAS NOT BEEN OF SOUND JUDGMENT SINCE HIS RETURN.
INCREASE GLOBAL SURVEILLANCE.

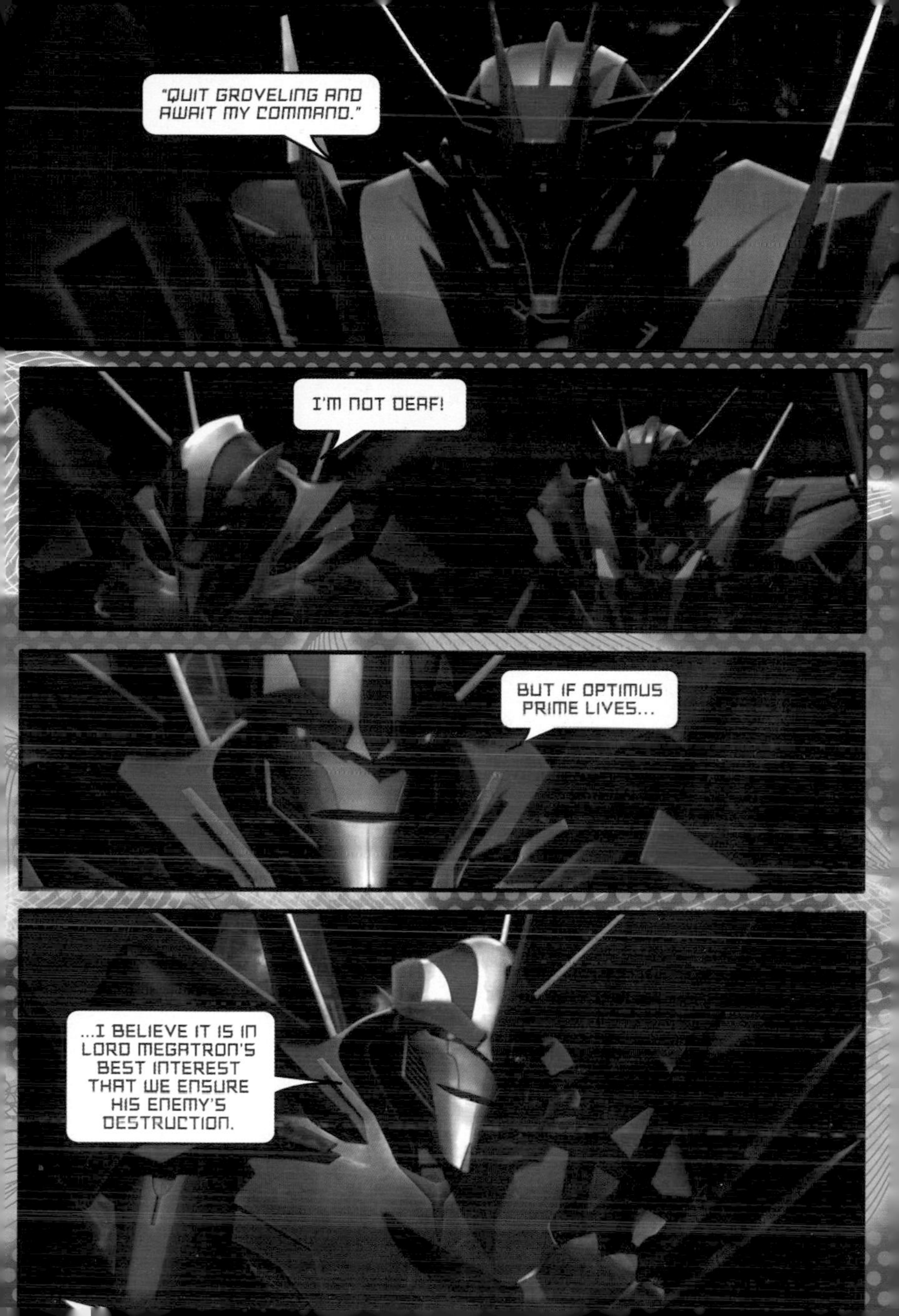
"QUIT GROVELING AND AWAIT MY COMMAND."
I'M NOT DEAF!
BUT IF OPTIMUS PRIME LIVES...
...I BELIEVE IT IS IN LORD MEGATRON'S BEST INTEREST THAT WE ENSURE HIS ENEMY'S DESTRUCTION.

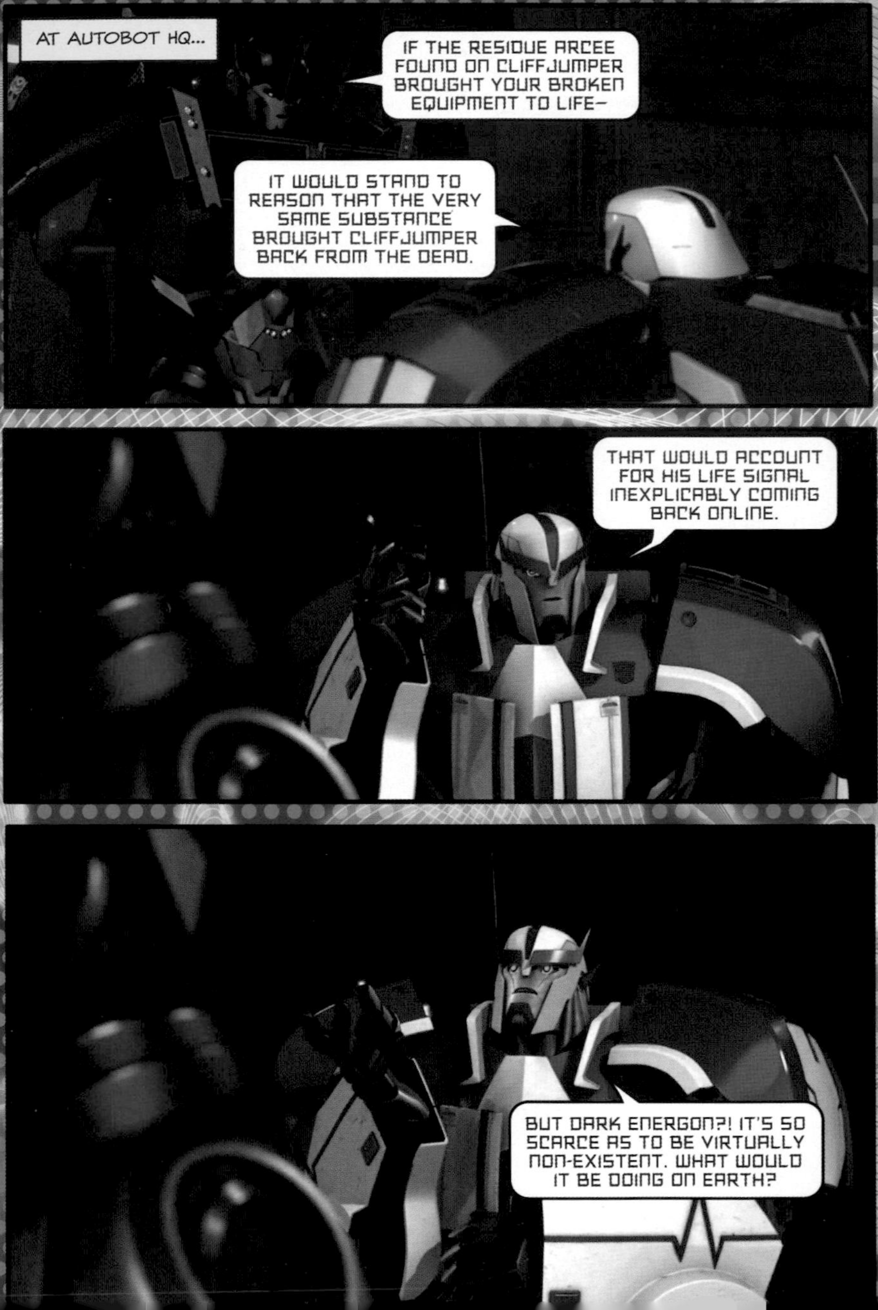
AT AUTOBOT HQ...
IF THE RESIDUE ARCEE FOUND ON CLIFFJUMPER BROUGHT YOUR BROKEN EQUIPMENT TO LIFE–
IT WOULD STAND TO REASON THAT THE VERY SAME SUBSTANCE BROUGHT CLIFFJUMPER BACK FROM THE DEAD.
THAT WOULD ACCOUNT FOR HIS LIFE SIGNAL INEXPLICABLY COMING BACK ONLINE.
BUT DARK ENERGON?! IT'S SO SCARCE AS TO BE VIRTUALLY NON-EXISTENT. WHAT WOULD IT BE DOING ON EARTH?

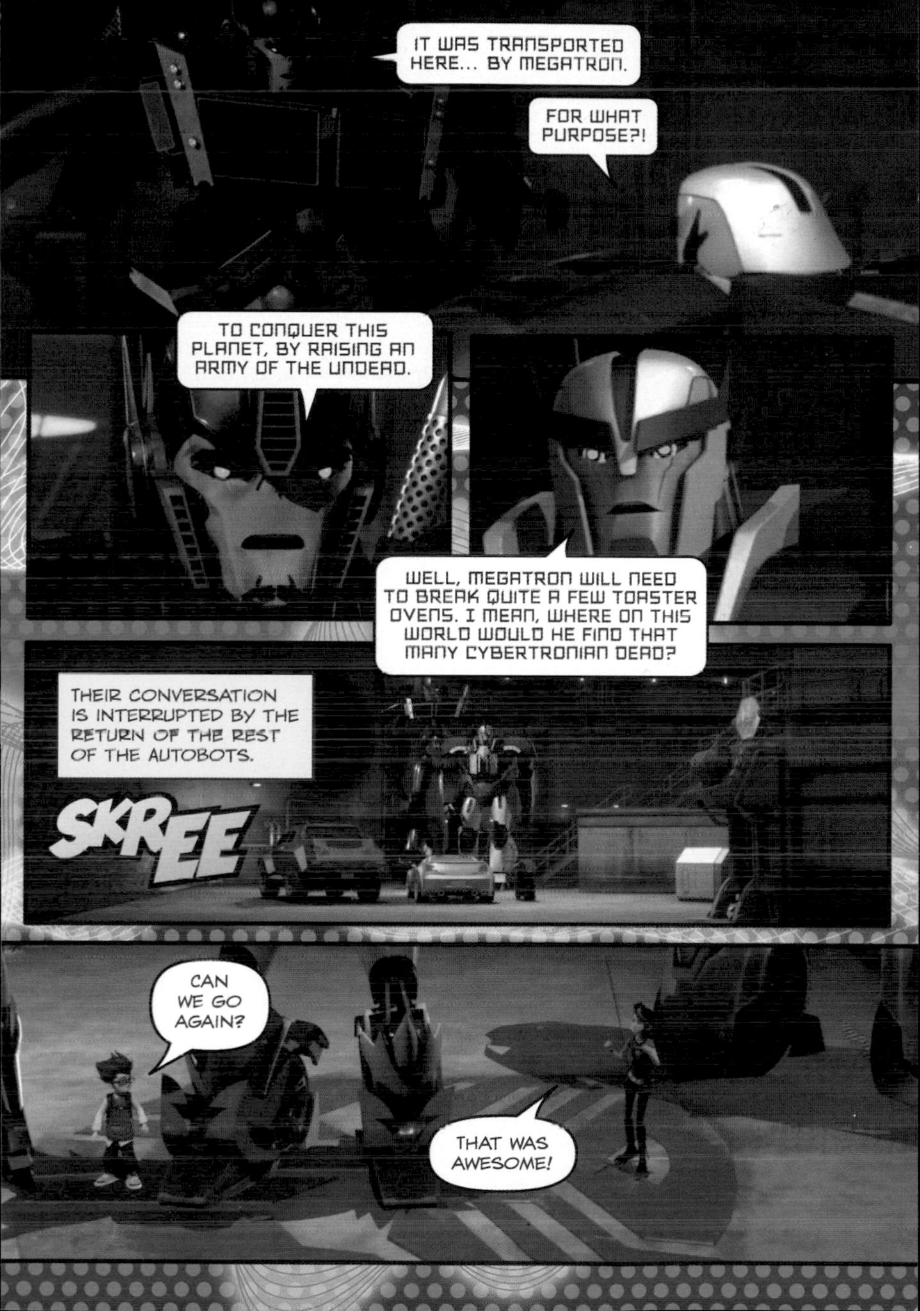
IT WAS TRANSPORTED HERE... BY MEGATRON.
FOR WHAT PURPOSE?!
TO CONQUER THIS PLANET, BY RAISING AN ARMY OF THE UNDEAD.
WELL, MEGATRON WILL NEED TO BREAK QUITE A FEW TOASTER OVENS. I MEAN, WHERE ON THIS WORLD WOULD HE FIND THAT MANY CYBERTRONIAN DEAD?
THEIR CONVERSATION IS INTERRUPTED BY THE RETURN OF THE REST OF THE AUTOBOTS.
SKREE
CAN WE GO AGAIN?
THAT WAS AWESOME!

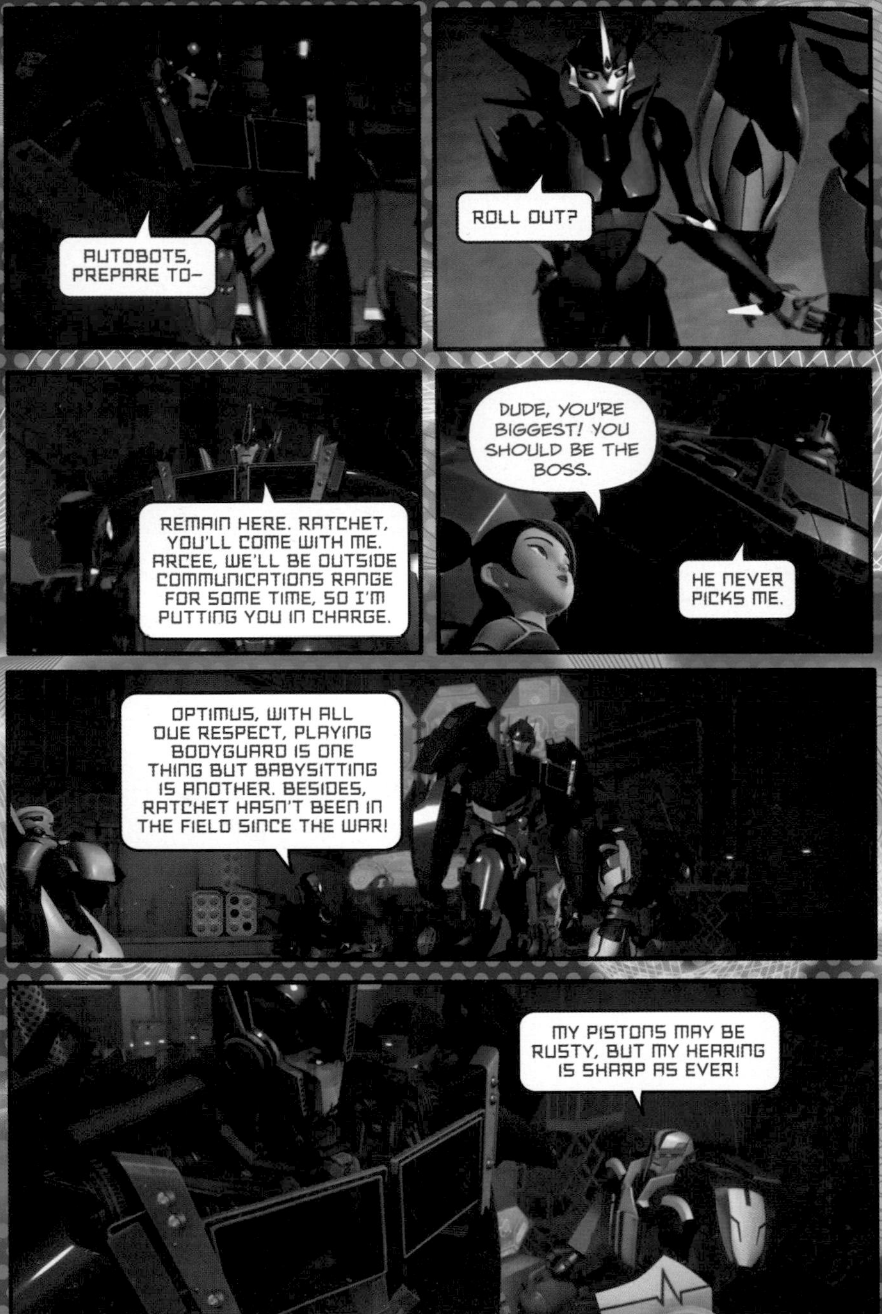
AUTOBOTS, PREPARE TO—
ROLL OUT?
REMAIN HERE. RATCHET, YOU'LL COME WITH ME. ARCEE, WE'LL BE OUTSIDE COMMUNICATIONS RANGE FOR SOME TIME, SO I'M PUTTING YOU IN CHARGE.
DUDE, YOU'RE BIGGEST! YOU SHOULD BE THE BOSS.
HE NEVER PICKS ME.
OPTIMUS, WITH ALL DUE RESPECT, PLAYING BODYGUARD IS ONE THING BUT BABYSITTING IS ANOTHER. BESIDES, RATCHET HASN'T BEEN IN THE FIELD SINCE THE WAR!
MY PISTONS MAY BE RUSTY, BUT MY HEARING IS SHARP AS EVER!

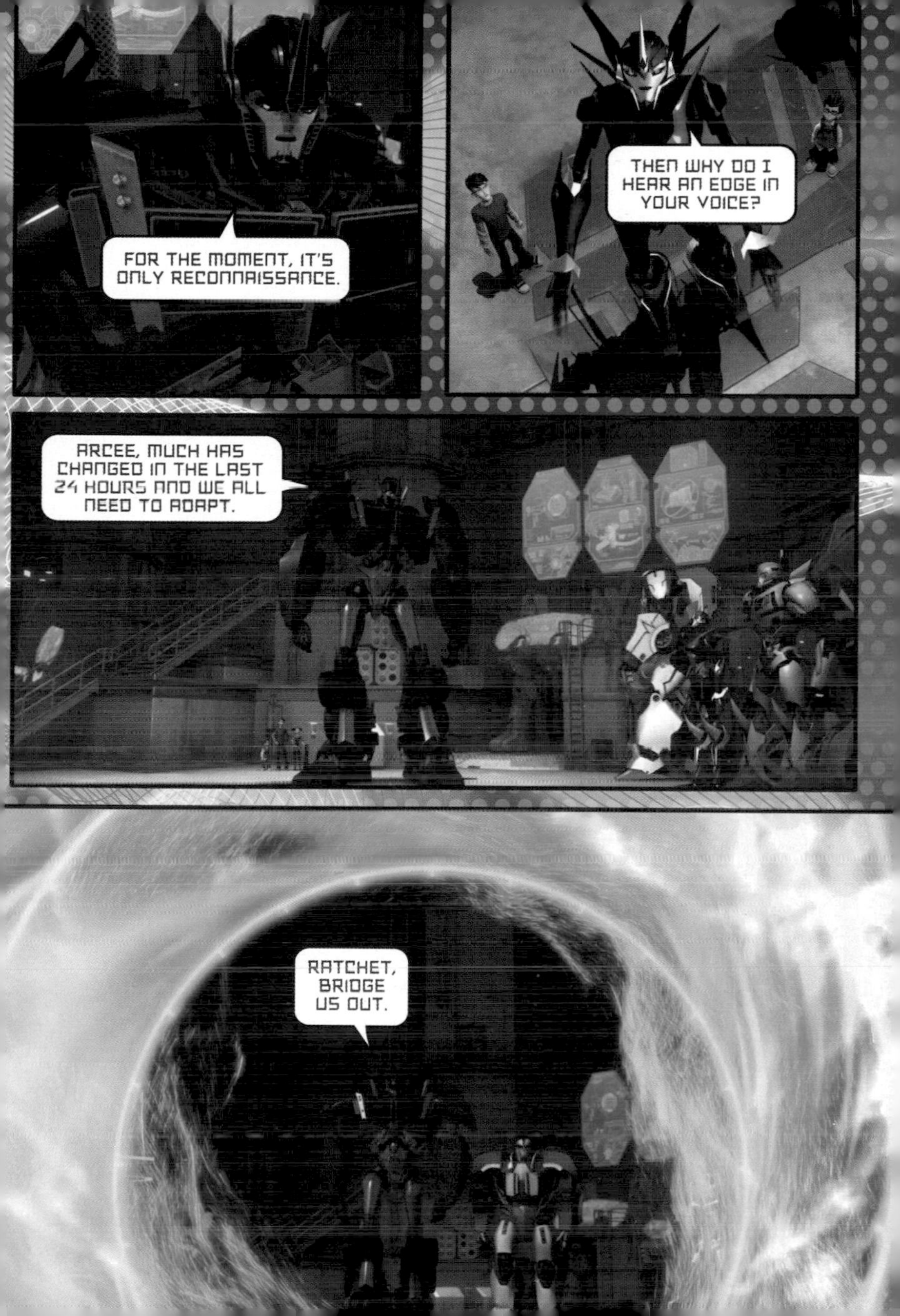
FOR THE MOMENT, IT'S ONLY RECONNAISSANCE.
THEN WHY DO I HEAR AN EDGE IN YOUR VOICE?
ARCEE, MUCH HAS CHANGED IN THE LAST 24 HOURS AND WE ALL NEED TO ADAPT.
RATCHET, BRIDGE US OUT.

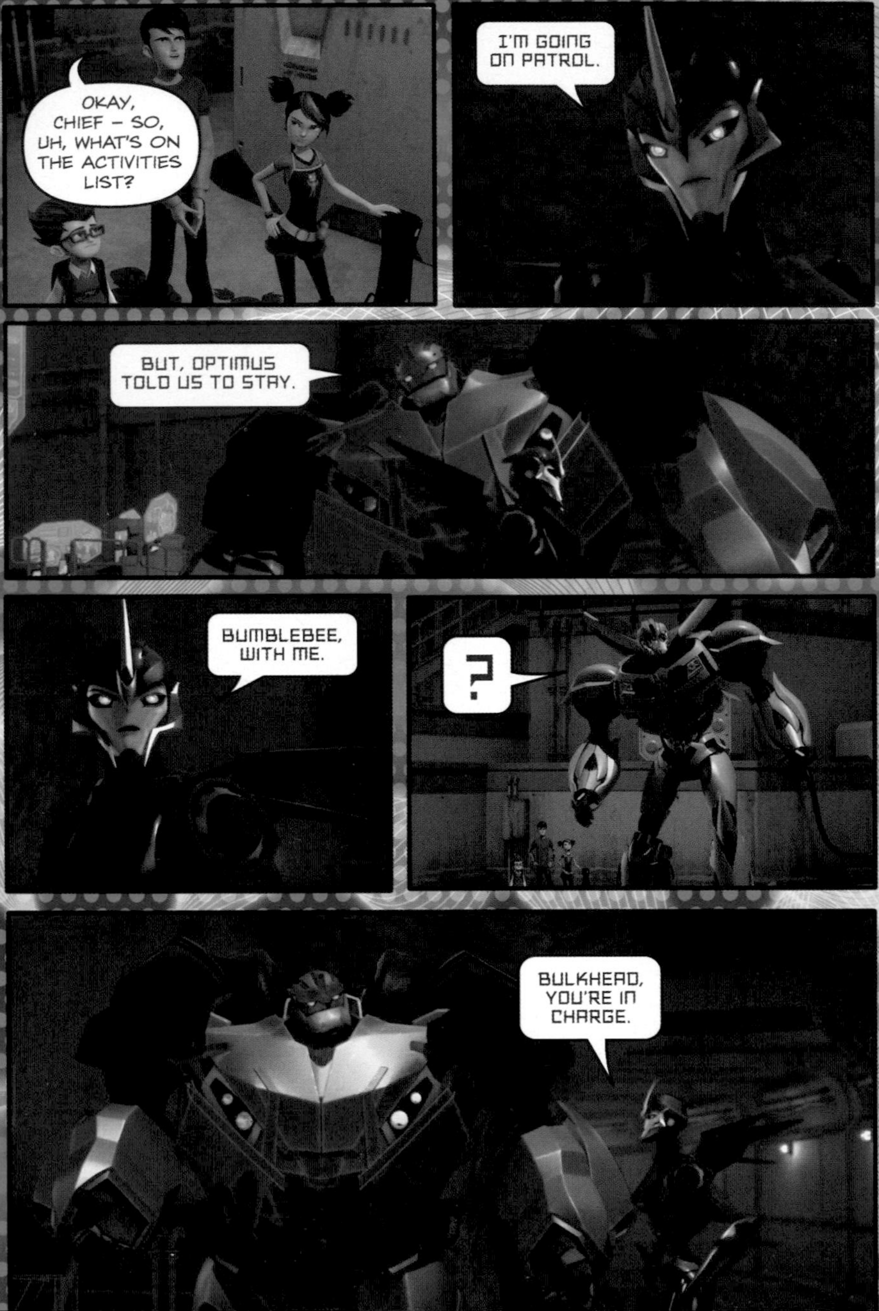
OKAY, CHIEF – SO, UH, WHAT'S ON THE ACTIVITIES LIST?
I'M GOING ON PATROL.
BUT, OPTIMUS TOLD US TO STAY.
BUMBLEBEE, WITH ME.
?
BULKHEAD, YOU'RE IN CHARGE.

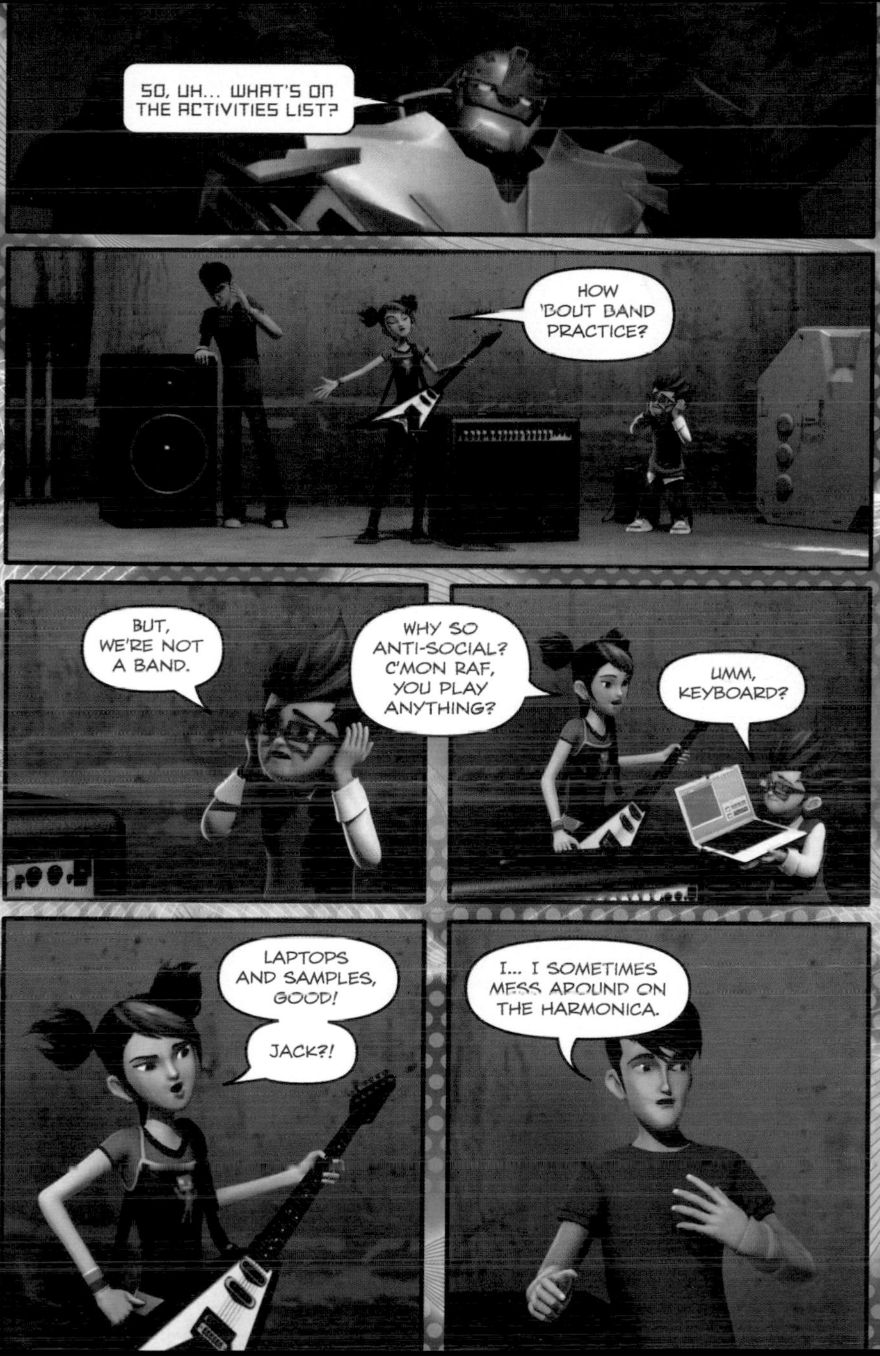
SO, UH... WHAT'S ON THE ACTIVITIES LIST?
HOW 'BOUT BAND PRACTICE?
BUT, WE'RE NOT A BAND.
WHY SO ANTI-SOCIAL? C'MON RAF, YOU PLAY ANYTHING?
UMM, KEYBOARD?
LAPTOPS AND SAMPLES, GOOD!
JACK?!
I... I SOMETIMES MESS AROUND ON THE HARMONICA.

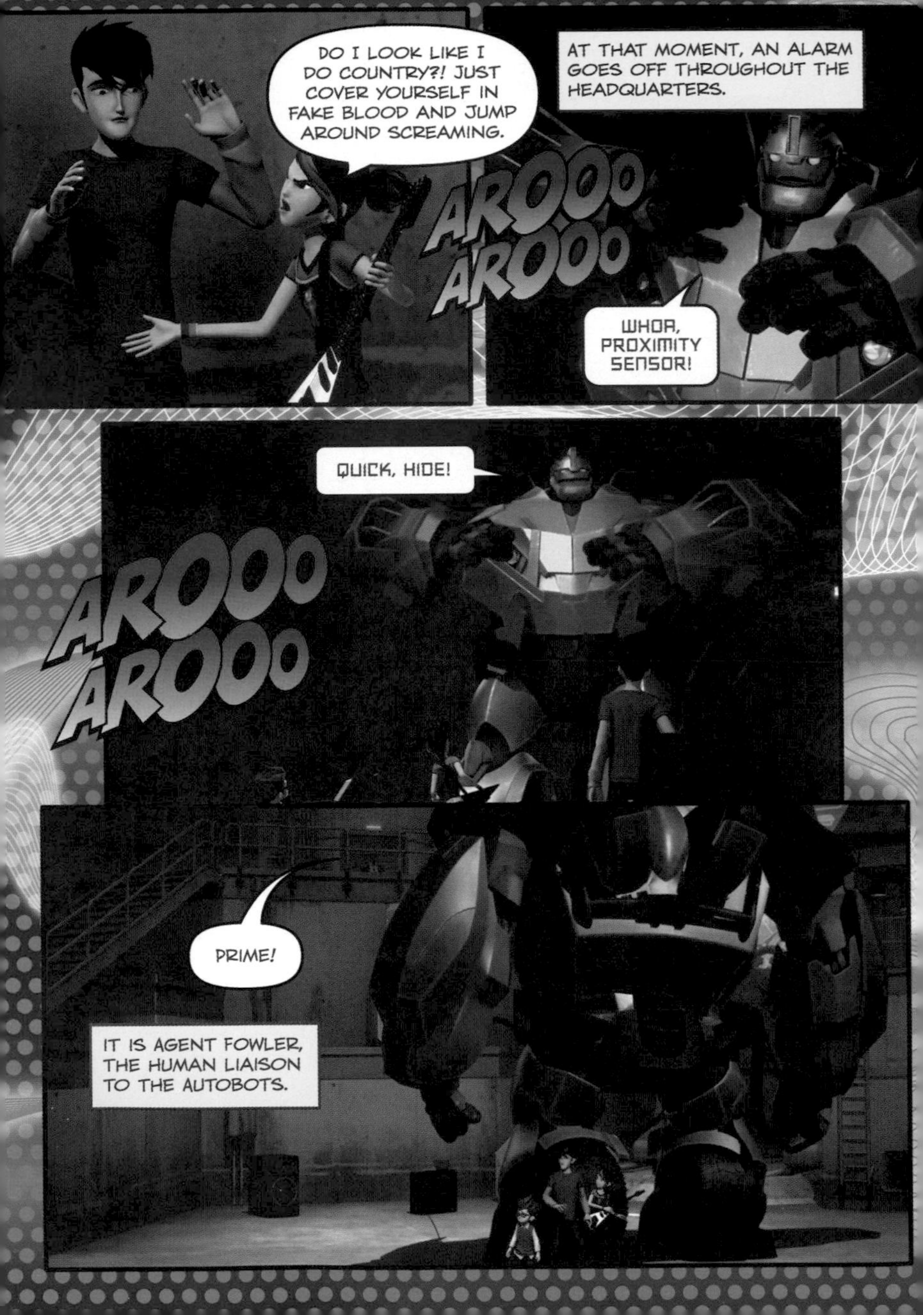
DO I LOOK LIKE I DO COUNTRY?! JUST COVER YOURSELF IN FAKE BLOOD AND JUMP AROUND SCREAMING.
AT THAT MOMENT, AN ALARM GOES OFF THROUGHOUT THE HEADQUARTERS.
AROOO AROOO
WHOA, PROXIMITY SENSOR!
QUICK, HIDE!
AROOO AROOO
PRIME!
IT IS AGENT FOWLER, THE HUMAN LIAISON TO THE AUTOBOTS.

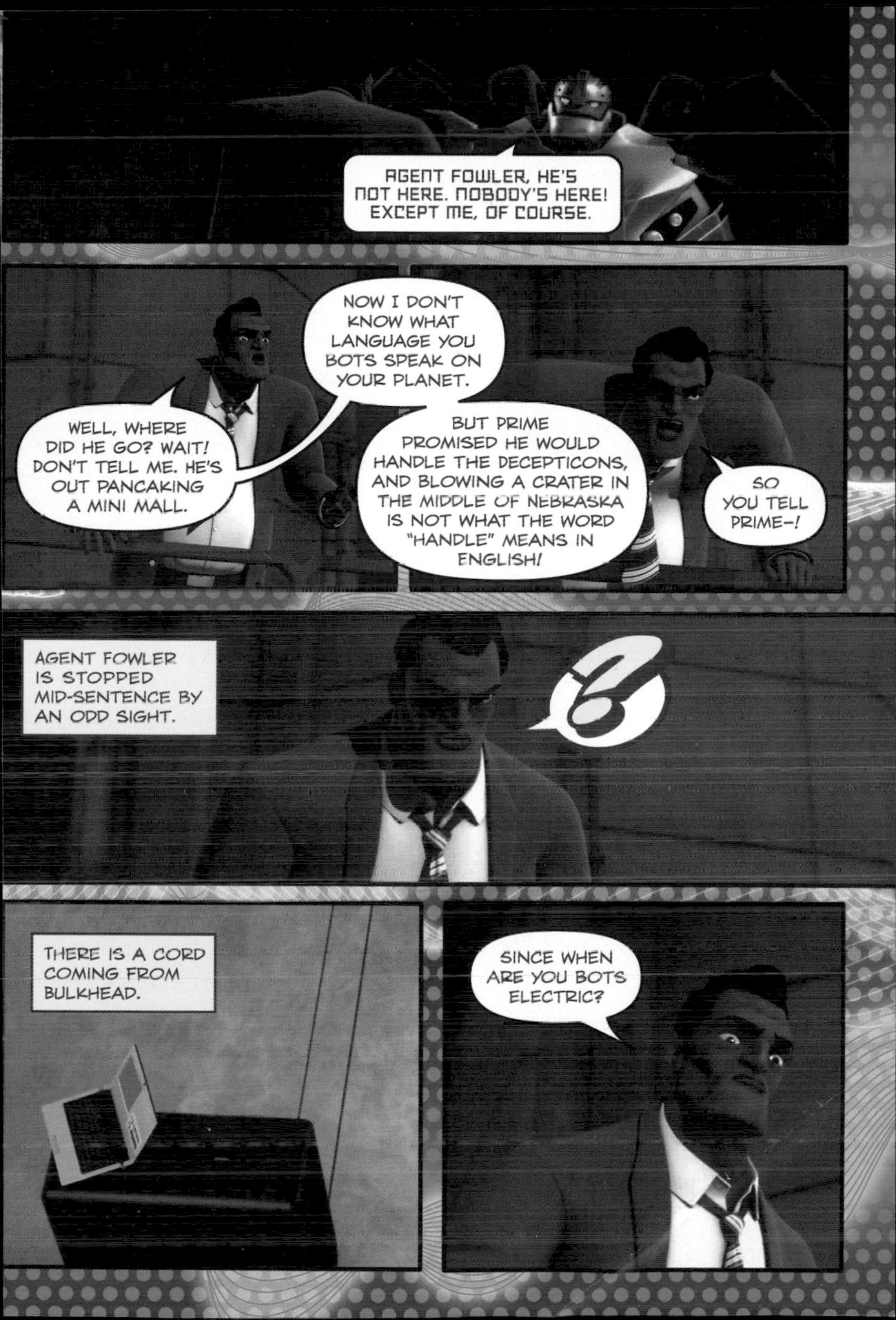
AGENT FOWLER, HE'S NOT HERE. NOBODY'S HERE! EXCEPT ME, OF COURSE.
WELL, WHERE DID HE GO? WAIT! DON'T TELL ME. HE'S OUT PANCAKING A MINI MALL.
NOW I DON'T KNOW WHAT LANGUAGE YOU BOTS SPEAK ON YOUR PLANET.
BUT PRIME PROMISED HE WOULD HANDLE THE DECEPTICONS, AND BLOWING A CRATER IN THE MIDDLE OF NEBRASKA IS NOT WHAT THE WORD "HANDLE" MEANS IN ENGLISH!
SO YOU TELL PRIME—!
AGENT FOWLER IS STOPPED MID-SENTENCE BY AN ODD SIGHT.
THERE IS A CORD COMING FROM BULKHEAD.
SINCE WHEN ARE YOU BOTS ELECTRIC?

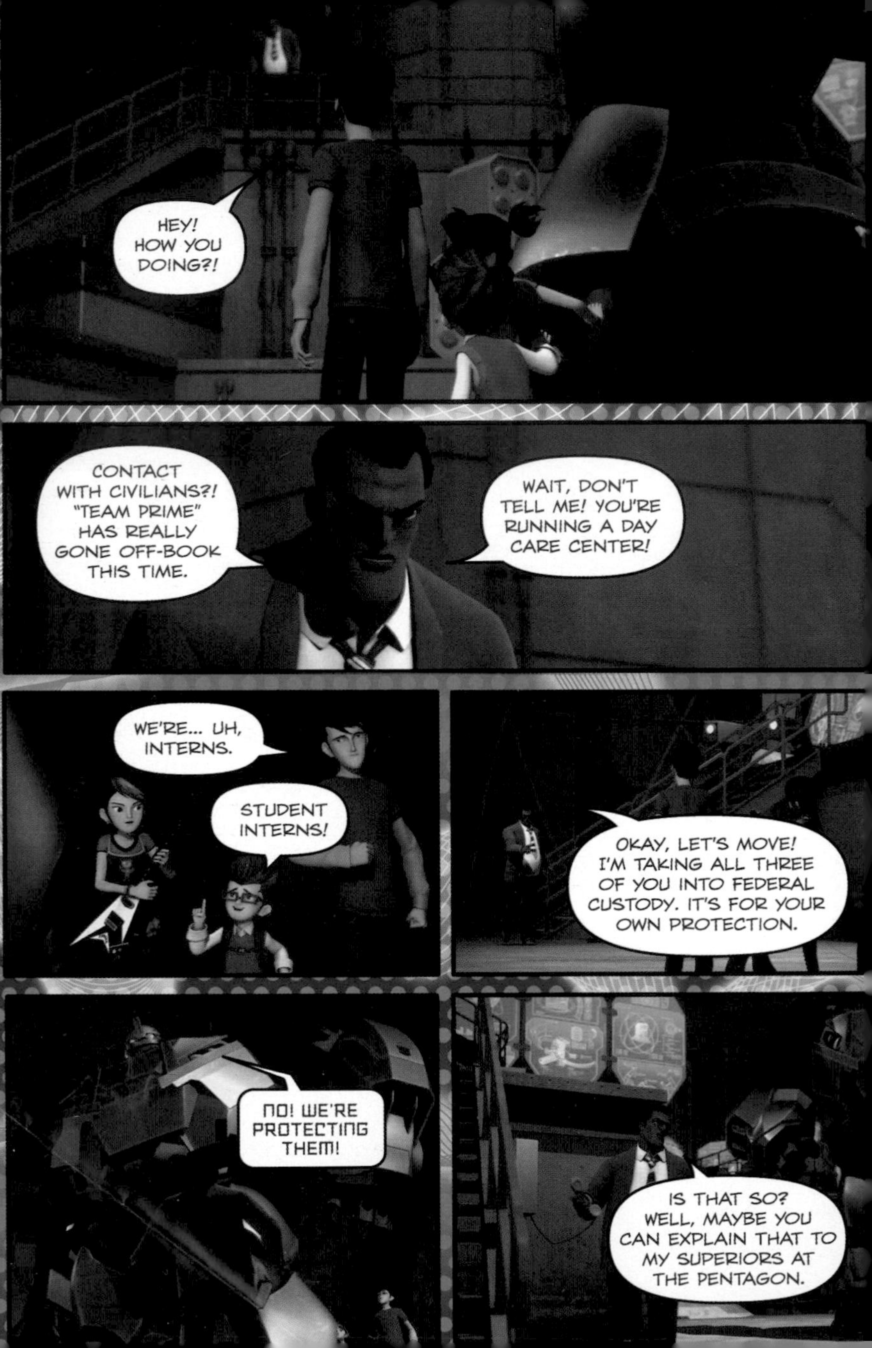
HEY! HOW YOU DOING?!
CONTACT WITH CIVILIANS?! "TEAM PRIME" HAS REALLY GONE OFF-BOOK THIS TIME.
WAIT, DON'T TELL ME! YOU'RE RUNNING A DAY CARE CENTER!
WE'RE... UH, INTERNS.
STUDENT INTERNS!
OKAY, LET'S MOVE! I'M TAKING ALL THREE OF YOU INTO FEDERAL CUSTODY. IT'S FOR YOUR OWN PROTECTION.
NO! WE'RE PROTECTING THEM!
IS THAT SO? WELL, MAYBE YOU CAN EXPLAIN THAT TO MY SUPERIORS AT THE PENTAGON.

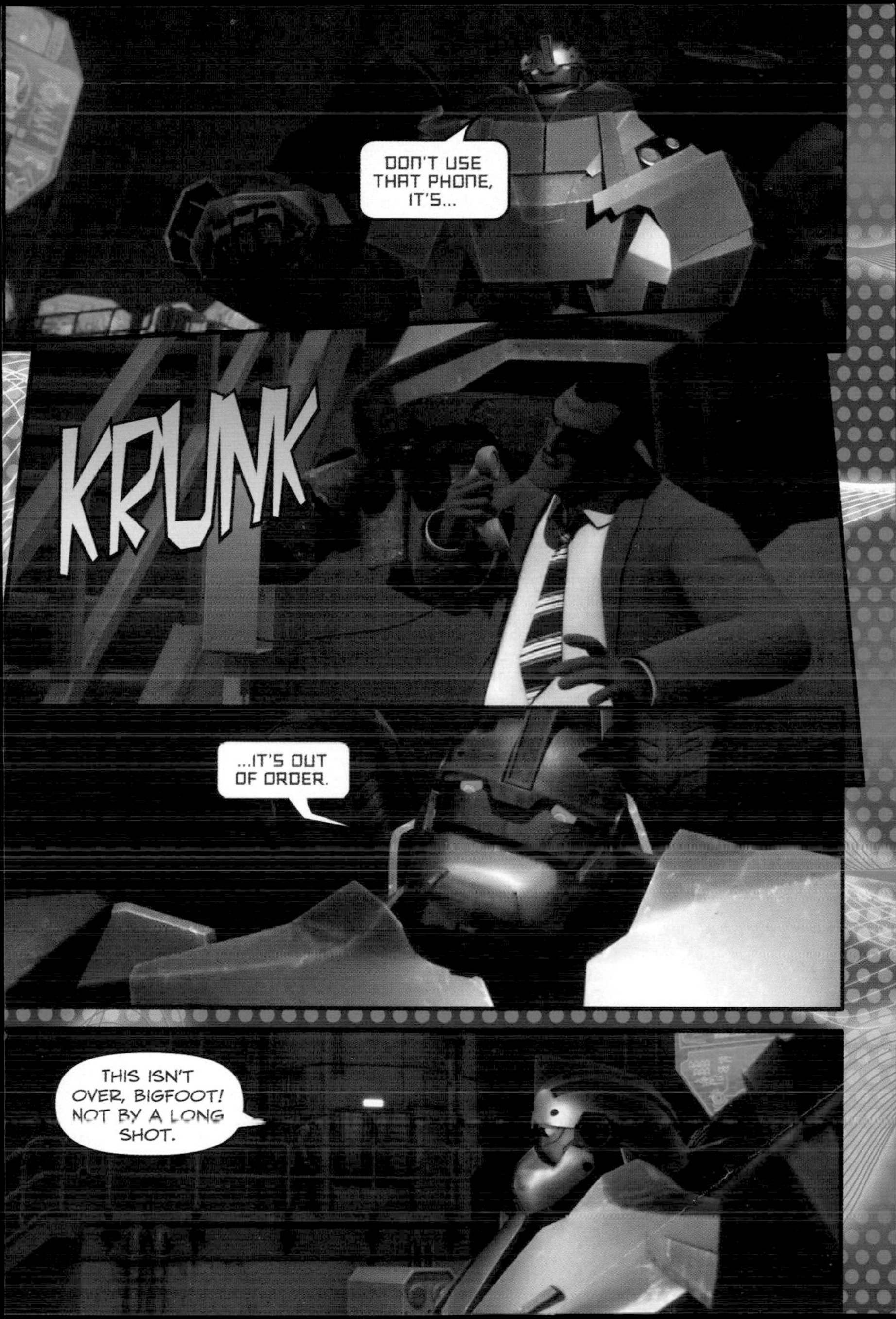
DON'T USE THAT PHONE, IT'S...
KRUNK
...IT'S OUT OF ORDER.
THIS ISN'T OVER, BIGFOOT! NOT BY A LONG SHOT.

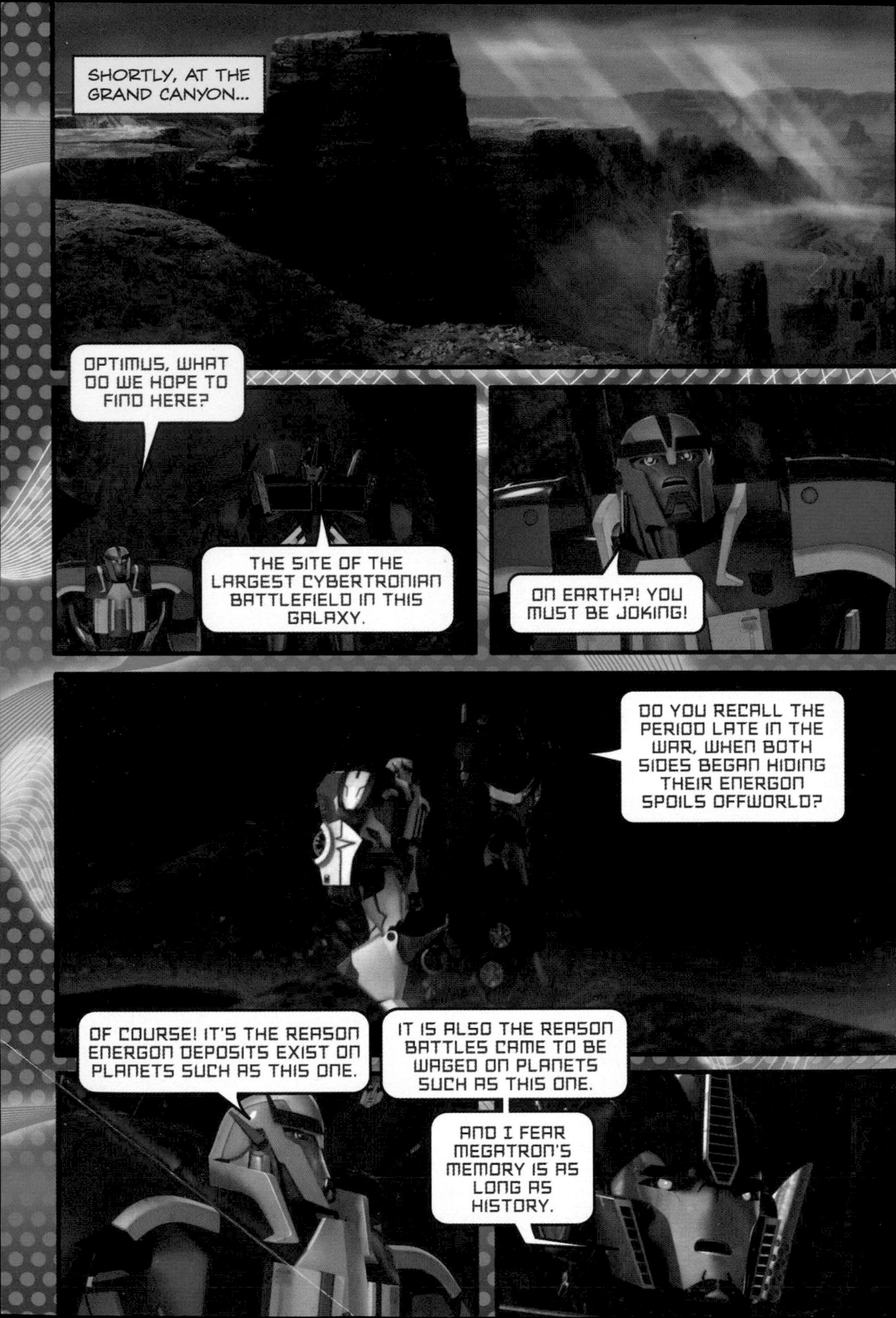
SHORTLY, AT THE GRAND CANYON...
OPTIMUS, WHAT DO WE HOPE TO FIND HERE?
THE SITE OF THE LARGEST CYBERTRONIAN BATTLEFIELD IN THIS GALAXY.
ON EARTH?! YOU MUST BE JOKING!
DO YOU RECALL THE PERIOD LATE IN THE WAR, WHEN BOTH SIDES BEGAN HIDING THEIR ENERGON SPOILS OFFWORLD?
OF COURSE! IT'S THE REASON ENERGON DEPOSITS EXIST ON PLANETS SUCH AS THIS ONE.
IT IS ALSO THE REASON BATTLES CAME TO BE WAGED ON PLANETS SUCH AS THIS ONE.
AND I FEAR MEGATRON'S MEMORY IS AS LONG AS HISTORY.

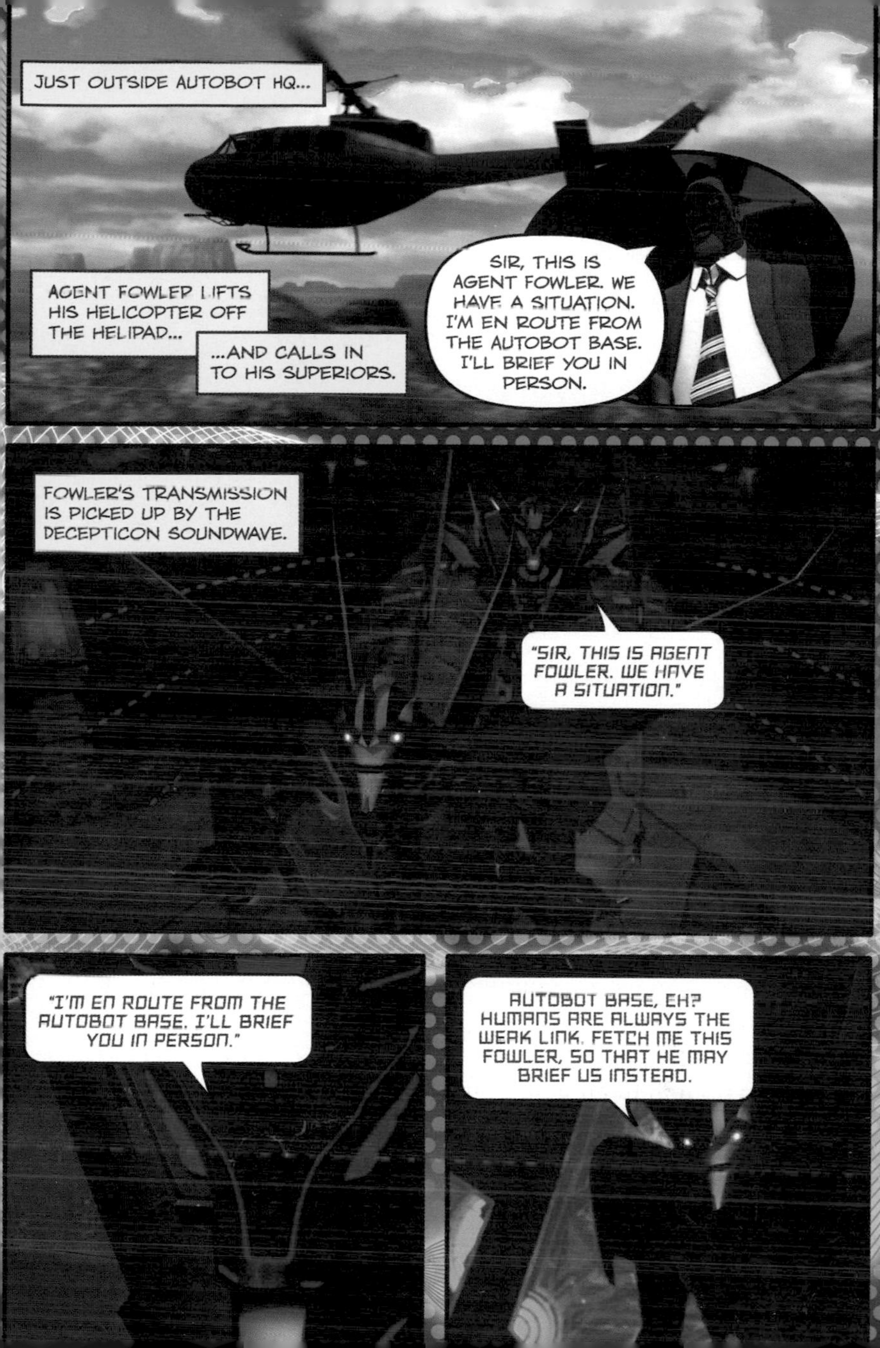
JUST OUTSIDE AUTOBOT HQ...
AGENT FOWLER LIFTS HIS HELICOPTER OFF THE HELIPAD...
...AND CALLS IN TO HIS SUPERIORS.
SIR, THIS IS AGENT FOWLER. WE HAVE A SITUATION. I'M EN ROUTE FROM THE AUTOBOT BASE. I'LL BRIEF YOU IN PERSON.
FOWLER'S TRANSMISSION IS PICKED UP BY THE DECEPTICON SOUNDWAVE.
"SIR, THIS IS AGENT FOWLER. WE HAVE A SITUATION."
"I'M EN ROUTE FROM THE AUTOBOT BASE. I'LL BRIEF YOU IN PERSON."
AUTOBOT BASE, EH? HUMANS ARE ALWAYS THE WEAK LINK. FETCH ME THIS FOWLER, SO THAT HE MAY BRIEF US INSTEAD.

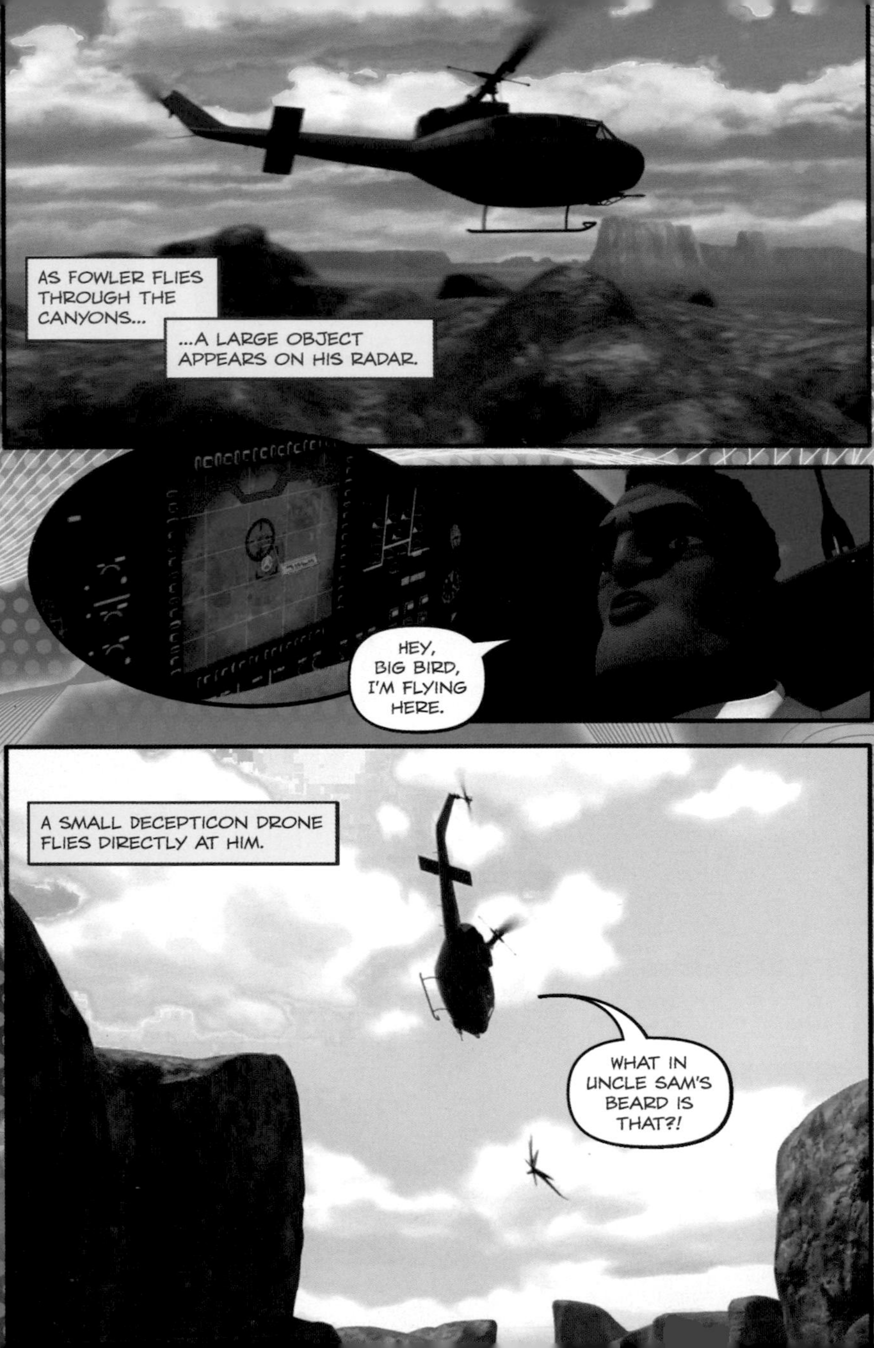
AS FOWLER FLIES THROUGH THE CANYONS...
...A LARGE OBJECT APPEARS ON HIS RADAR.
HEY, BIG BIRD, I'M FLYING HERE.
A SMALL DECEPTICON DRONE FLIES DIRECTLY AT HIM.
WHAT IN UNCLE SAM'S BEARD IS THAT?!

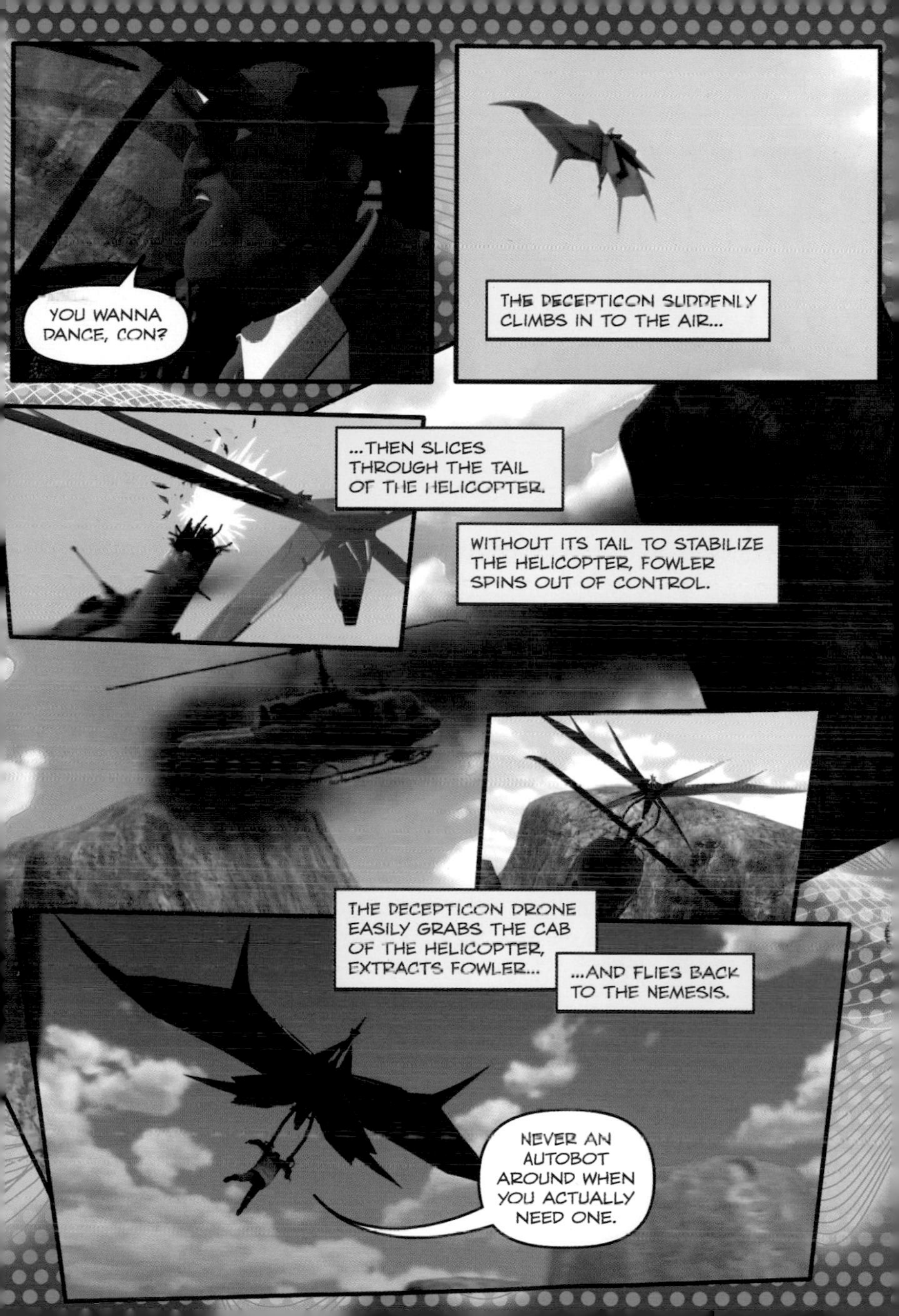
YOU WANNA DANCE, CON?
THE DECEPTICON SUDDENLY CLIMBS IN TO THE AIR...
...THEN SLICES THROUGH THE TAIL OF THE HELICOPTER.
WITHOUT ITS TAIL TO STABILIZE THE HELICOPTER, FOWLER SPINS OUT OF CONTROL.
THE DECEPTICON DRONE EASILY GRABS THE CAB OF THE HELICOPTER, EXTRACTS FOWLER...
...AND FLIES BACK TO THE NEMESIS.
NEVER AN AUTOBOT AROUND WHEN YOU ACTUALLY NEED ONE.

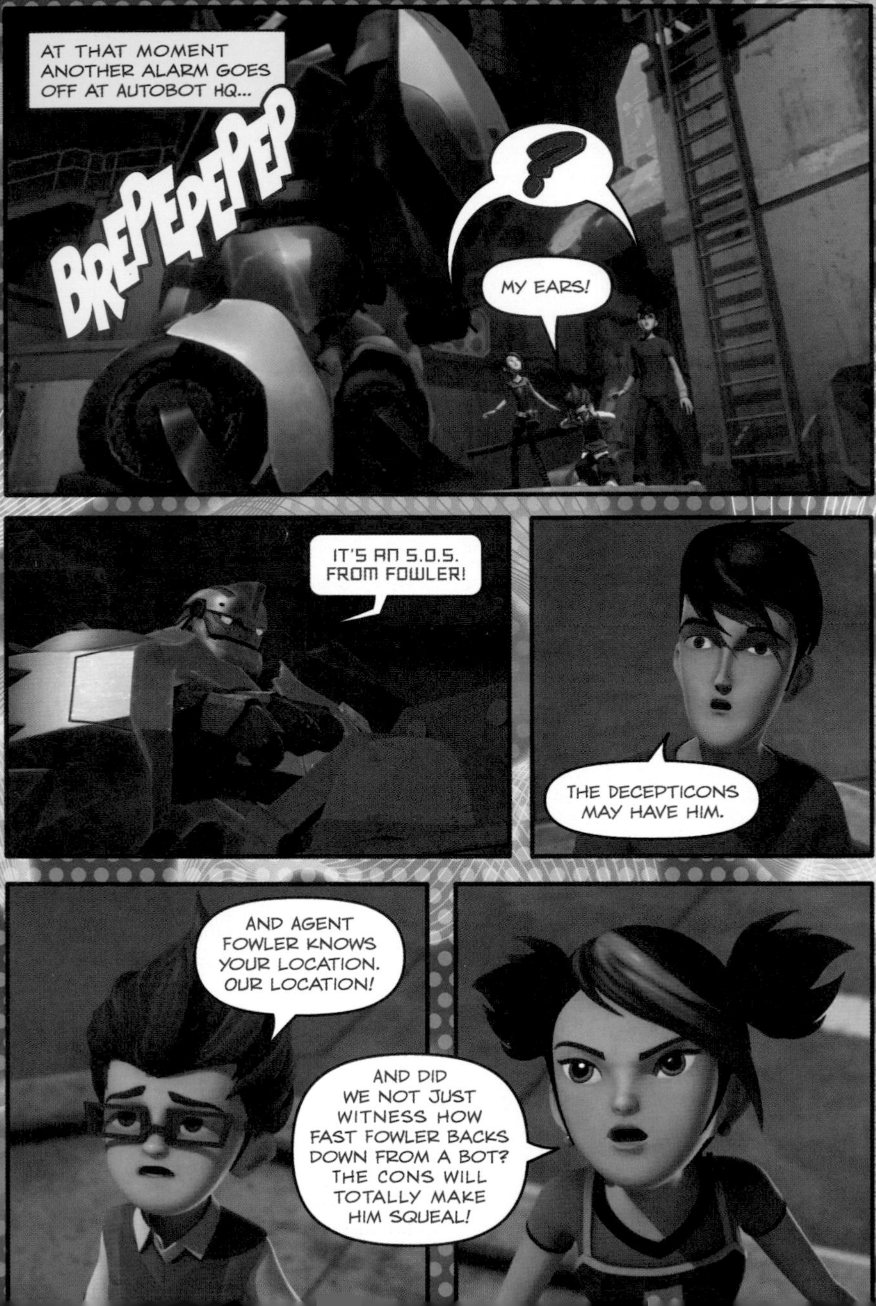
AT THAT MOMENT ANOTHER ALARM GOES OFF AT AUTOBOT HQ...
BREPEPEPEP
?
MY EARS!
IT'S AN S.O.S. FROM FOWLER!
THE DECEPTICONS MAY HAVE HIM.
AND AGENT FOWLER KNOWS YOUR LOCATION. OUR LOCATION!
AND DID WE NOT JUST WITNESS HOW FAST FOWLER BACKS DOWN FROM A BOT? THE CONS WILL TOTALLY MAKE HIM SQUEAL!

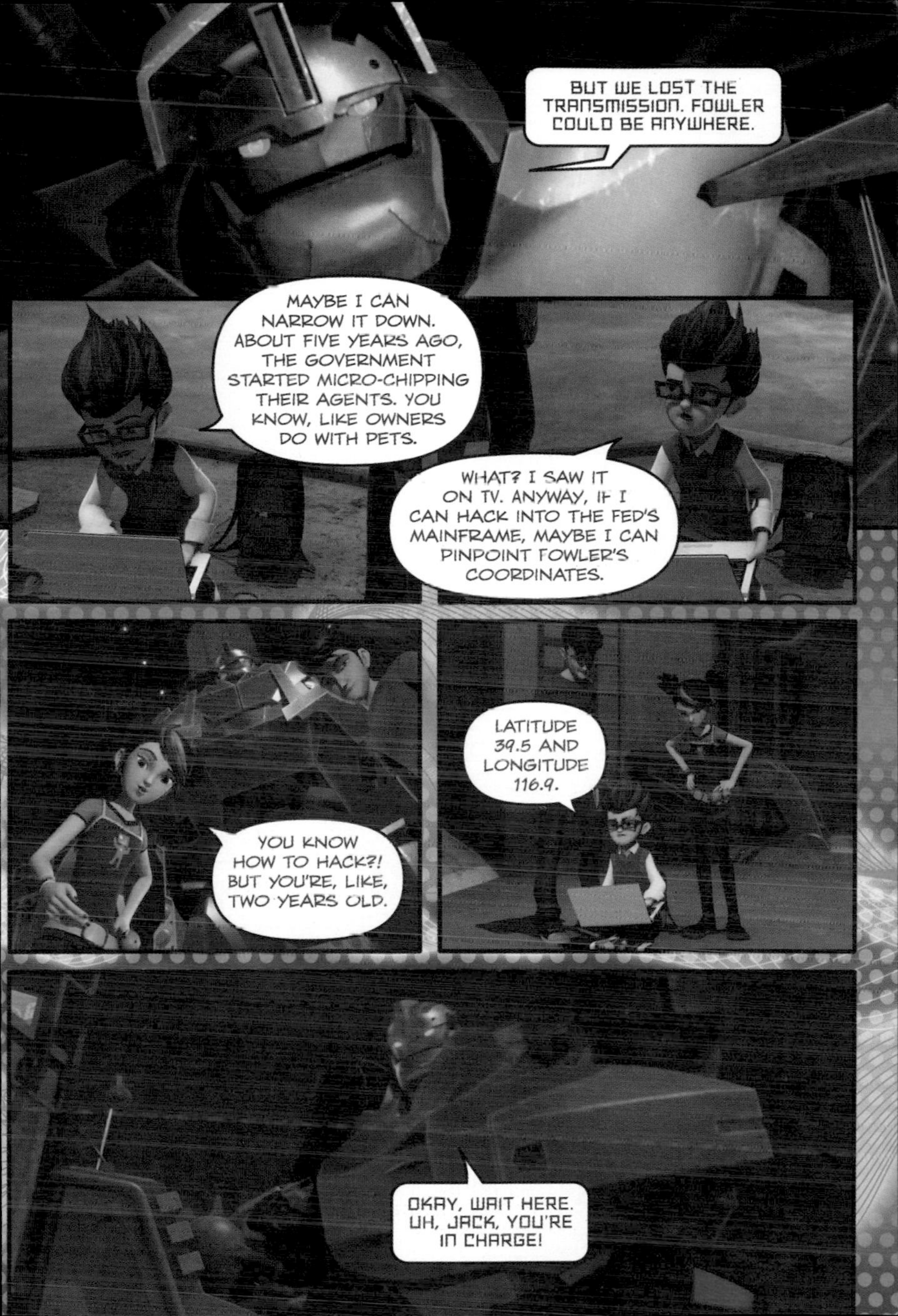
BUT WE LOST THE TRANSMISSION. FOWLER COULD BE ANYWHERE.
MAYBE I CAN NARROW IT DOWN. ABOUT FIVE YEARS AGO, THE GOVERNMENT STARTED MICRO-CHIPPING THEIR AGENTS. YOU KNOW, LIKE OWNERS DO WITH PETS.
WHAT? I SAW IT ON TV. ANYWAY, IF I CAN HACK INTO THE FED'S MAINFRAME, MAYBE I CAN PINPOINT FOWLER'S COORDINATES.
YOU KNOW HOW TO HACK?! BUT YOU'RE, LIKE, TWO YEARS OLD.
LATITUDE 39.5 AND LONGITUDE 116.9.
OKAY, WAIT HERE. UH, JACK, YOU'RE IN CHARGE!

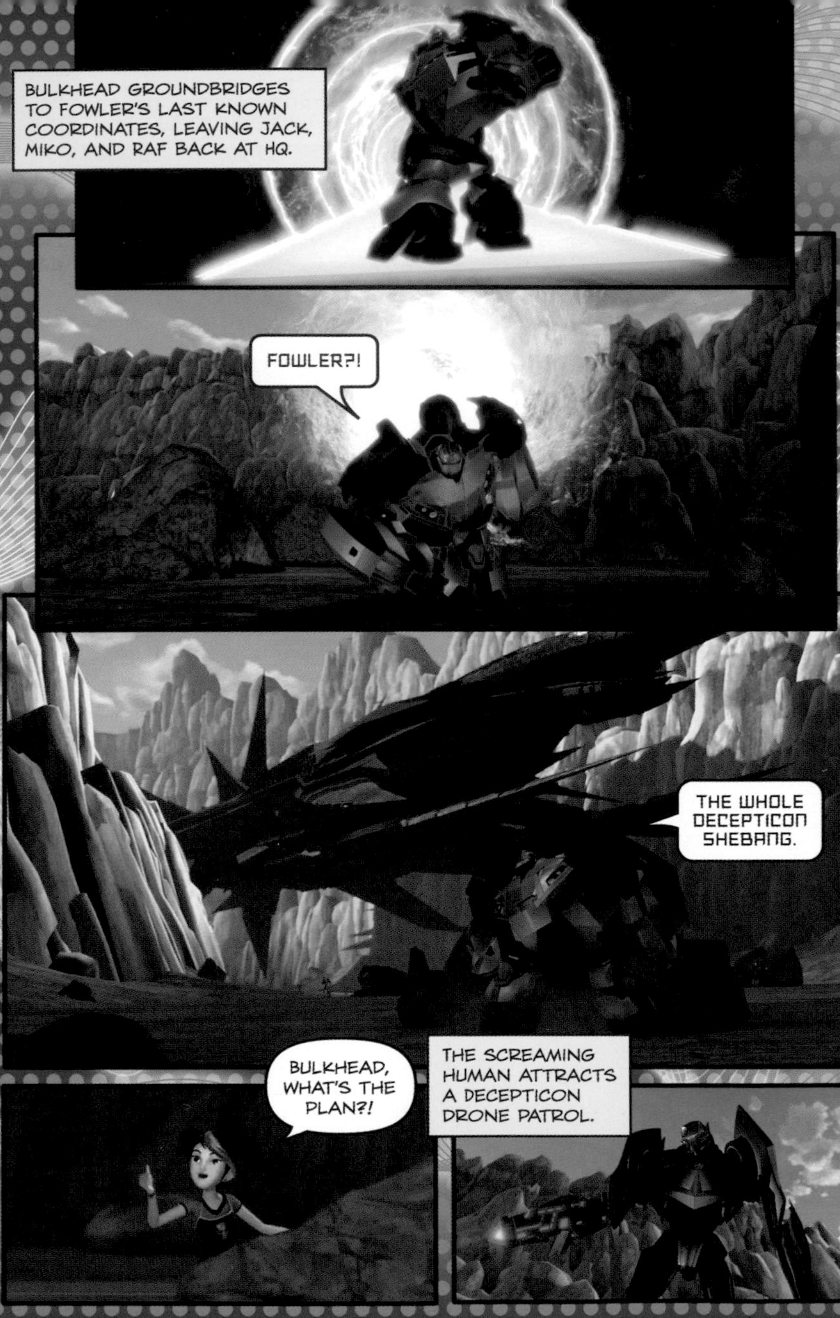
BULKHEAD GROUNDBRIDGES TO FOWLER'S LAST KNOWN COORDINATES, LEAVING JACK, MIKO, AND RAF BACK AT HQ.
FOWLER?!
THE WHOLE DECEPTICON SHEBANG.
BULKHEAD, WHAT'S THE PLAN?!
THE SCREAMING HUMAN ATTRACTS A DECEPTICON DRONE PATROL.

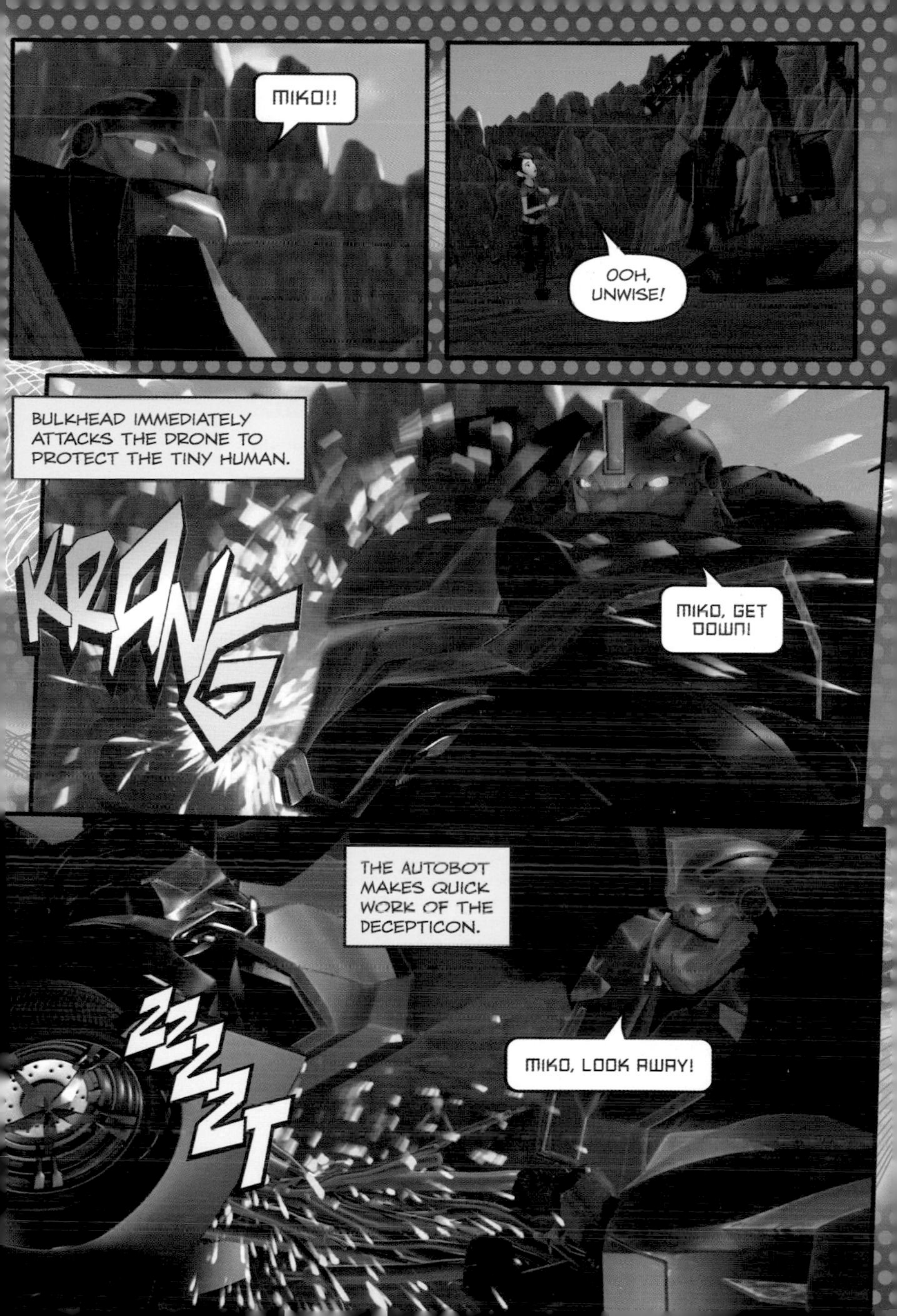
MIKO!!
OOH, UNWISE!
BULKHEAD IMMEDIATELY ATTACKS THE DRONE TO PROTECT THE TINY HUMAN.
KRANG
MIKO, GET DOWN!
THE AUTOBOT MAKES QUICK WORK OF THE DECEPTICON.
ZZZZT
MIKO, LOOK AWAY!

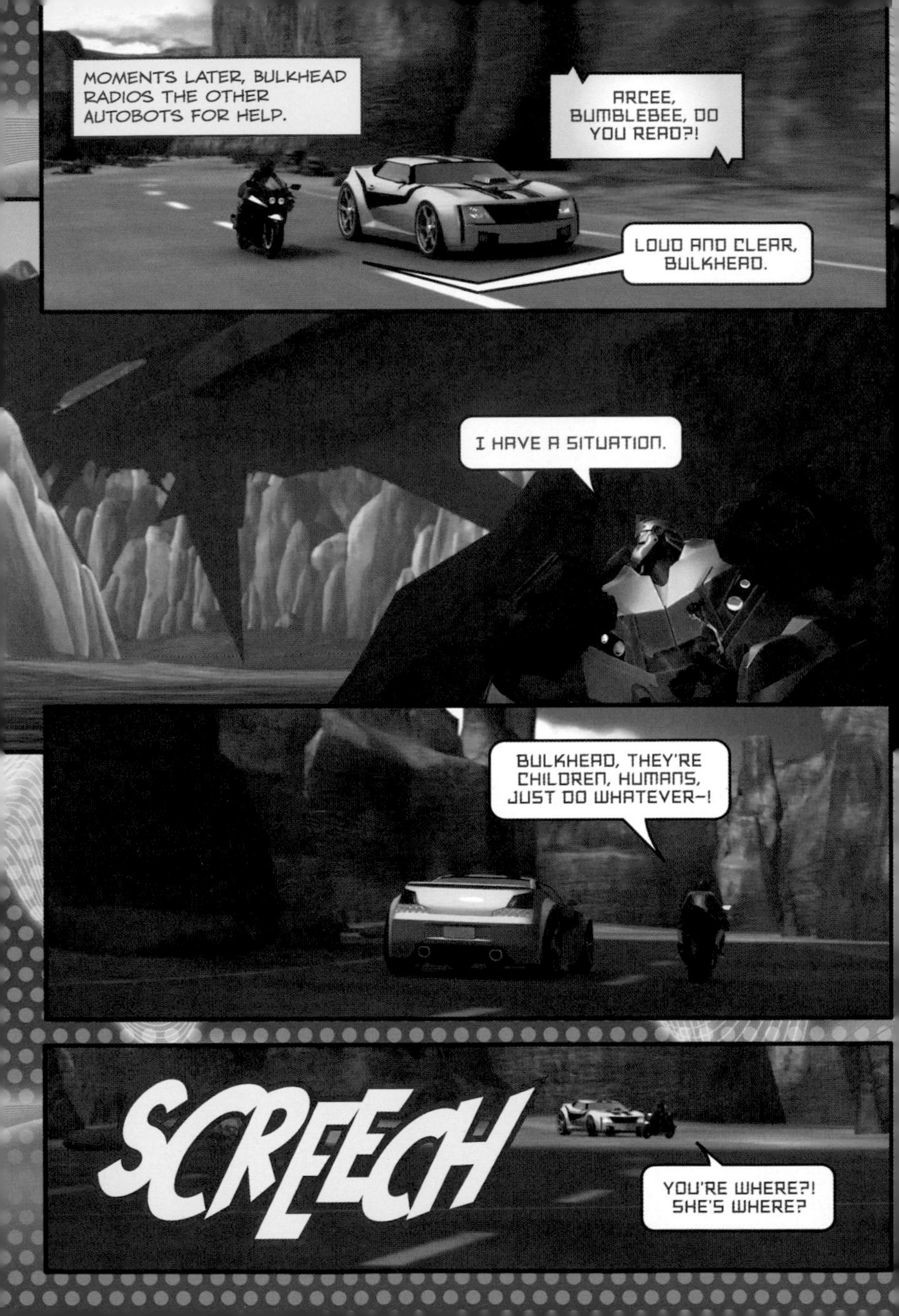
MOMENTS LATER, BULKHEAD RADIOS THE OTHER AUTOBOTS FOR HELP.
ARCEE, BUMBLEBEE, DO YOU READ?!
LOUD AND CLEAR, BULKHEAD.
I HAVE A SITUATION.
BULKHEAD, THEY'RE CHILDREN, HUMANS, JUST DO WHATEVER—!
SCREECH
YOU'RE WHERE?! SHE'S WHERE?

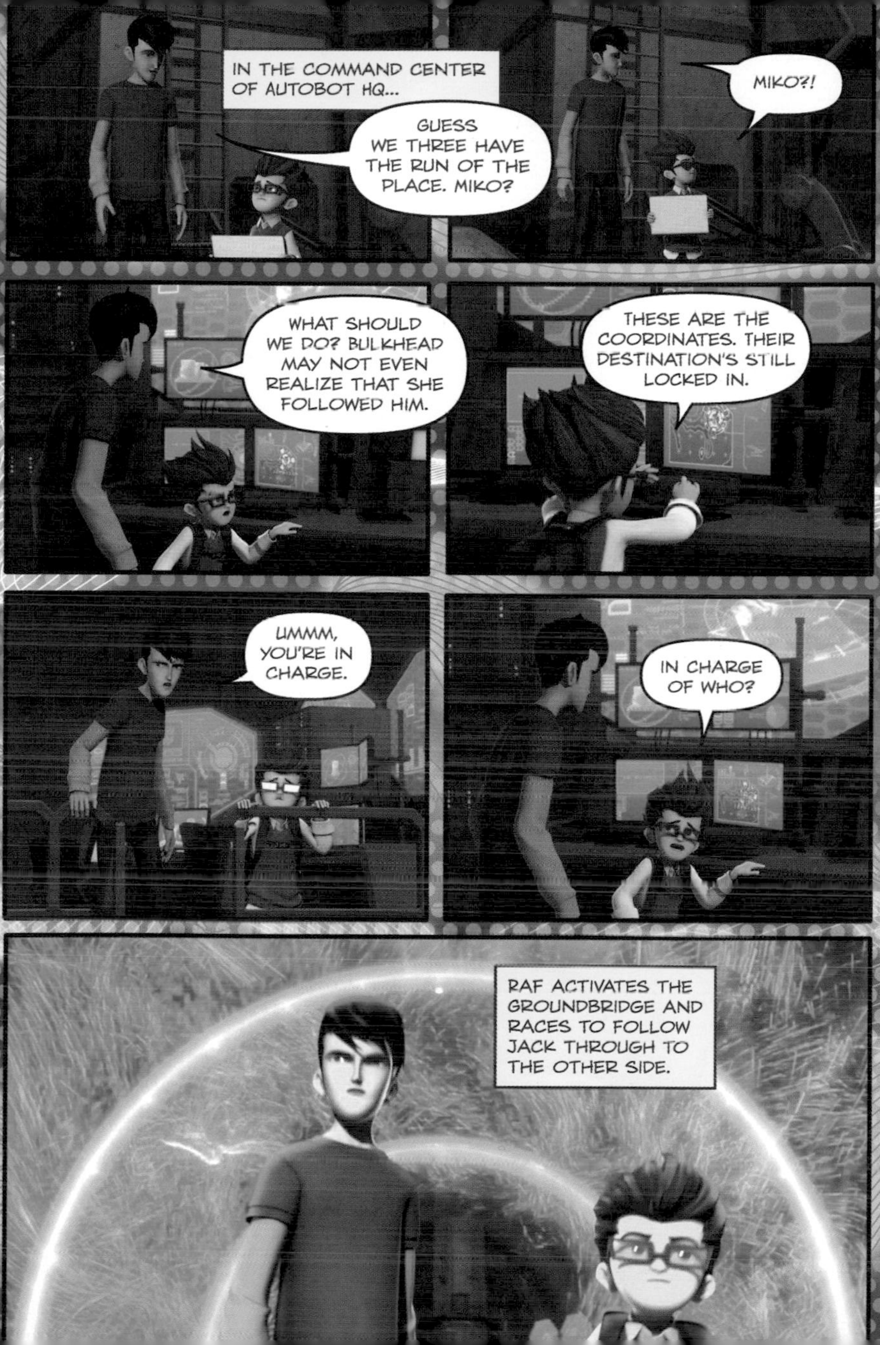
IN THE COMMAND CENTER OF AUTOBOT HQ...
GUESS WE THREE HAVE THE RUN OF THE PLACE. MIKO?
MIKO?!
WHAT SHOULD WE DO? BULKHEAD MAY NOT EVEN REALIZE THAT SHE FOLLOWED HIM.
THESE ARE THE COORDINATES. THEIR DESTINATION'S STILL LOCKED IN.
UMMM, YOU'RE IN CHARGE.
IN CHARGE OF WHO?
RAF ACTIVATES THE GROUNDBRIDGE AND RACES TO FOLLOW JACK THROUGH TO THE OTHER SIDE.

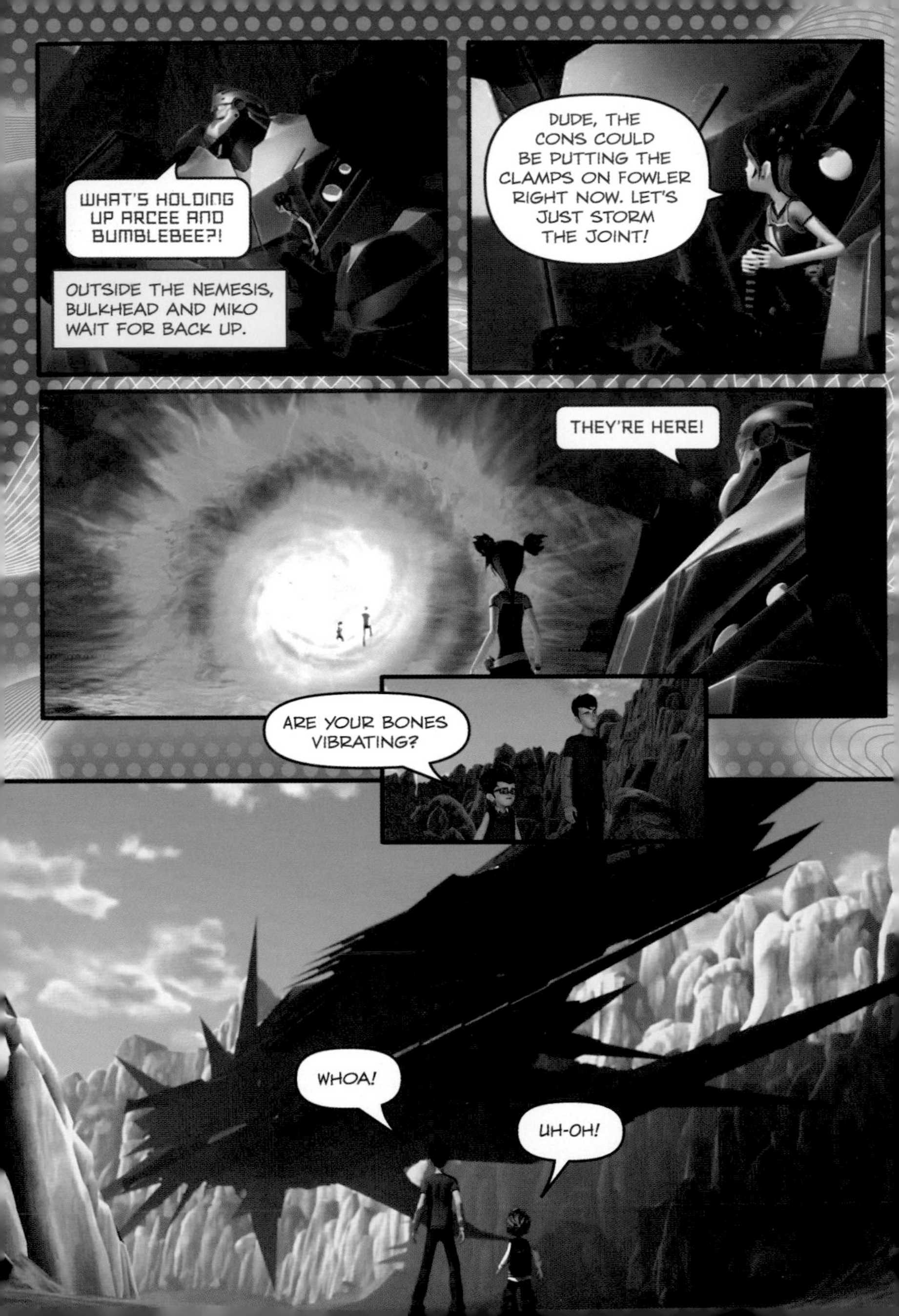
OUTSIDE THE NEMESIS, BULKHEAD AND MIKO WAIT FOR BACK UP.
WHAT'S HOLDING UP ARCEE AND BUMBLEBEE?!
DUDE, THE CONS COULD BE PUTTING THE CLAMPS ON FOWLER RIGHT NOW. LET'S JUST STORM THE JOINT!
THEY'RE HERE!
ARE YOUR BONES VIBRATING?
WHOA!
UH-OH!

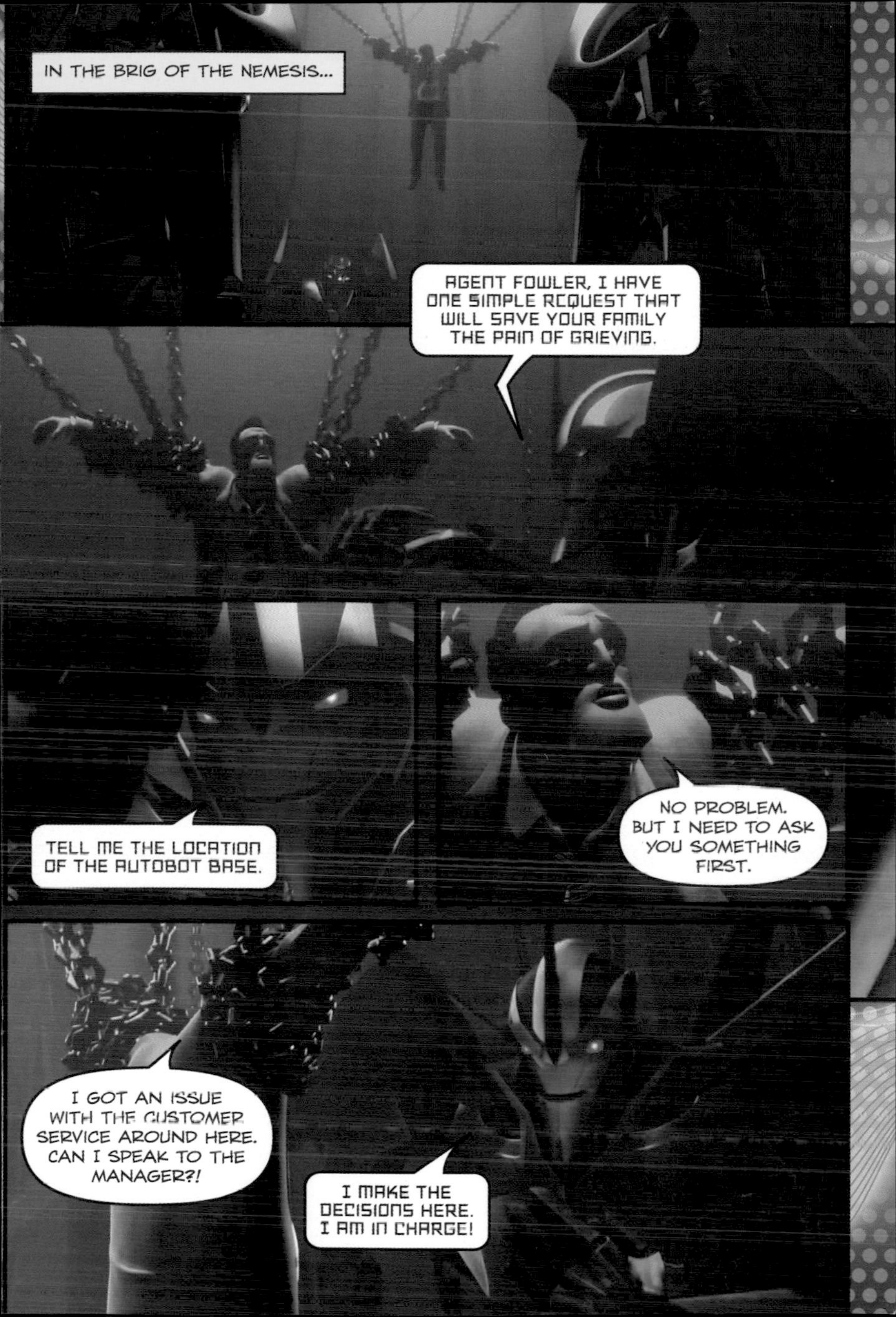
IN THE BRIG OF THE NEMESIS...
AGENT FOWLER, I HAVE ONE SIMPLE REQUEST THAT WILL SAVE YOUR FAMILY THE PAIN OF GRIEVING.
TELL ME THE LOCATION OF THE AUTOBOT BASE.
NO PROBLEM. BUT I NEED TO ASK YOU SOMETHING FIRST.
I GOT AN ISSUE WITH THE CUSTOMER SERVICE AROUND HERE. CAN I SPEAK TO THE MANAGER?!
I MAKE THE DECISIONS HERE. I AM IN CHARGE!

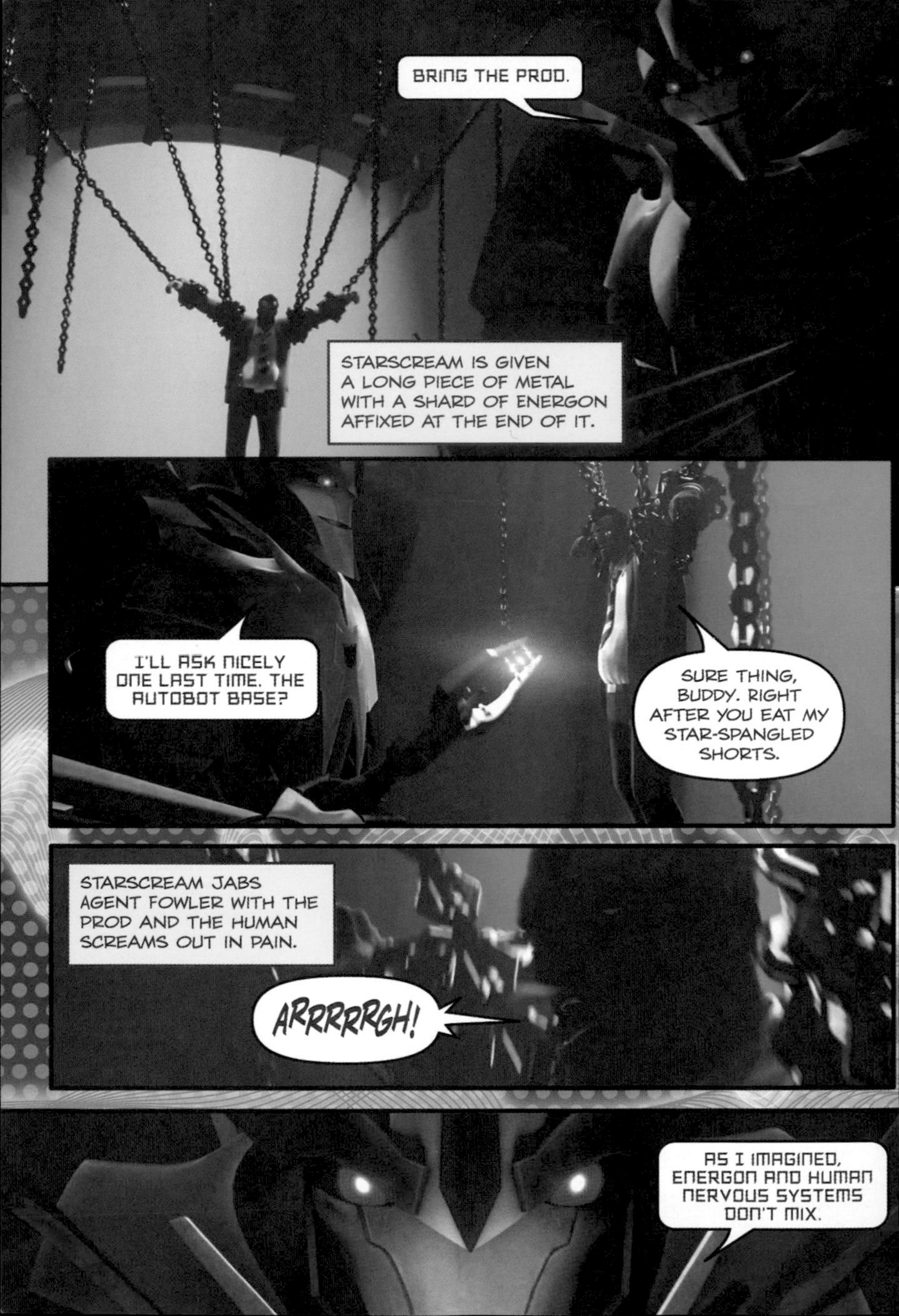
BRING THE PROD.
STARSCREAM IS GIVEN A LONG PIECE OF METAL WITH A SHARD OF ENERGON AFFIXED AT THE END OF IT.
I'LL ASK NICELY ONE LAST TIME. THE AUTOBOT BASE?
SURE THING, BUDDY. RIGHT AFTER YOU EAT MY STAR-SPANGLED SHORTS.
STARSCREAM JABS AGENT FOWLER WITH THE PROD AND THE HUMAN SCREAMS OUT IN PAIN.
ARRRRRGH!
AS I IMAGINED, ENERGON AND HUMAN NERVOUS SYSTEMS DON'T MIX.

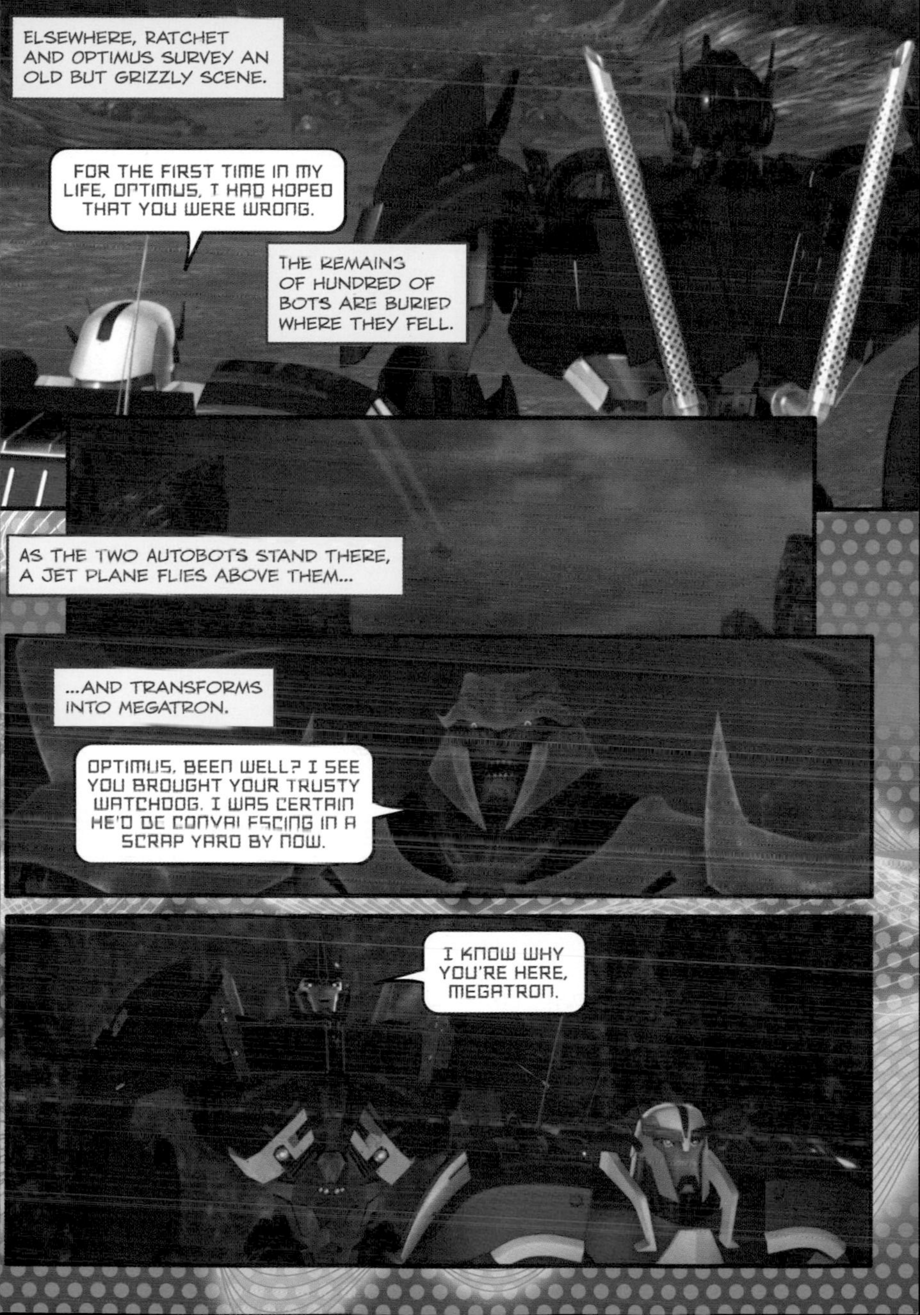

ELSEWHERE, RATCHET AND OPTIMUS SURVEY AN OLD BUT GRIZZLY SCENE.
FOR THE FIRST TIME IN MY LIFE, OPTIMUS, I HAD HOPED THAT YOU WERE WRONG.
THE REMAINS OF HUNDRED OF BOTS ARE BURIED WHERE THEY FELL.
AS THE TWO AUTOBOTS STAND THERE, A JET PLANE FLIES ABOVE THEM...
...AND TRANSFORMS INTO MEGATRON.
OPTIMUS, BEEN WELL? I SEE YOU BROUGHT YOUR TRUSTY WATCHDOG. I WAS CERTAIN HE'D BE CONVALESCING IN A SCRAP YARD BY NOW.
I KNOW WHY YOU'RE HERE, MEGATRON.

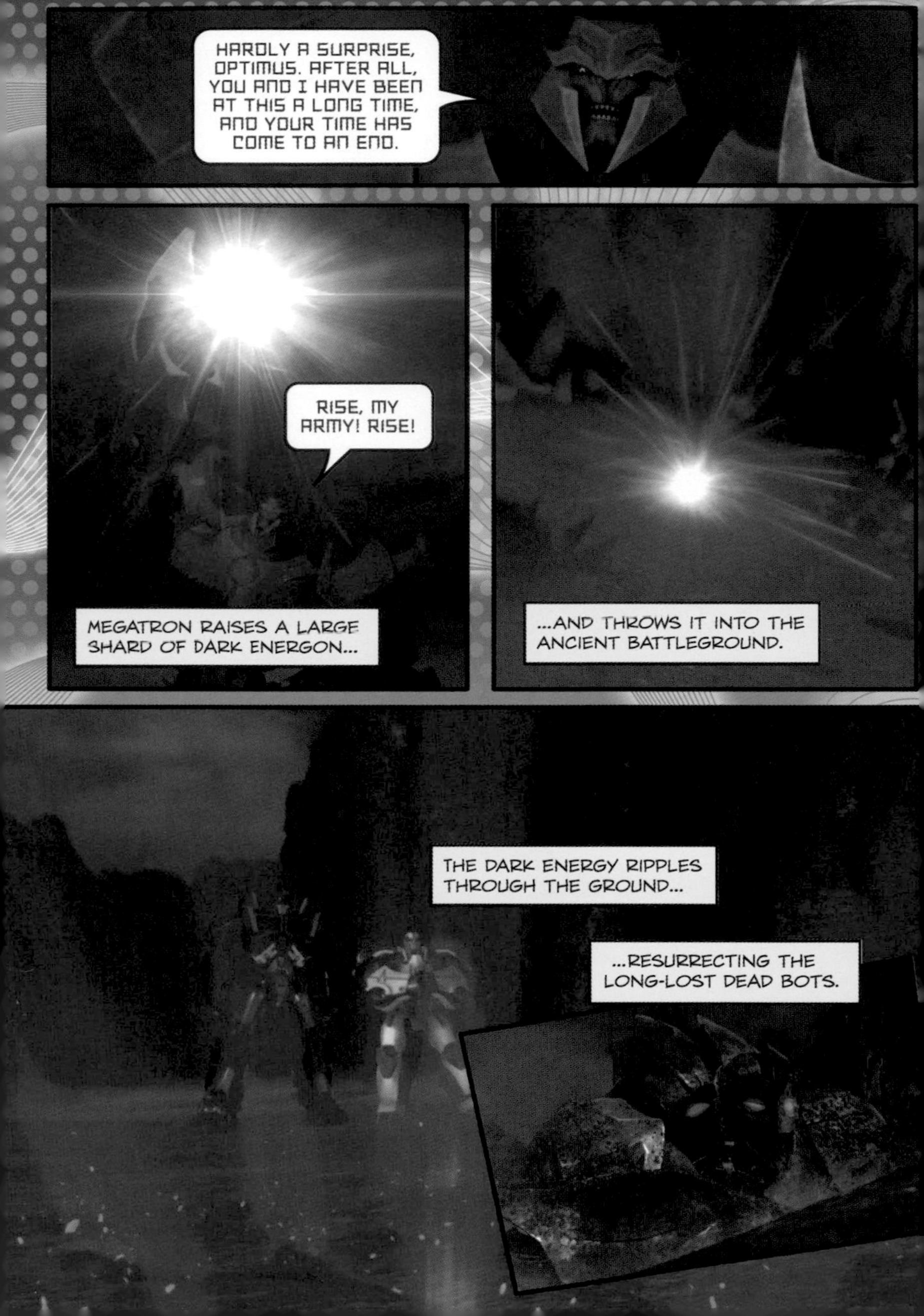
HARDLY A SURPRISE, OPTIMUS. AFTER ALL, YOU AND I HAVE BEEN AT THIS A LONG TIME, AND YOUR TIME HAS COME TO AN END.
RISE, MY ARMY! RISE!
MEGATRON RAISES A LARGE SHARD OF DARK ENERGON...
...AND THROWS IT INTO THE ANCIENT BATTLEGROUND.
THE DARK ENERGY RIPPLES THROUGH THE GROUND...
...RESURRECTING THE LONG-LOST DEAD BOTS.

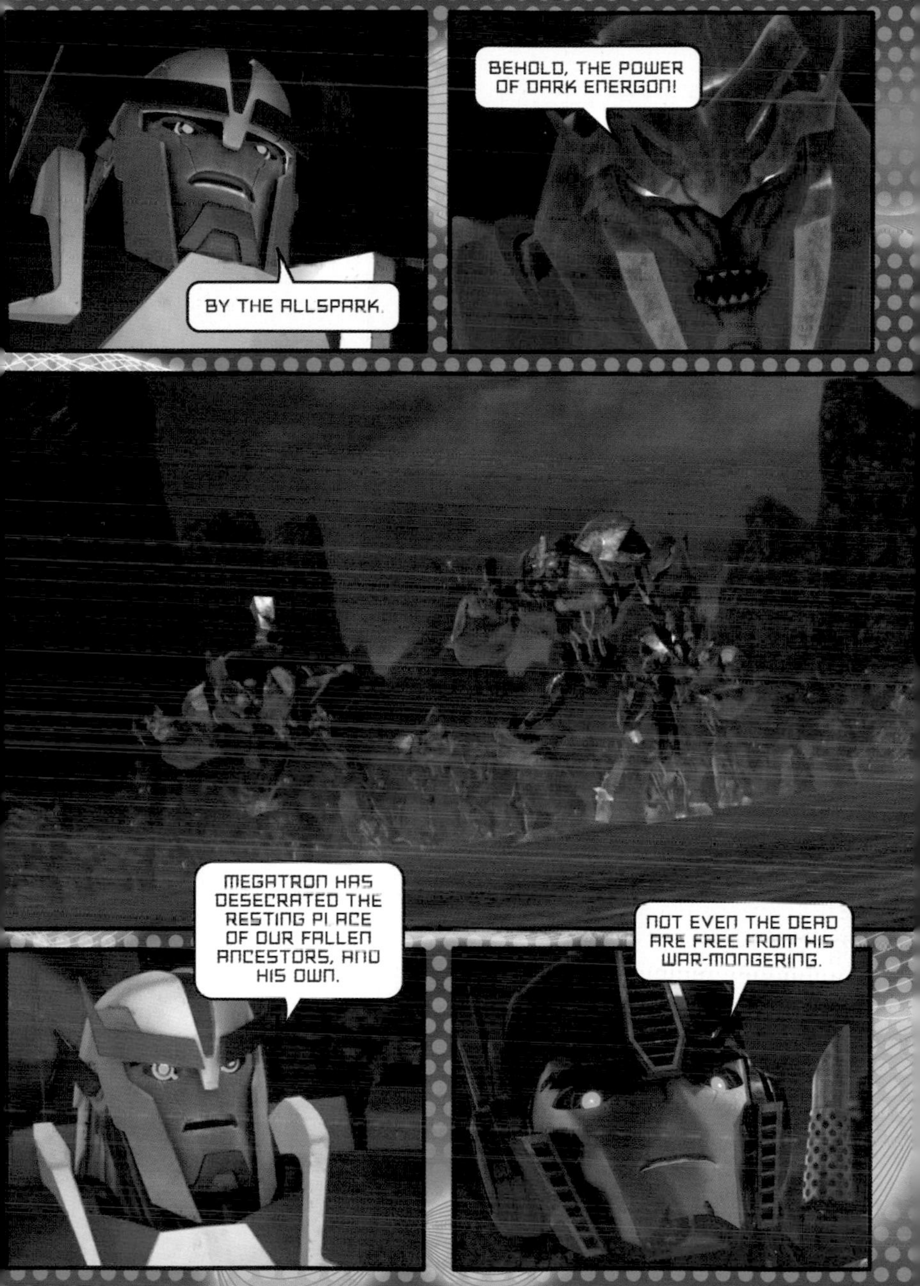
BY THE ALLSPARK.
BEHOLD, THE POWER OF DARK ENERGON!
MEGATRON HAS DESECRATED THE RESTING PLACE OF OUR FALLEN ANCESTORS, AND HIS OWN.
NOT EVEN THE DEAD ARE FREE FROM HIS WAR-MONGERING.

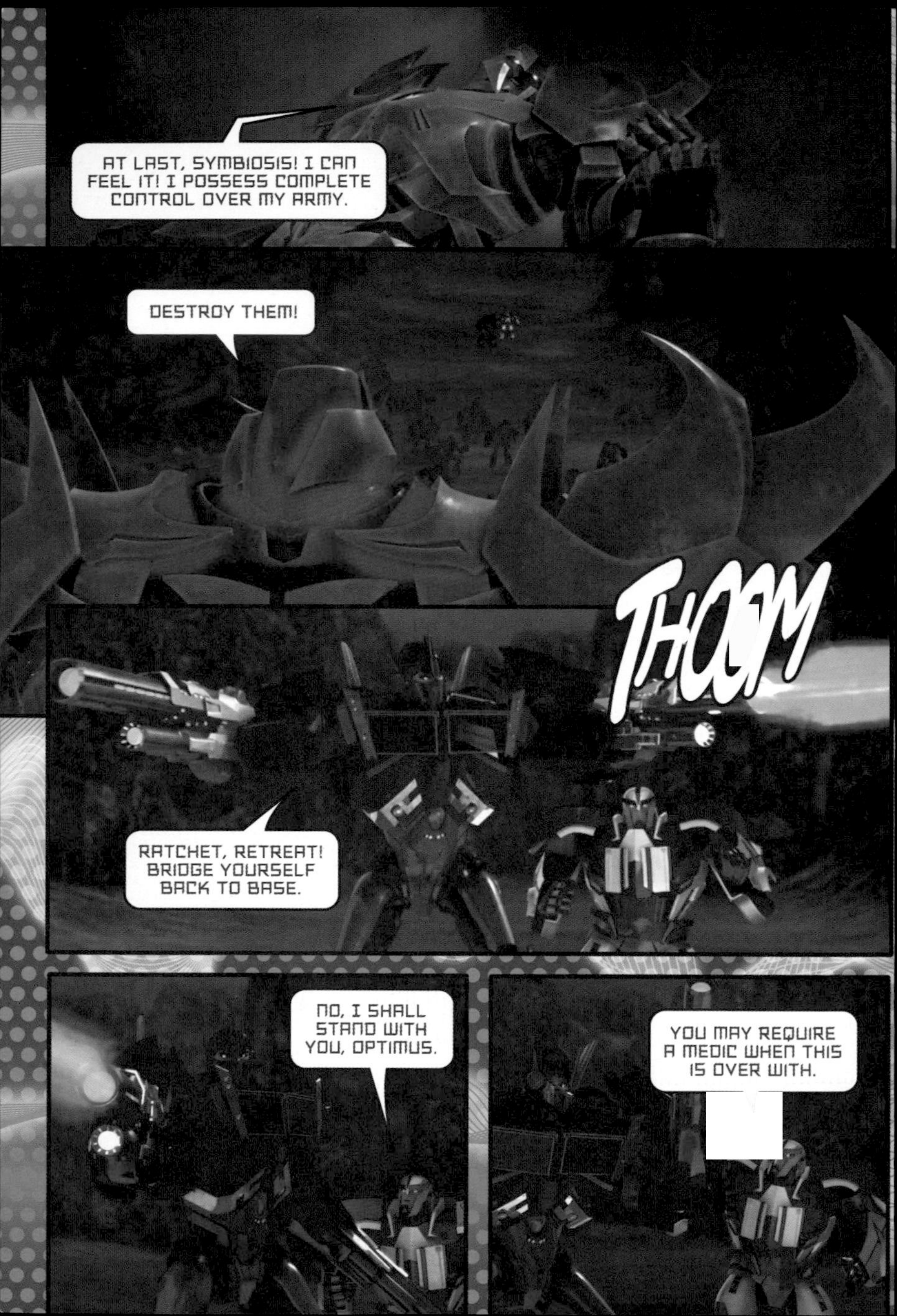
AT LAST, SYMBIOSIS! I CAN FEEL IT! I POSSESS COMPLETE CONTROL OVER MY ARMY.
DESTROY THEM!
THOOM
RATCHET, RETREAT! BRIDGE YOURSELF BACK TO BASE.
NO, I SHALL STAND WITH YOU, OPTIMUS.
YOU MAY REQUIRE A MEDIC WHEN THIS IS OVER WITH.

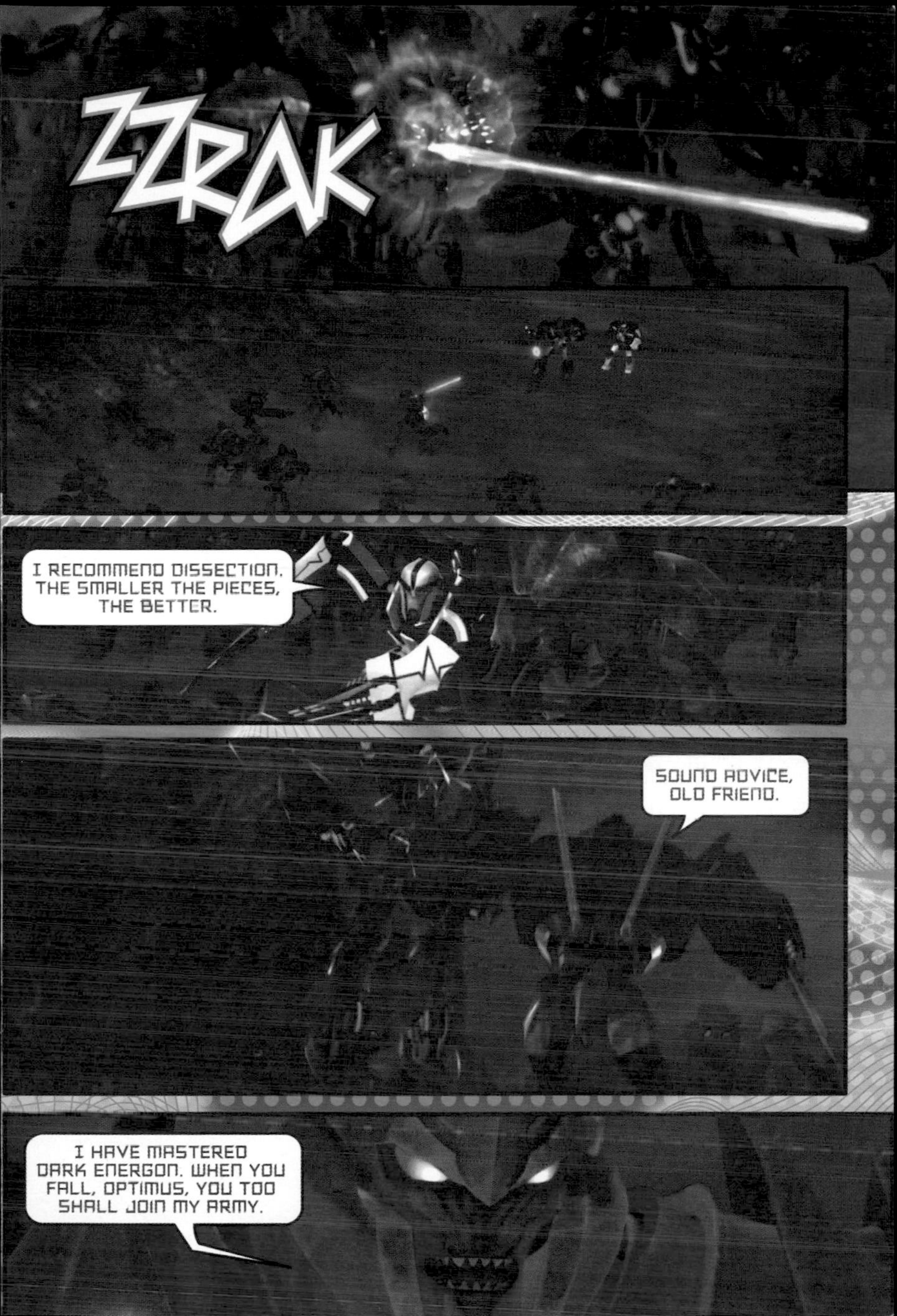
ZZRAK
I RECOMMEND DISSECTION. THE SMALLER THE PIECES, THE BETTER.
SOUND ADVICE, OLD FRIEND.
I HAVE MASTERED DARK ENERGON. WHEN YOU FALL, OPTIMUS, YOU TOO SHALL JOIN MY ARMY.

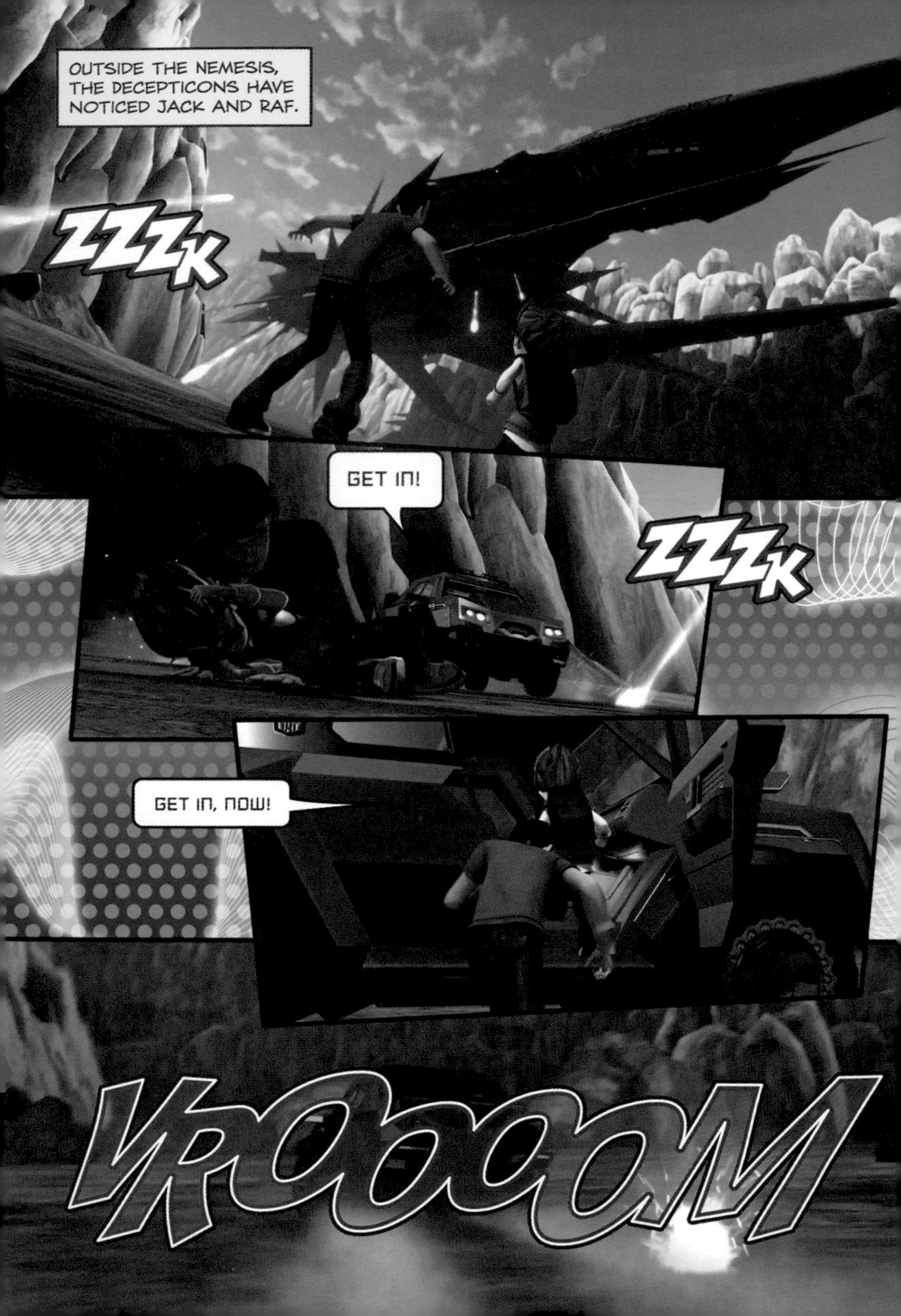
OUTSIDE THE NEMESIS, THE DECEPTICONS HAVE NOTICED JACK AND RAF.
ZZZK
GET IN!
ZZZK
GET IN, NOW!
VROOOOM

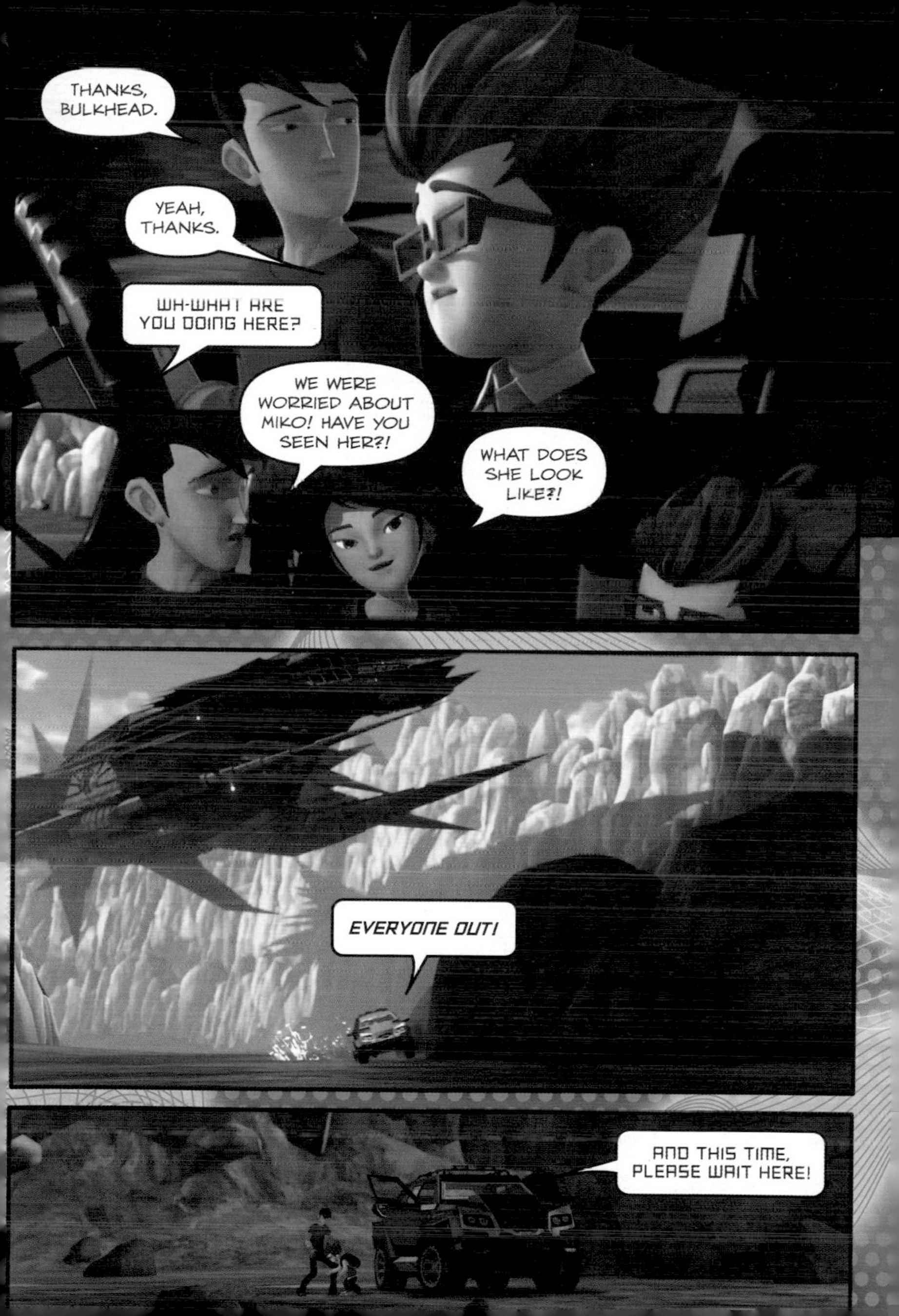
THANKS, BULKHEAD.
YEAH, THANKS.
WH-WHAT ARE YOU DOING HERE?
WE WERE WORRIED ABOUT MIKO! HAVE YOU SEEN HER?!
WHAT DOES SHE LOOK LIKE?!
EVERYONE OUT!
AND THIS TIME, PLEASE WAIT HERE!

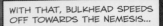

WITH THAT, BULKHEAD SPEEDS OFF TOWARDS THE NEMESIS...

VVRRR

...HE JUMPS ONTO A CLIFF NEXT TO THE SHIP...

...AND CLIMBS ONTO THE NOSE.

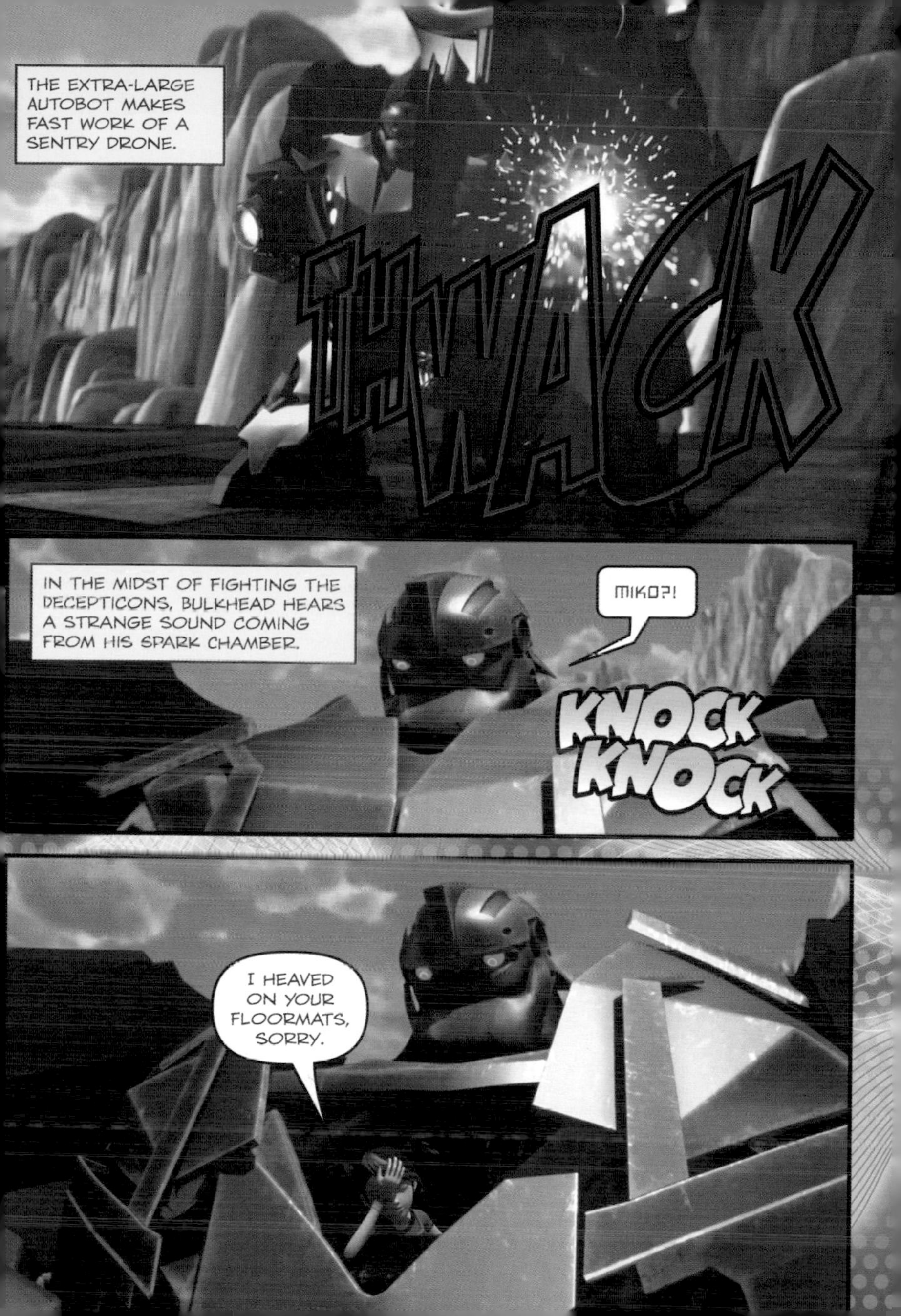
THE EXTRA-LARGE AUTOBOT MAKES FAST WORK OF A SENTRY DRONE.
THWACK
IN THE MIDST OF FIGHTING THE DECEPTICONS, BULKHEAD HEARS A STRANGE SOUND COMING FROM HIS SPARK CHAMBER.
MIKO?!
KNOCK KNOCK
I HEAVED ON YOUR FLOORMATS, SORRY.

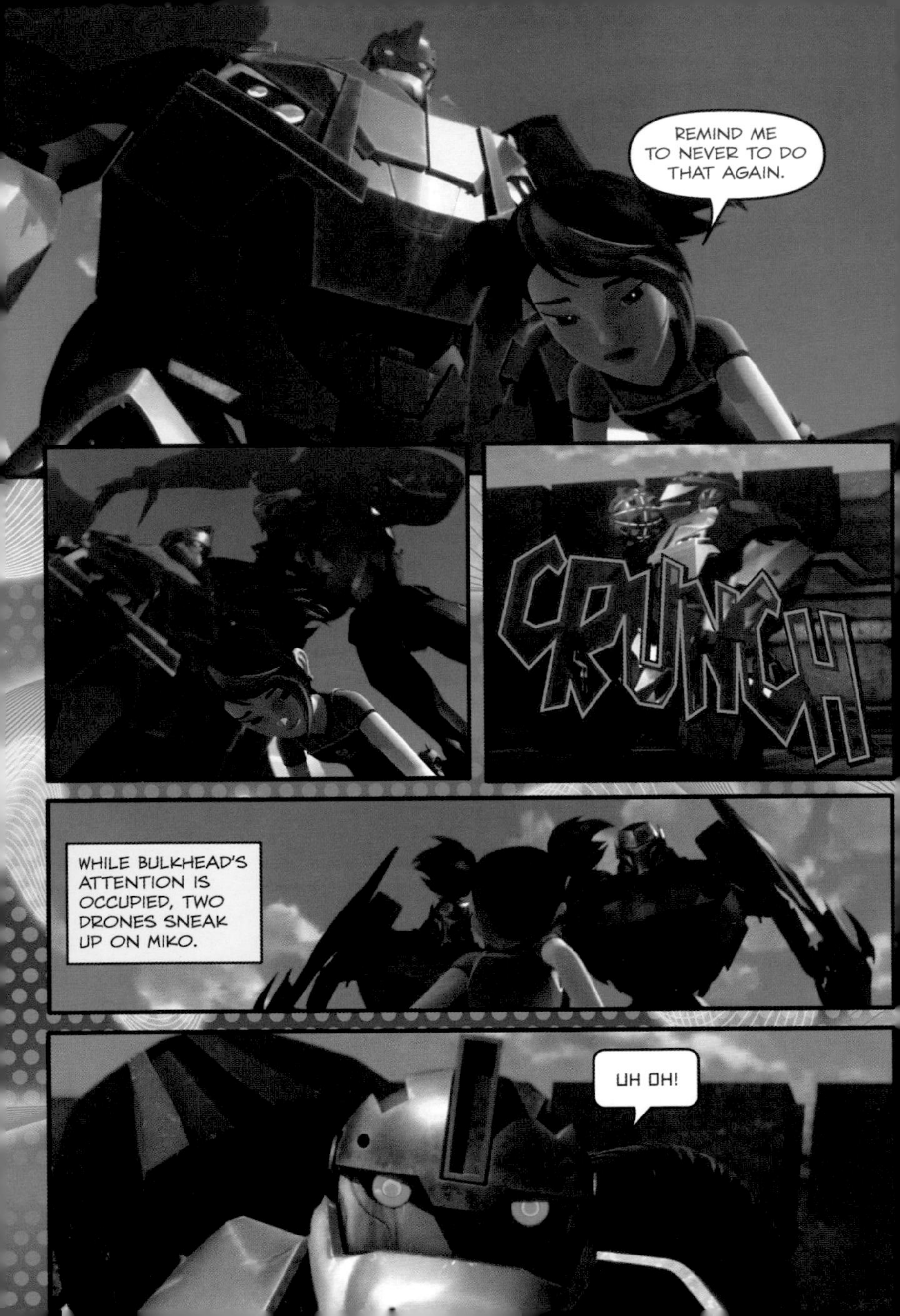
REMIND ME TO NEVER TO DO THAT AGAIN.
CRUNCH
WHILE BULKHEAD'S ATTENTION IS OCCUPIED, TWO DRONES SNEAK UP ON MIKO.
UH OH!

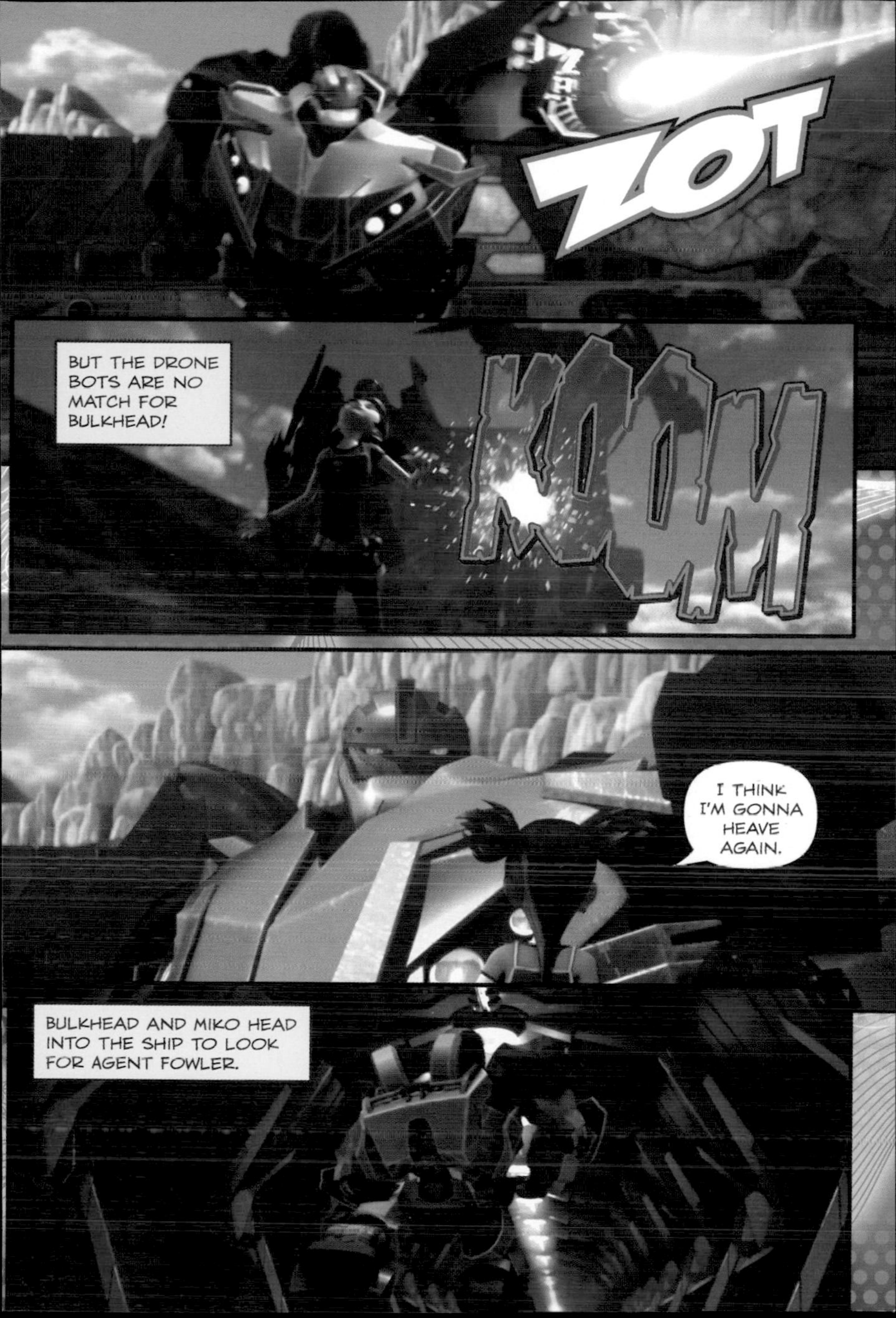
ZOT
BUT THE DRONE BOTS ARE NO MATCH FOR BULKHEAD!
KOOM
I THINK I'M GONNA HEAVE AGAIN.
BULKHEAD AND MIKO HEAD INTO THE SHIP TO LOOK FOR AGENT FOWLER.

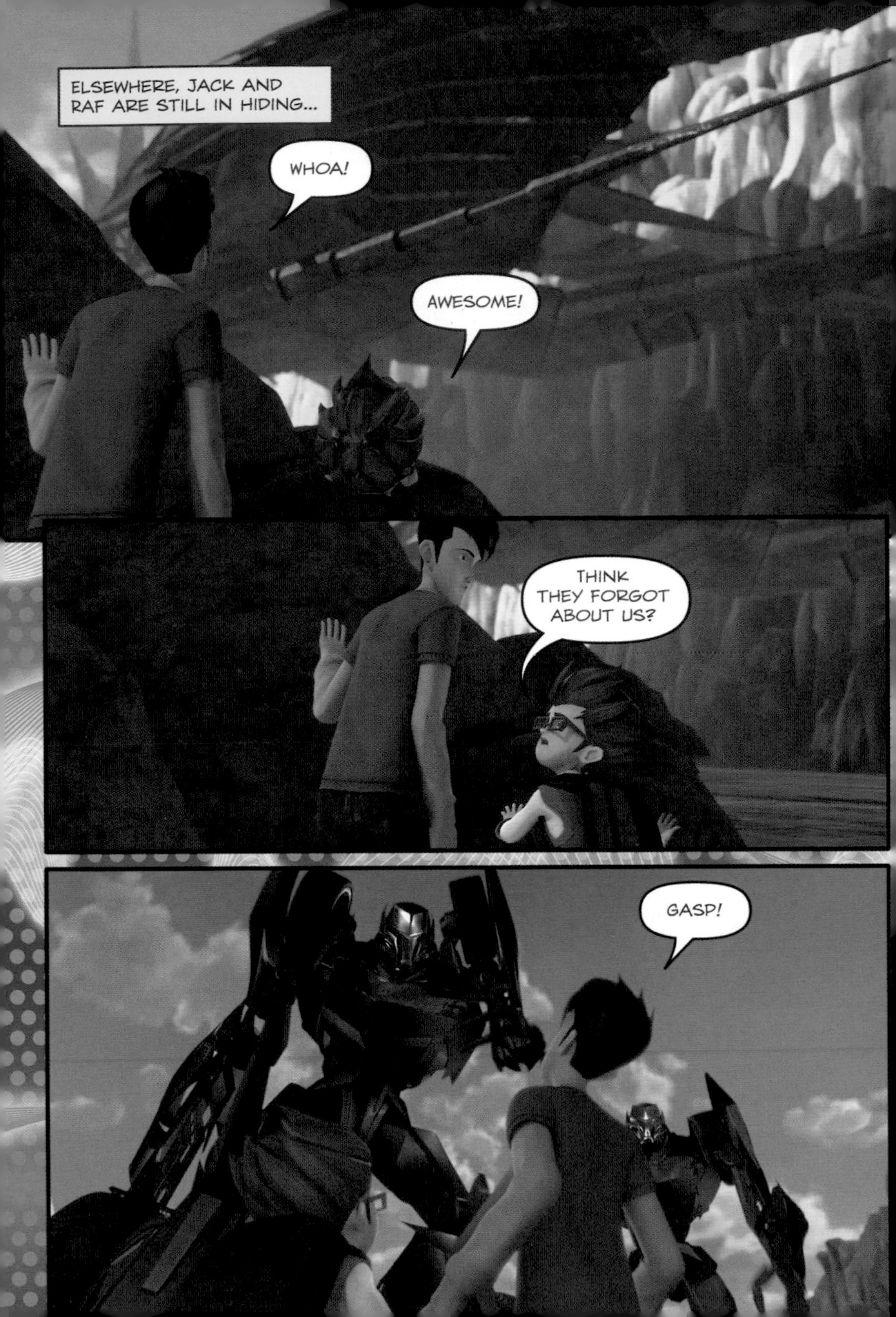
ELSEWHERE, JACK AND RAF ARE STILL IN HIDING...
WHOA!
AWESOME!
THINK THEY FORGOT ABOUT US?
GASP!

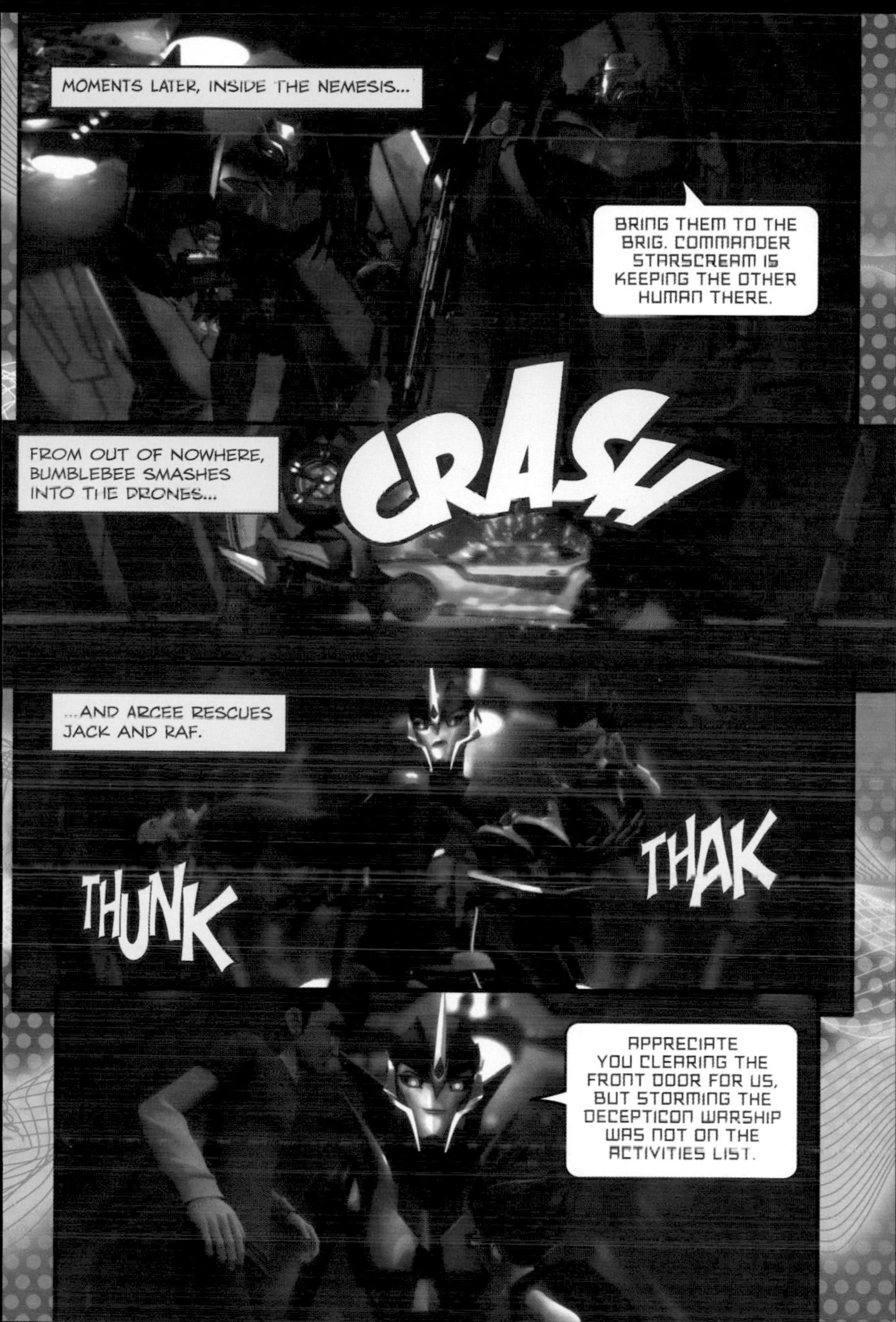

MOMENTS LATER, INSIDE THE NEMESIS...
BRING THEM TO THE BRIG. COMMANDER STARSCREAM IS KEEPING THE OTHER HUMAN THERE.
FROM OUT OF NOWHERE, BUMBLEBEE SMASHES INTO THE DRONES...
CRASH
...AND ARCEE RESCUES JACK AND RAF.
THUNK
THAK
APPRECIATE YOU CLEARING THE FRONT DOOR FOR US, BUT STORMING THE DECEPTICON WARSHIP WAS NOT ON THE ACTIVITIES LIST.

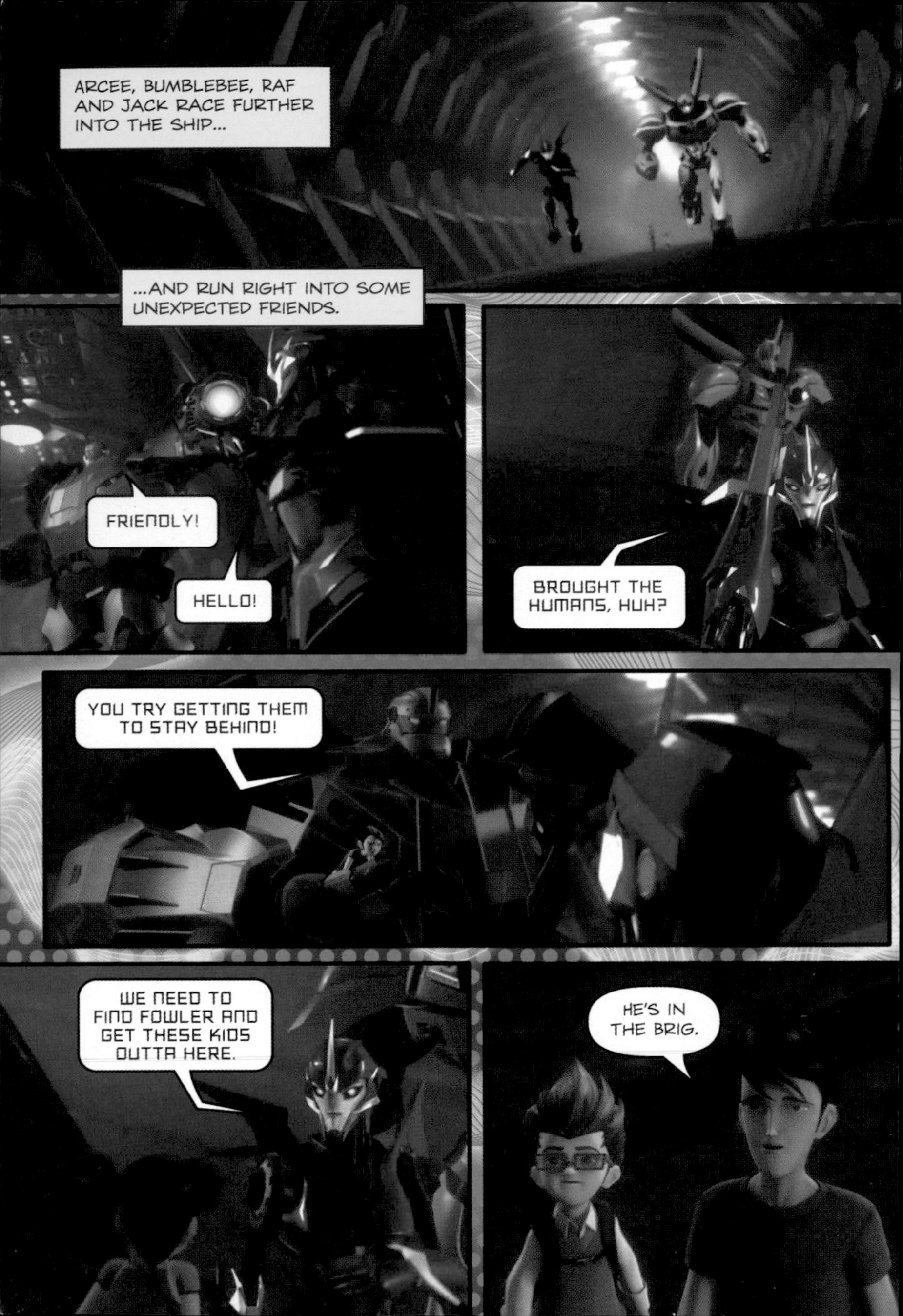

ARCEE, BUMBLEBEE, RAF AND JACK RACE FURTHER INTO THE SHIP...
...AND RUN RIGHT INTO SOME UNEXPECTED FRIENDS.
FRIENDLY!
HELLO!
BROUGHT THE HUMANS, HUH?
YOU TRY GETTING THEM TO STAY BEHIND!
WE NEED TO FIND FOWLER AND GET THESE KIDS OUTTA HERE.
HE'S IN THE BRIG.

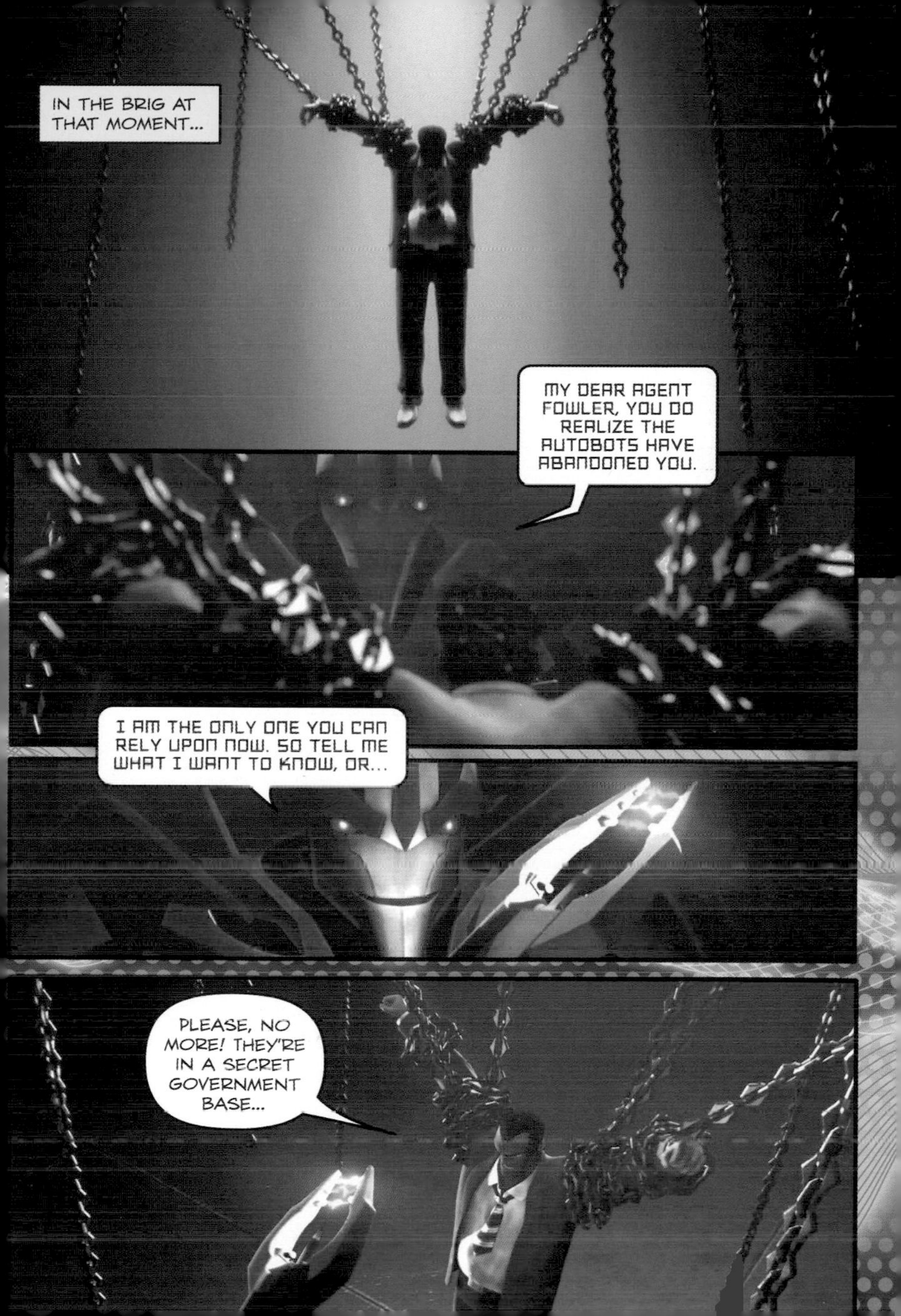
IN THE BRIG AT THAT MOMENT...
MY DEAR AGENT FOWLER, YOU DO REALIZE THE AUTOBOTS HAVE ABANDONED YOU.
I AM THE ONLY ONE YOU CAN RELY UPON NOW. SO TELL ME WHAT I WANT TO KNOW, OR...
PLEASE, NO MORE! THEY'RE IN A SECRET GOVERNMENT BASE...

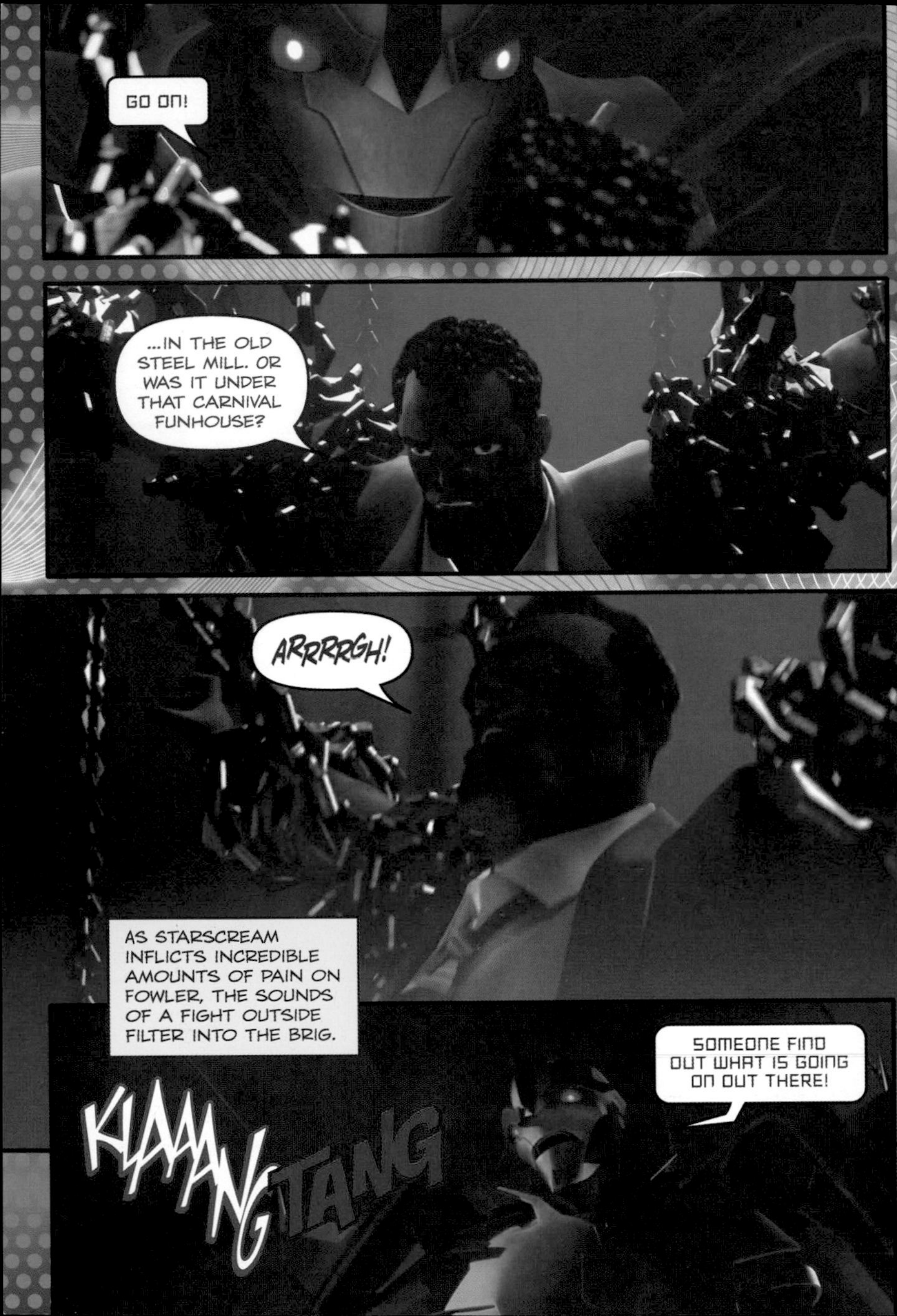
GO ON!
...IN THE OLD STEEL MILL. OR WAS IT UNDER THAT CARNIVAL FUNHOUSE?
ARRRRGH!
AS STARSCREAM INFLICTS INCREDIBLE AMOUNTS OF PAIN ON FOWLER, THE SOUNDS OF A FIGHT OUTSIDE FILTER INTO THE BRIG.
KLAAANG
TANG
SOMEONE FIND OUT WHAT IS GOING ON OUT THERE!

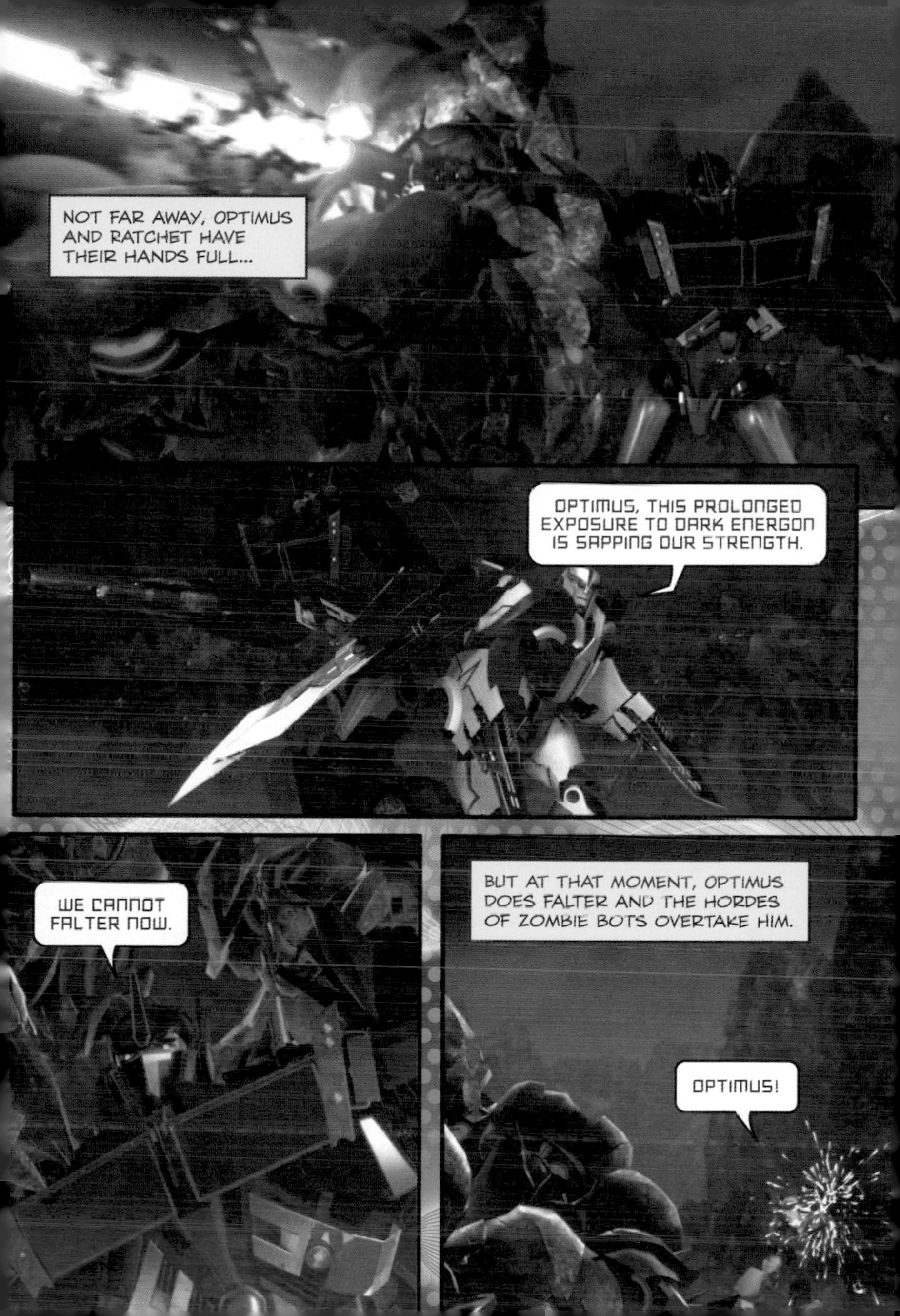
NOT FAR AWAY, OPTIMUS AND RATCHET HAVE THEIR HANDS FULL...
OPTIMUS, THIS PROLONGED EXPOSURE TO DARK ENERGON IS SAPPING OUR STRENGTH.
WE CANNOT FALTER NOW.
BUT AT THAT MOMENT, OPTIMUS DOES FALTER AND THE HORDES OF ZOMBIE BOTS OVERTAKE HIM.
OPTIMUS!

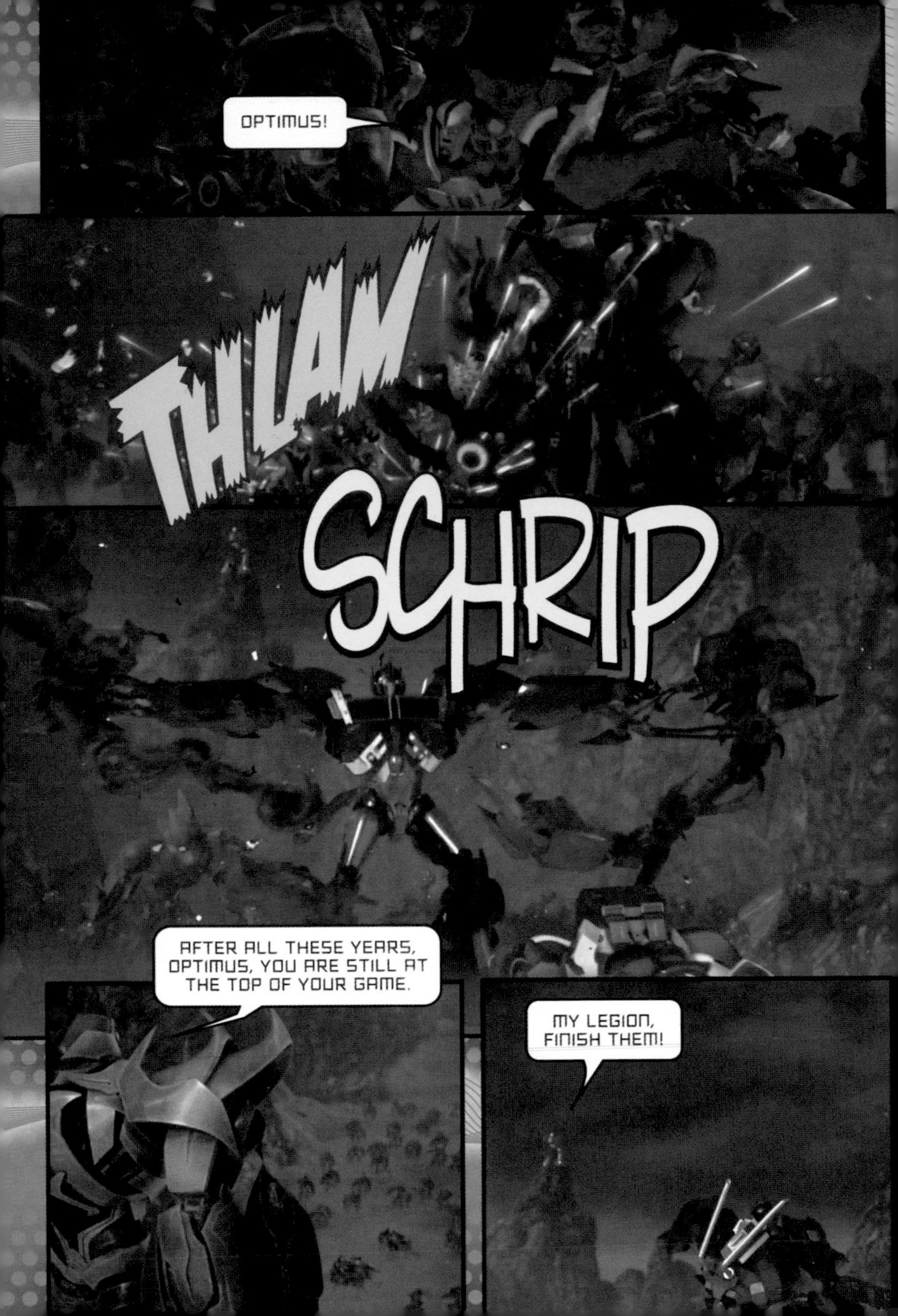
OPTIMUS!
THLAM
SCHRIP
AFTER ALL THESE YEARS, OPTIMUS, YOU ARE STILL AT THE TOP OF YOUR GAME.
MY LEGION, FINISH THEM!

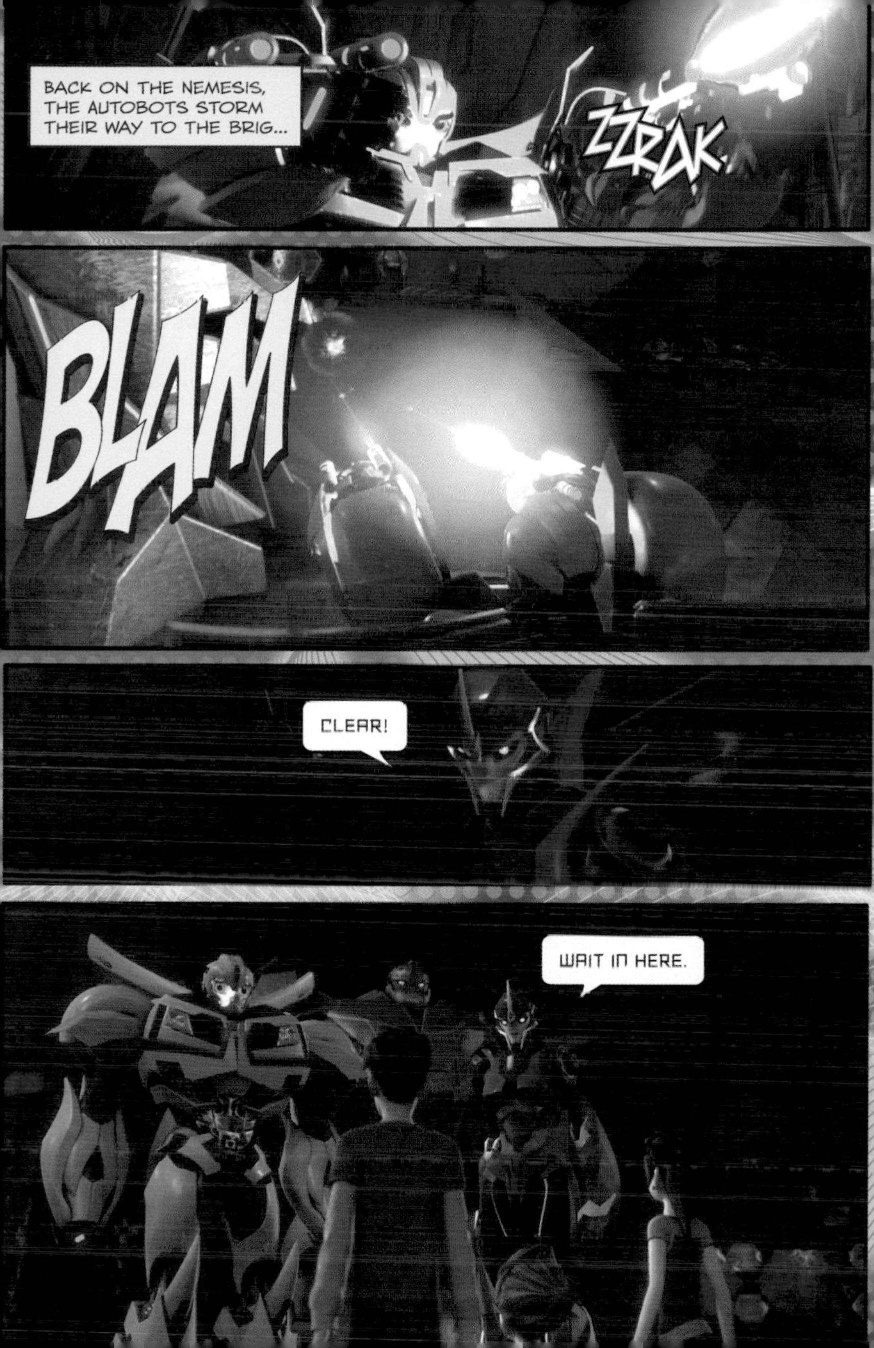
BACK ON THE NEMESIS, THE AUTOBOTS STORM THEIR WAY TO THE BRIG...
ZZRAK
BLAM
CLEAR!
WAIT IN HERE.

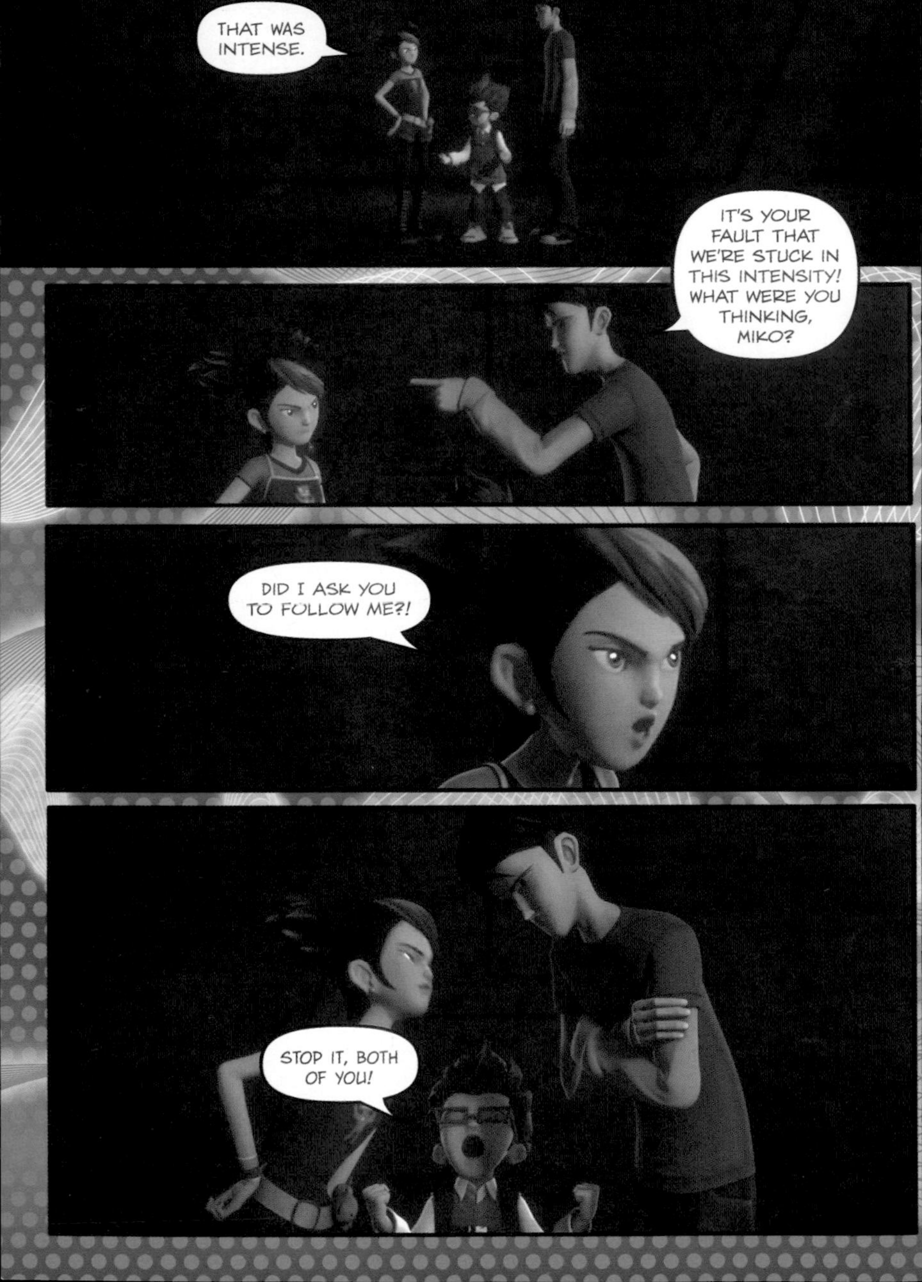
THAT WAS INTENSE.
IT'S YOUR FAULT THAT WE'RE STUCK IN THIS INTENSITY! WHAT WERE YOU THINKING, MIKO?
DID I ASK YOU TO FOLLOW ME?!
STOP IT, BOTH OF YOU!

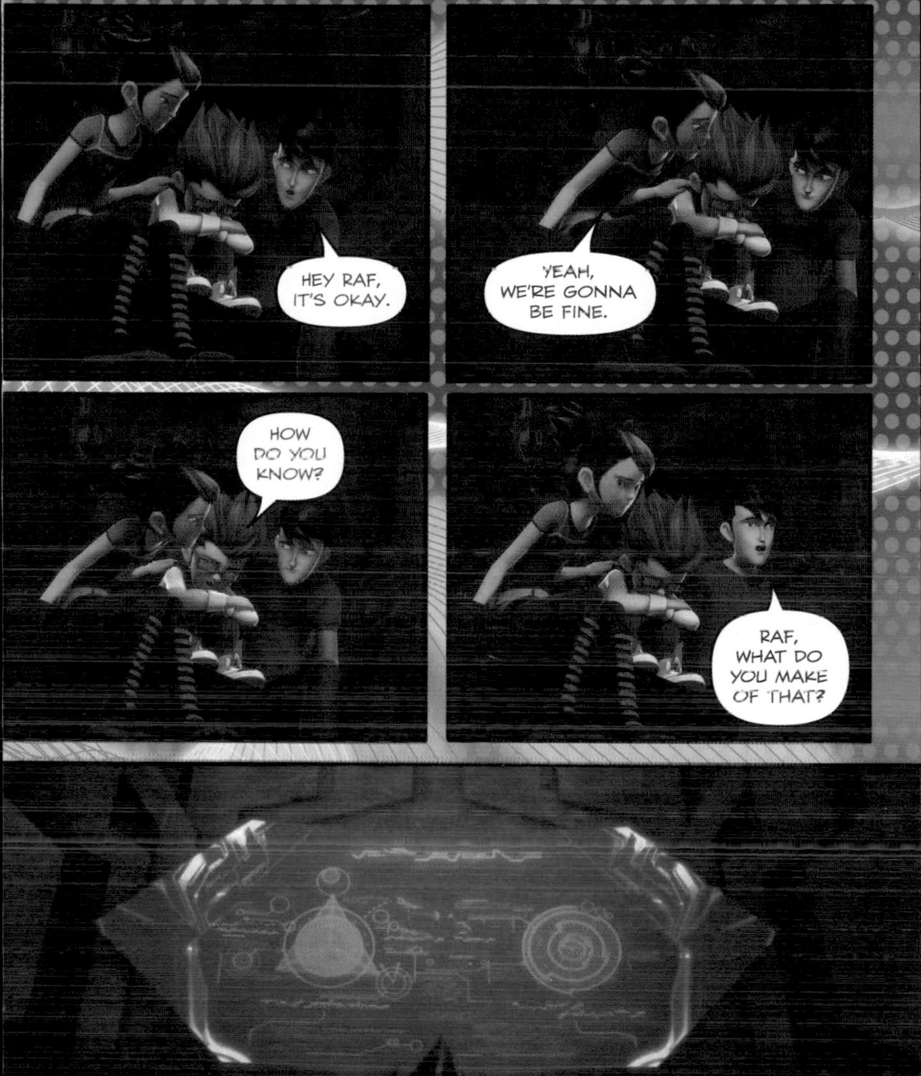
HEY RAF, IT'S OKAY.
YEAH, WE'RE GONNA BE FINE.
HOW DO YOU KNOW?
RAF, WHAT DO YOU MAKE OF THAT?

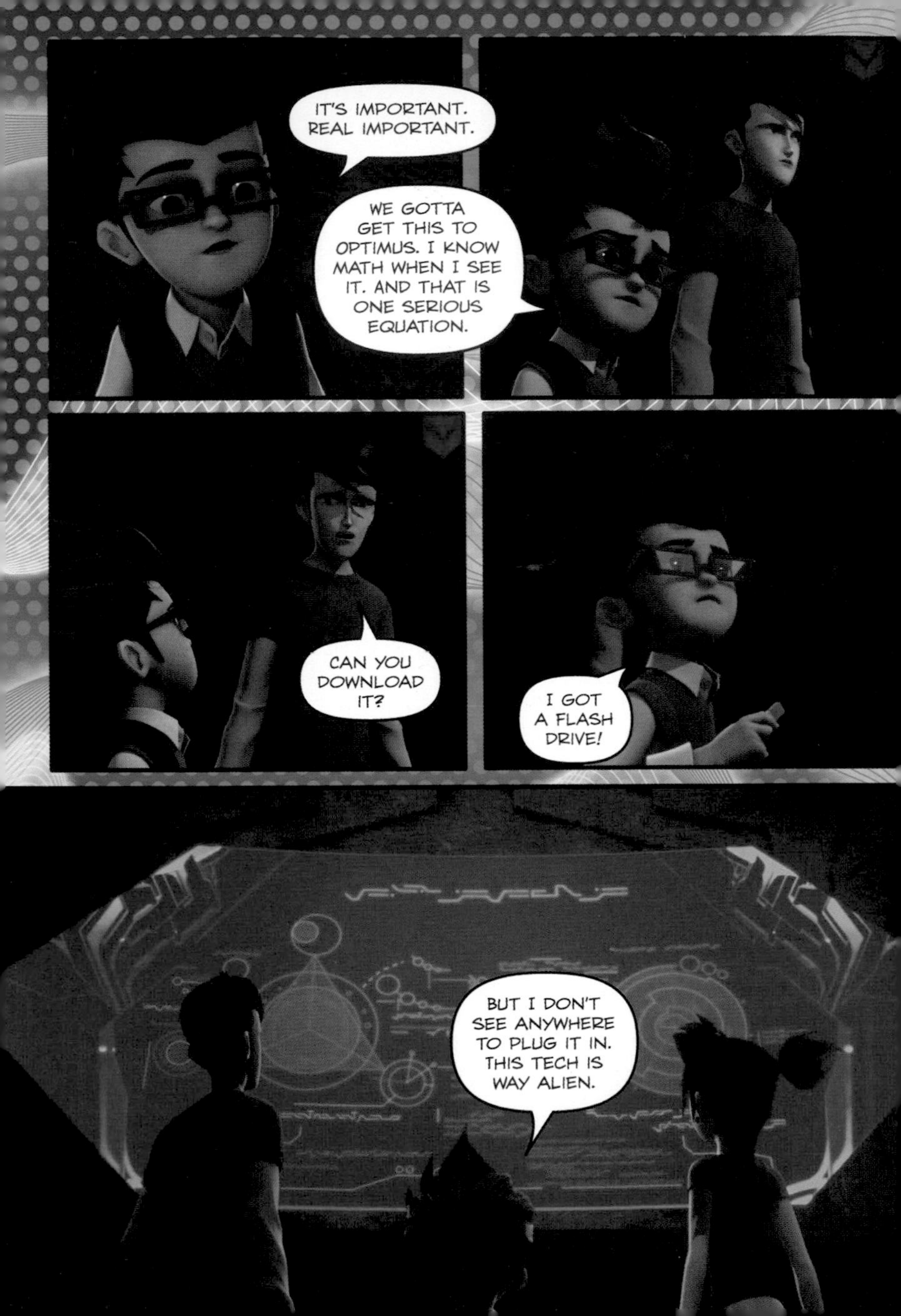
IT'S IMPORTANT. REAL IMPORTANT.
WE GOTTA GET THIS TO OPTIMUS. I KNOW MATH WHEN I SEE IT. AND THAT IS ONE SERIOUS EQUATION.
CAN YOU DOWNLOAD IT?
I GOT A FLASH DRIVE!
BUT I DON'T SEE ANYWHERE TO PLUG IT IN. THIS TECH IS WAY ALIEN.

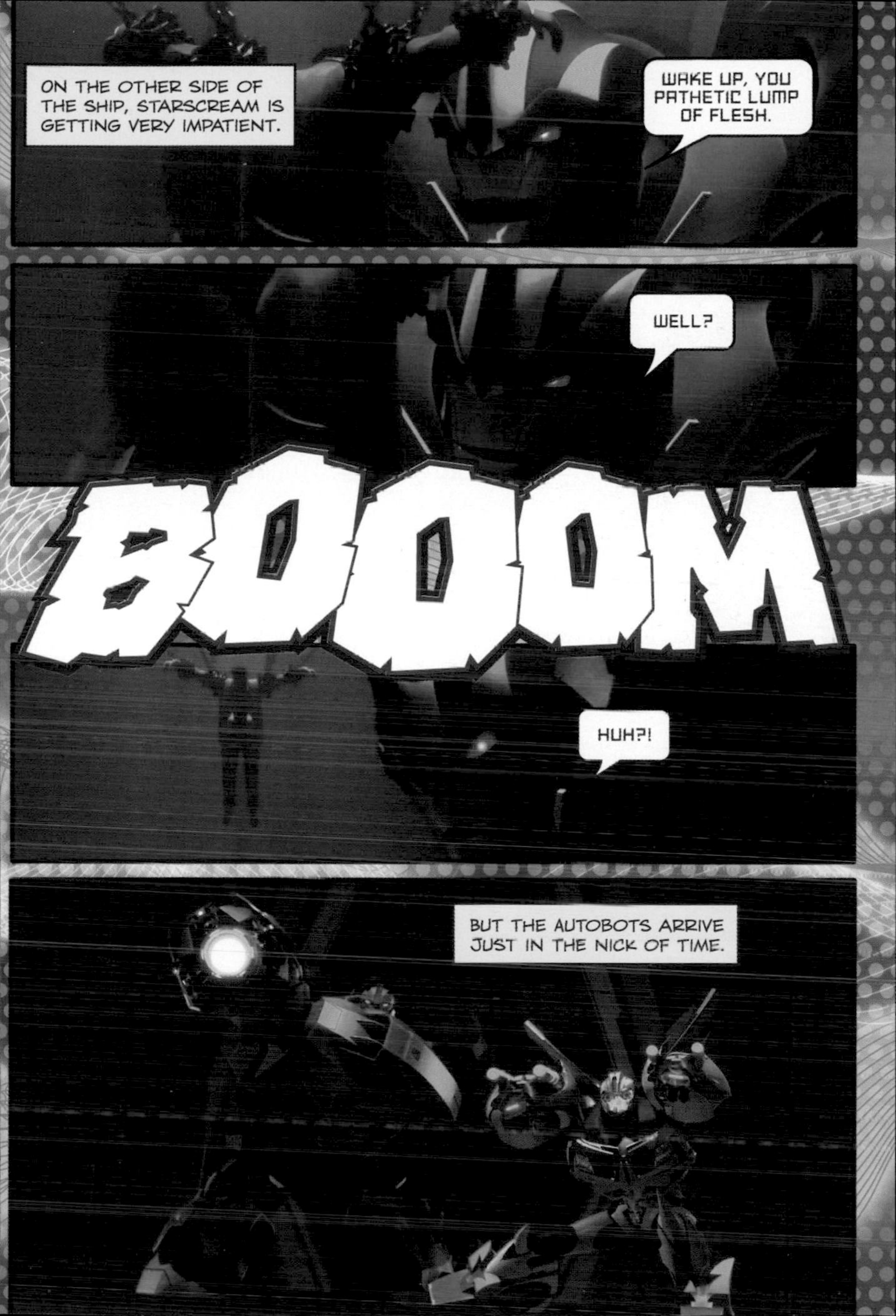
ON THE OTHER SIDE OF THE SHIP, STARSCREAM IS GETTING VERY IMPATIENT.
WAKE UP, YOU PATHETIC LUMP OF FLESH.
WELL?
BOOOM
HUH?!
BUT THE AUTOBOTS ARRIVE JUST IN THE NICK OF TIME.

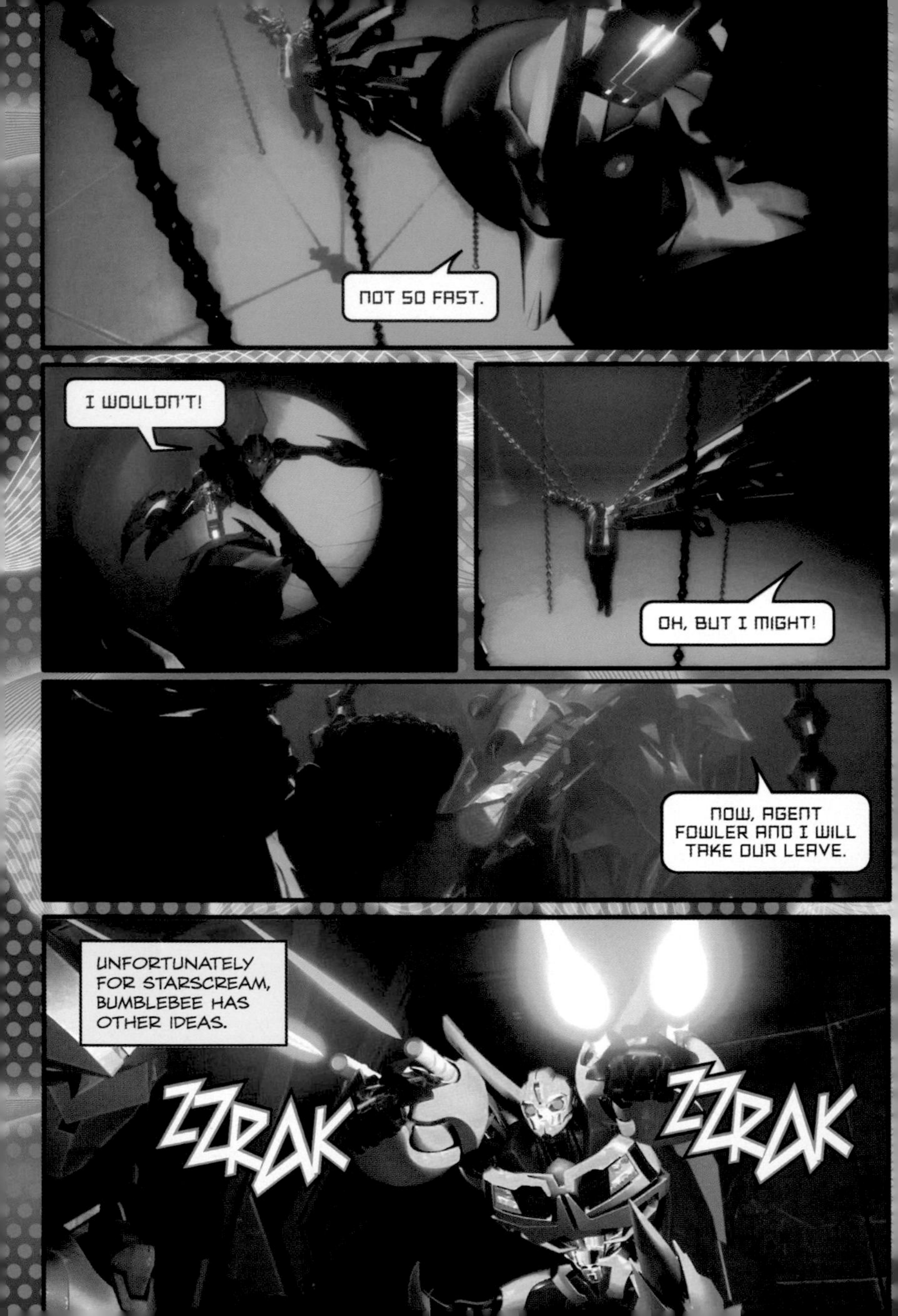
NOT SO FAST.
I WOULDN'T!
OH, BUT I MIGHT!
NOW, AGENT FOWLER AND I WILL TAKE OUR LEAVE.
UNFORTUNATELY FOR STARSCREAM, BUMBLEBEE HAS OTHER IDEAS.
ZZRAK
ZZRAK

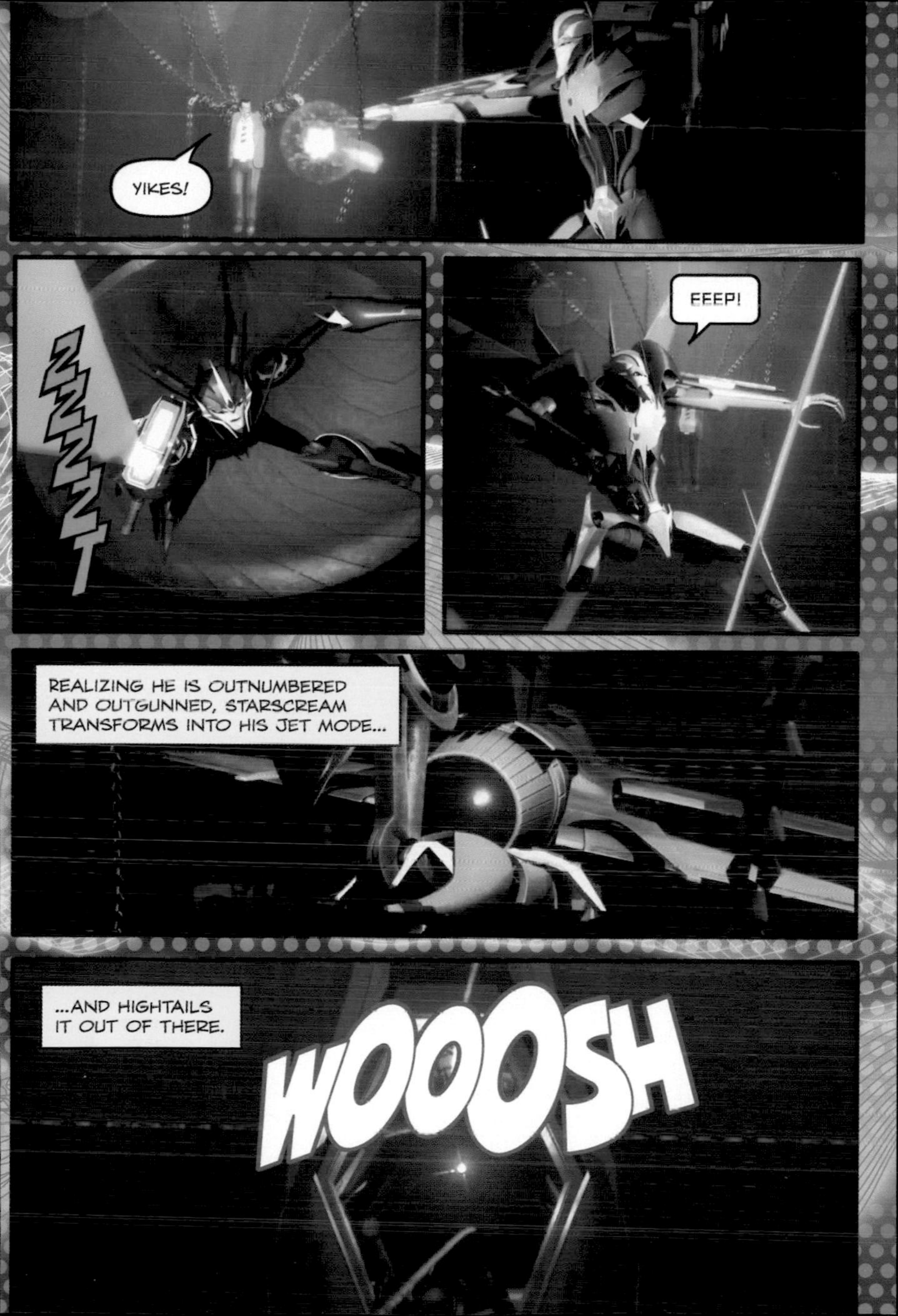
YIKES!
ZZZZZT
EEEP!
REALIZING HE IS OUTNUMBERED AND OUTGUNNED, STARSCREAM TRANSFORMS INTO HIS JET MODE...
...AND HIGHTAILS IT OUT OF THERE.
WOOOSH

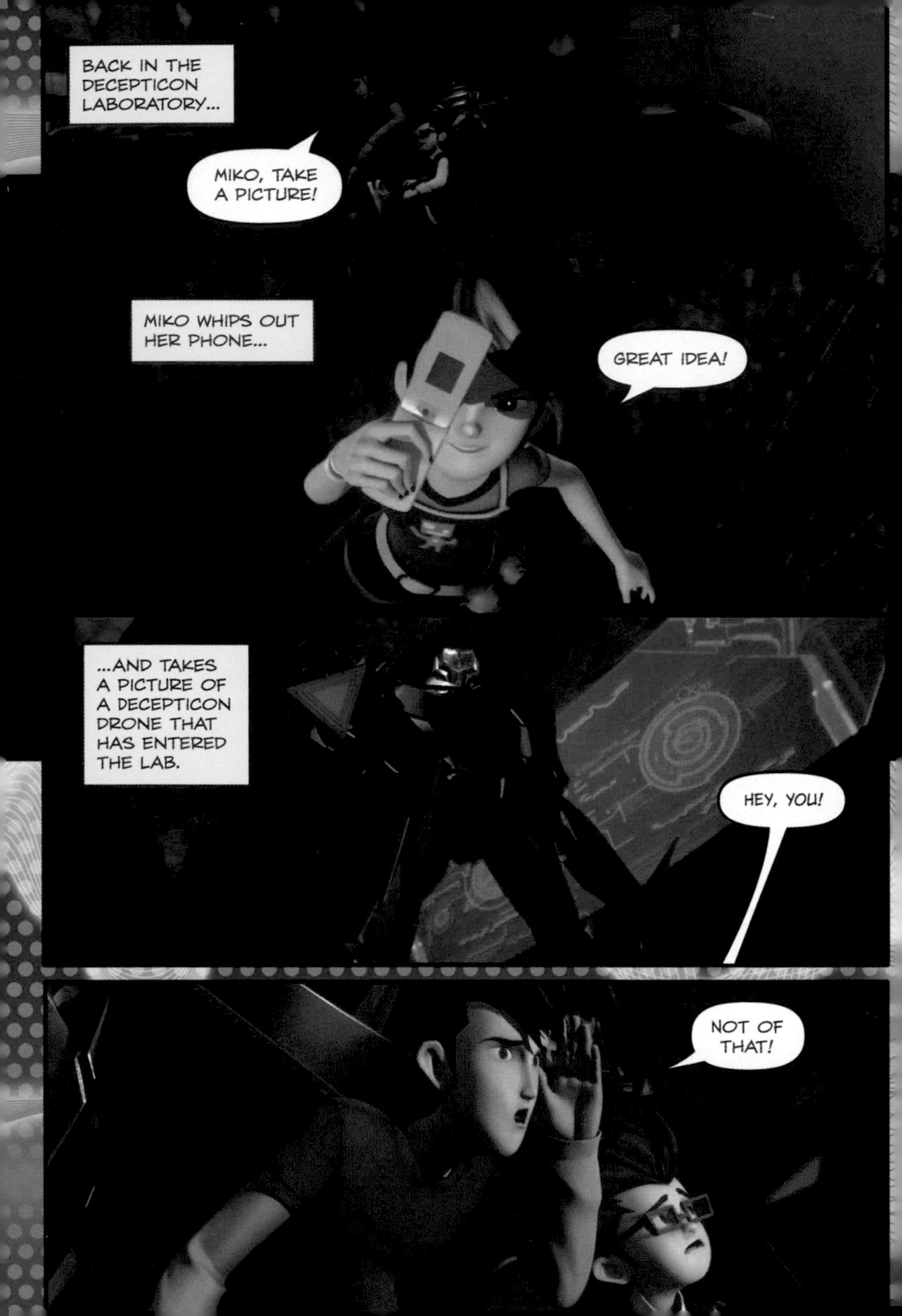
BACK IN THE DECEPTICON LABORATORY...
MIKO, TAKE A PICTURE!
MIKO WHIPS OUT HER PHONE...
GREAT IDEA!
...AND TAKES A PICTURE OF A DECEPTICON DRONE THAT HAS ENTERED THE LAB.
HEY, YOU!
NOT OF THAT!

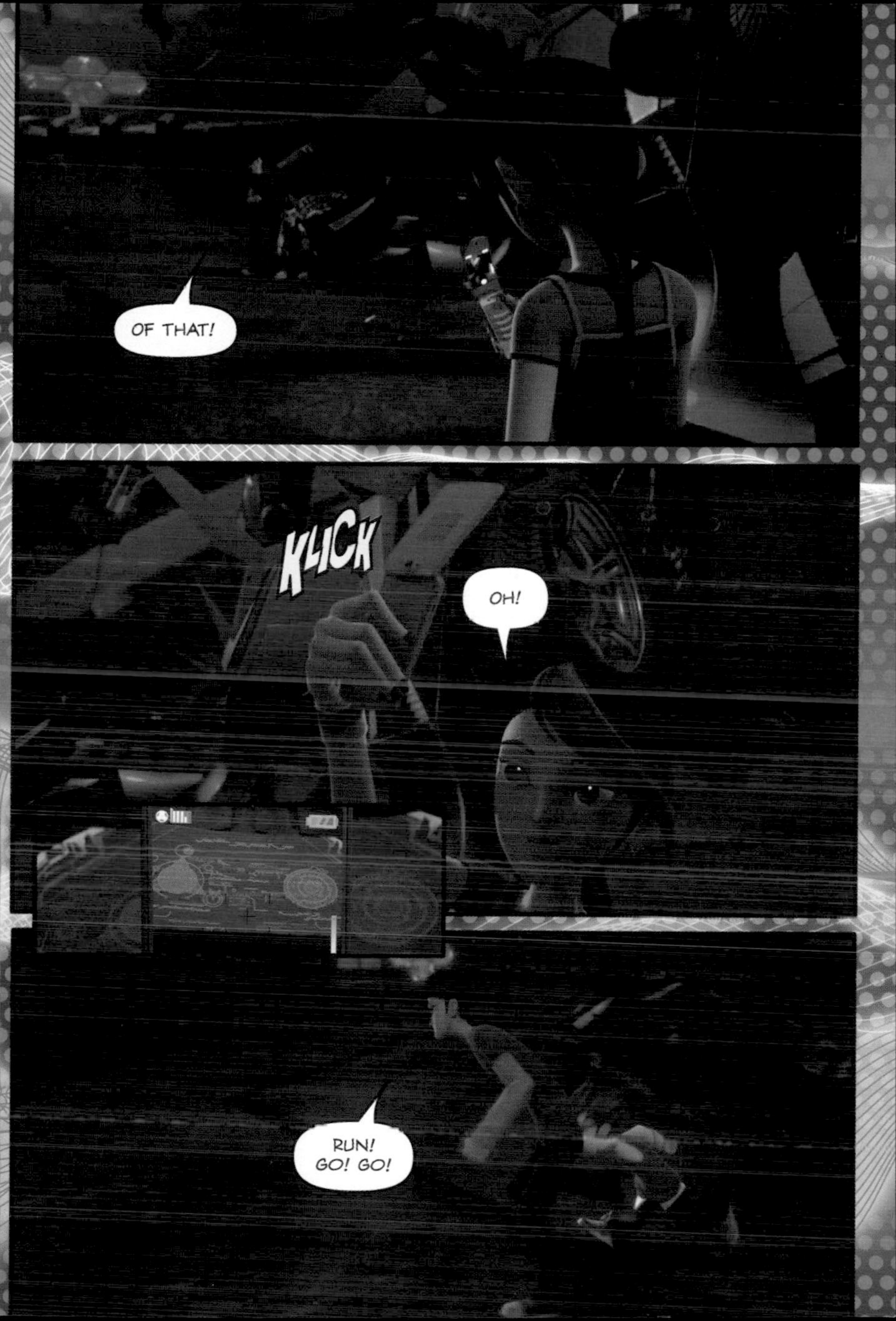
OF THAT!
KLICK
OH!
RUN!
GO! GO!

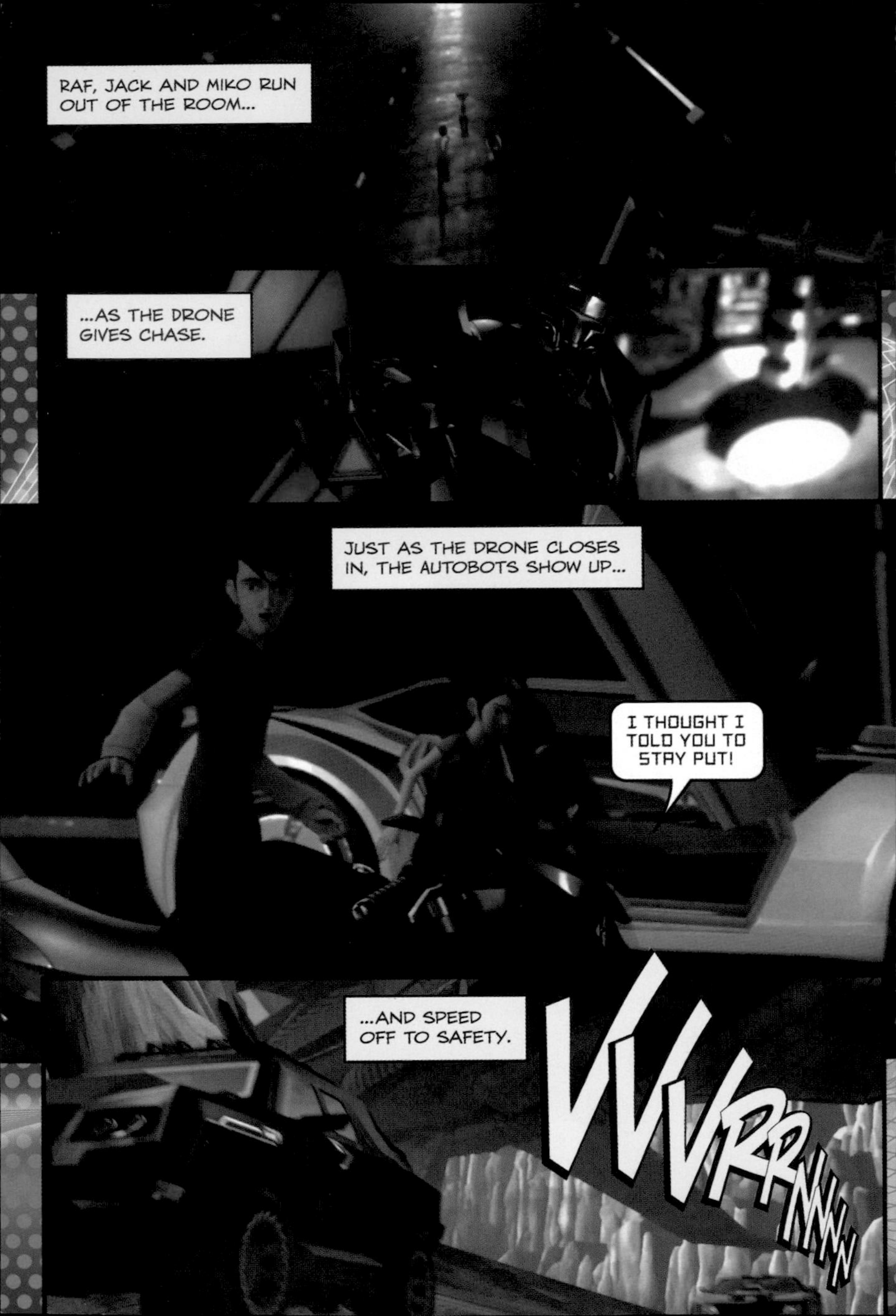
RAF, JACK AND MIKO RUN OUT OF THE ROOM...
...AS THE DRONE GIVES CHASE.
JUST AS THE DRONE CLOSES IN, THE AUTOBOTS SHOW UP...
I THOUGHT I TOLD YOU TO STAY PUT!
...AND SPEED OFF TO SAFETY.
VVVRRRNNNN

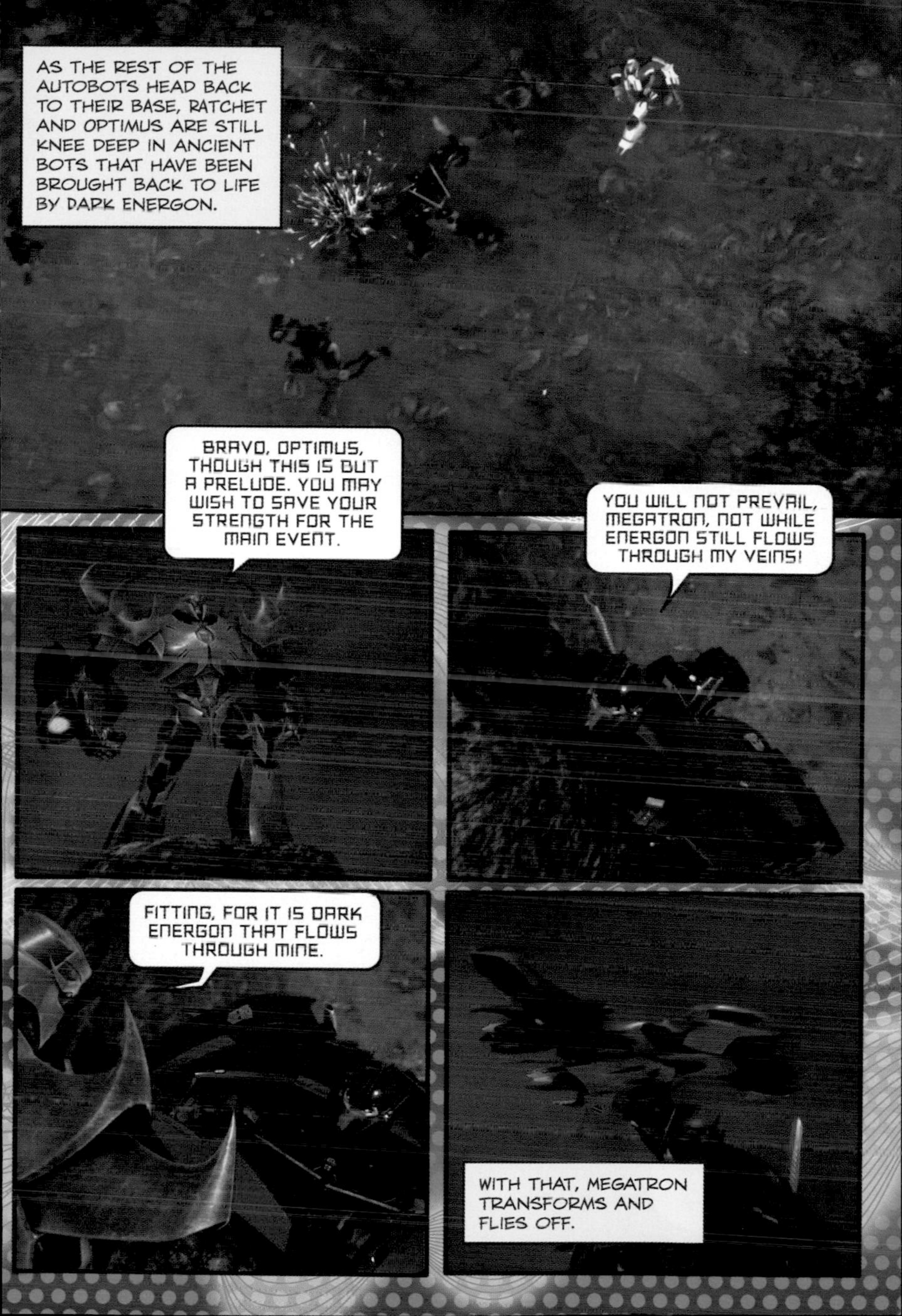
AS THE REST OF THE AUTOBOTS HEAD BACK TO THEIR BASE, RATCHET AND OPTIMUS ARE STILL KNEE DEEP IN ANCIENT BOTS THAT HAVE BEEN BROUGHT BACK TO LIFE BY DARK ENERGON.
BRAVO, OPTIMUS, THOUGH THIS IS BUT A PRELUDE. YOU MAY WISH TO SAVE YOUR STRENGTH FOR THE MAIN EVENT.
YOU WILL NOT PREVAIL, MEGATRON, NOT WHILE ENERGON STILL FLOWS THROUGH MY VEINS!
FITTING, FOR IT IS DARK ENERGON THAT FLOWS THROUGH MINE.
WITH THAT, MEGATRON TRANSFORMS AND FLIES OFF.

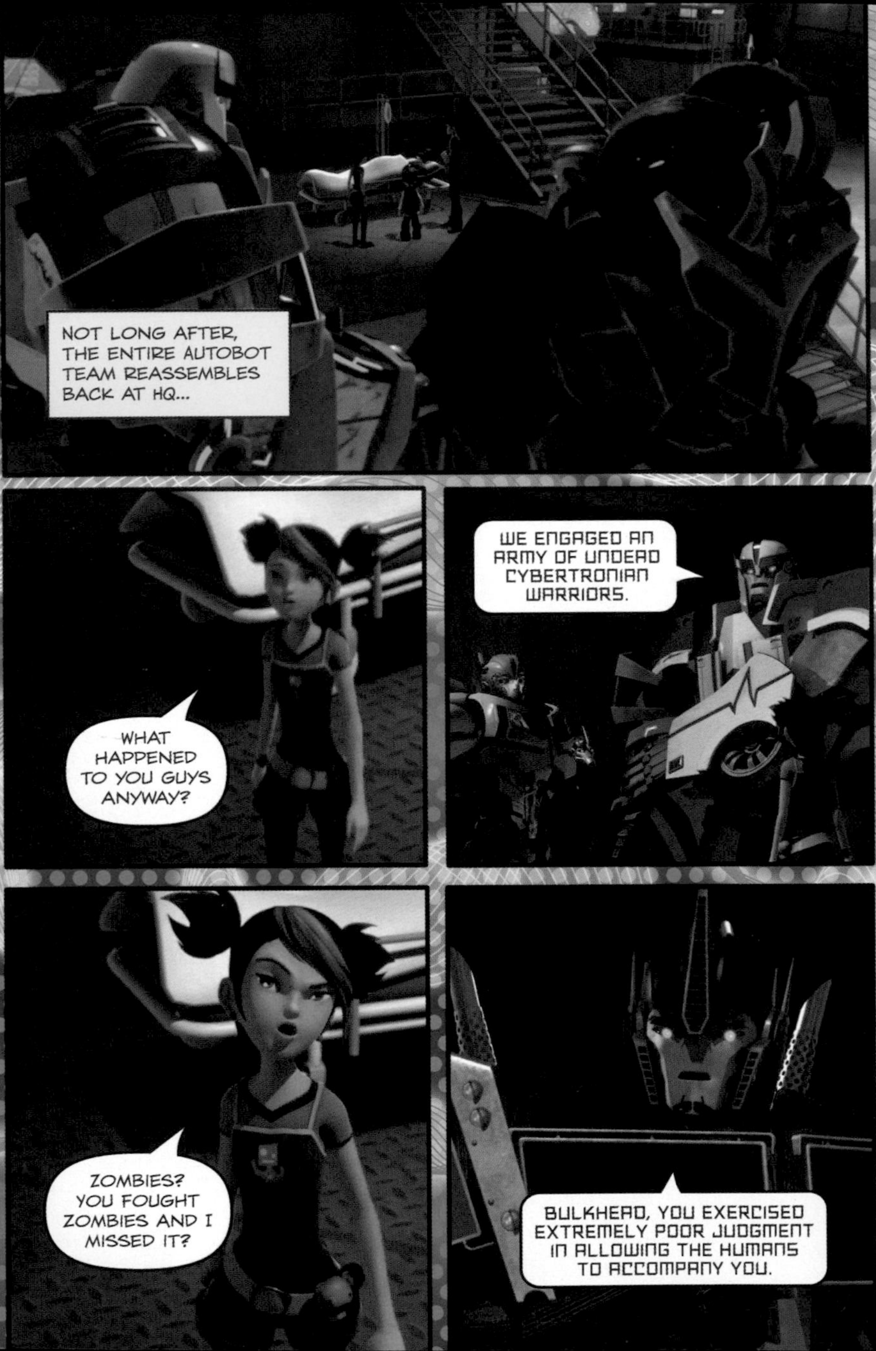
NOT LONG AFTER, THE ENTIRE AUTOBOT TEAM REASSEMBLES BACK AT HQ...
WHAT HAPPENED TO YOU GUYS ANYWAY?
WE ENGAGED AN ARMY OF UNDEAD CYBERTRONIAN WARRIORS.
ZOMBIES? YOU FOUGHT ZOMBIES AND I MISSED IT?
BULKHEAD, YOU EXERCISED EXTREMELY POOR JUDGMENT IN ALLOWING THE HUMANS TO ACCOMPANY YOU.

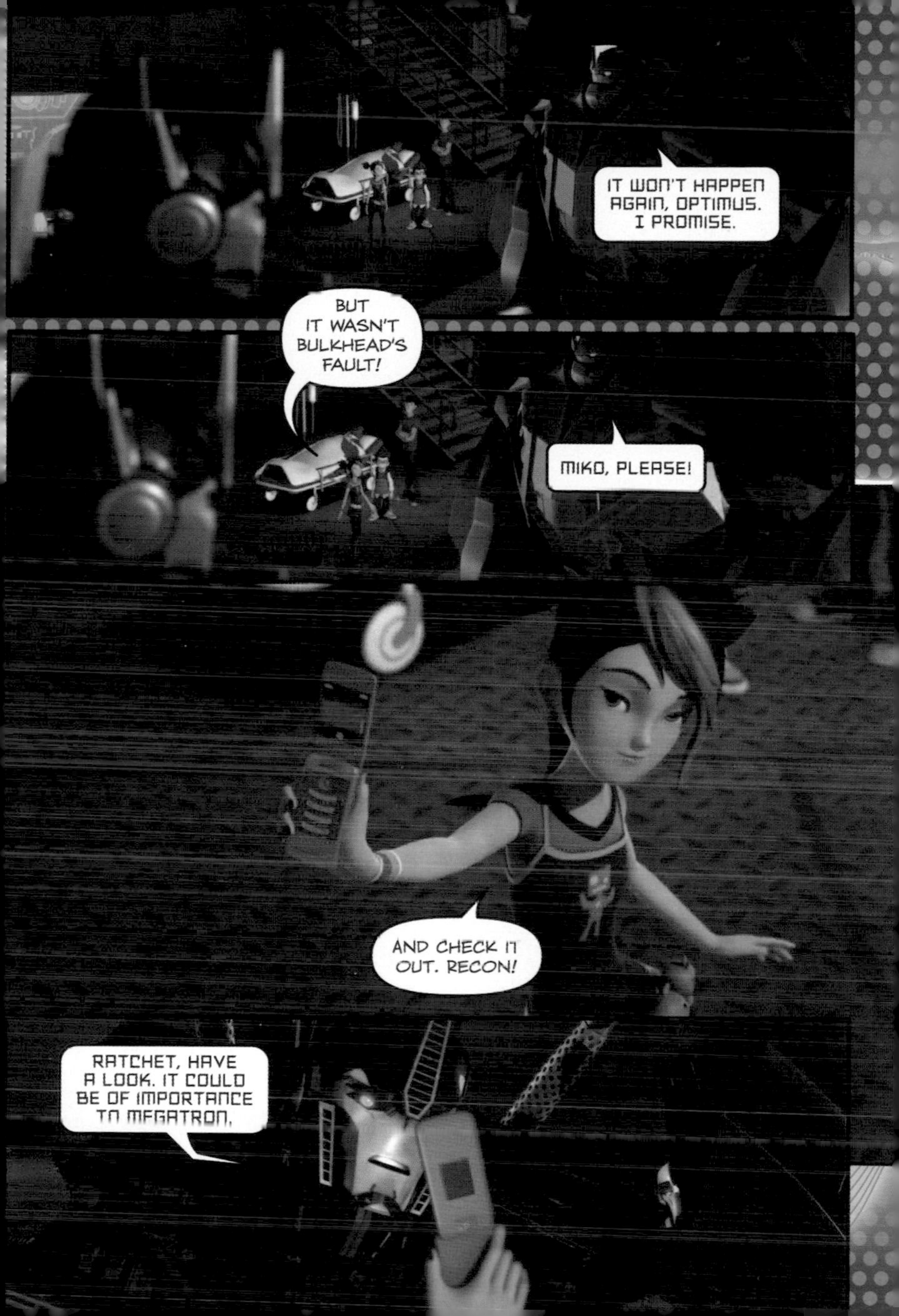
IT WON'T HAPPEN AGAIN, OPTIMUS. I PROMISE.
BUT IT WASN'T BULKHEAD'S FAULT!
MIKO, PLEASE!
AND CHECK IT OUT. RECON!
RATCHET, HAVE A LOOK. IT COULD BE OF IMPORTANCE TO MEGATRON.

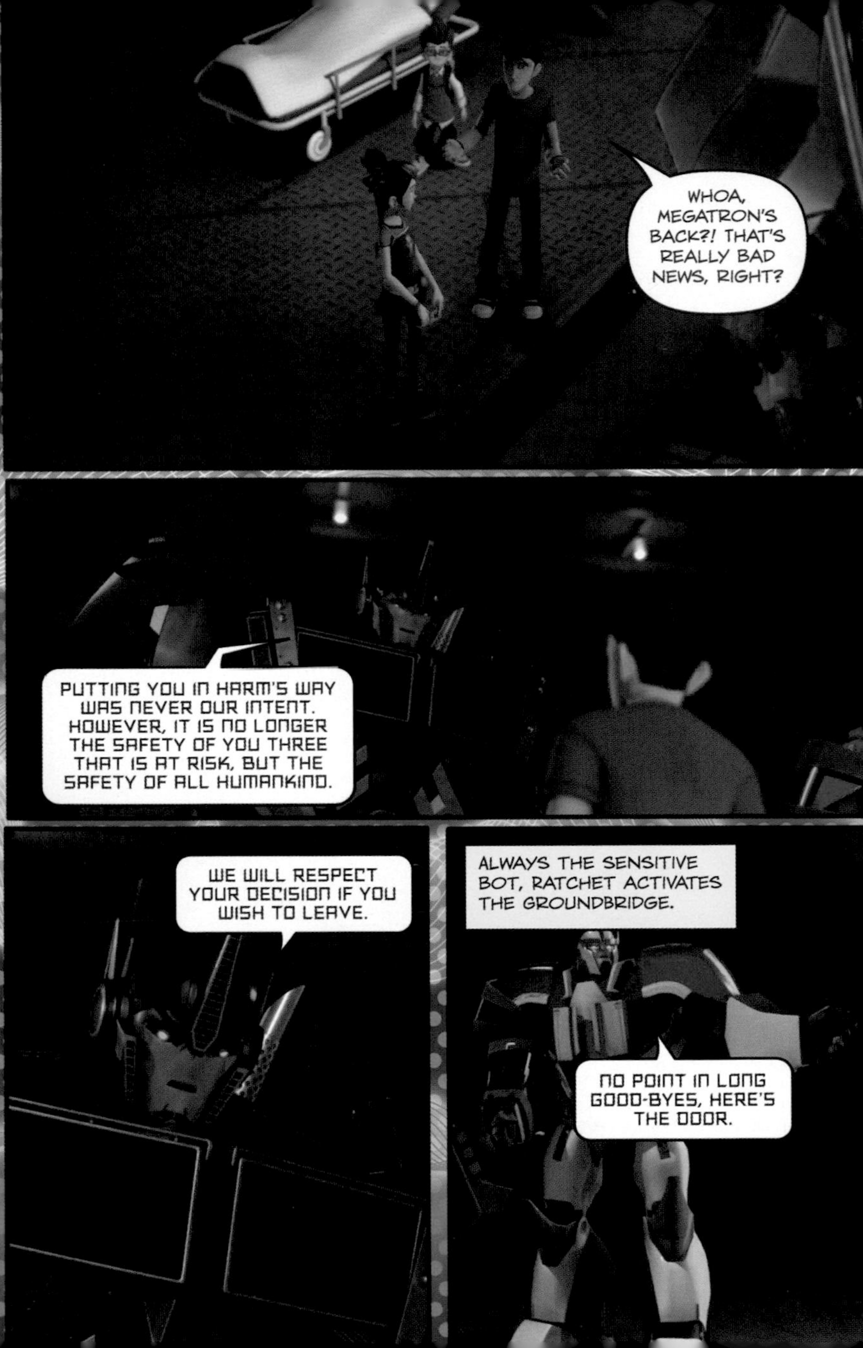
WHOA, MEGATRON'S BACK?! THAT'S REALLY BAD NEWS, RIGHT?
PUTTING YOU IN HARM'S WAY WAS NEVER OUR INTENT. HOWEVER, IT IS NO LONGER THE SAFETY OF YOU THREE THAT IS AT RISK, BUT THE SAFETY OF ALL HUMANKIND.
WE WILL RESPECT YOUR DECISION IF YOU WISH TO LEAVE.
ALWAYS THE SENSITIVE BOT, RATCHET ACTIVATES THE GROUNDBRIDGE.
NO POINT IN LONG GOOD-BYES, HERE'S THE DOOR.

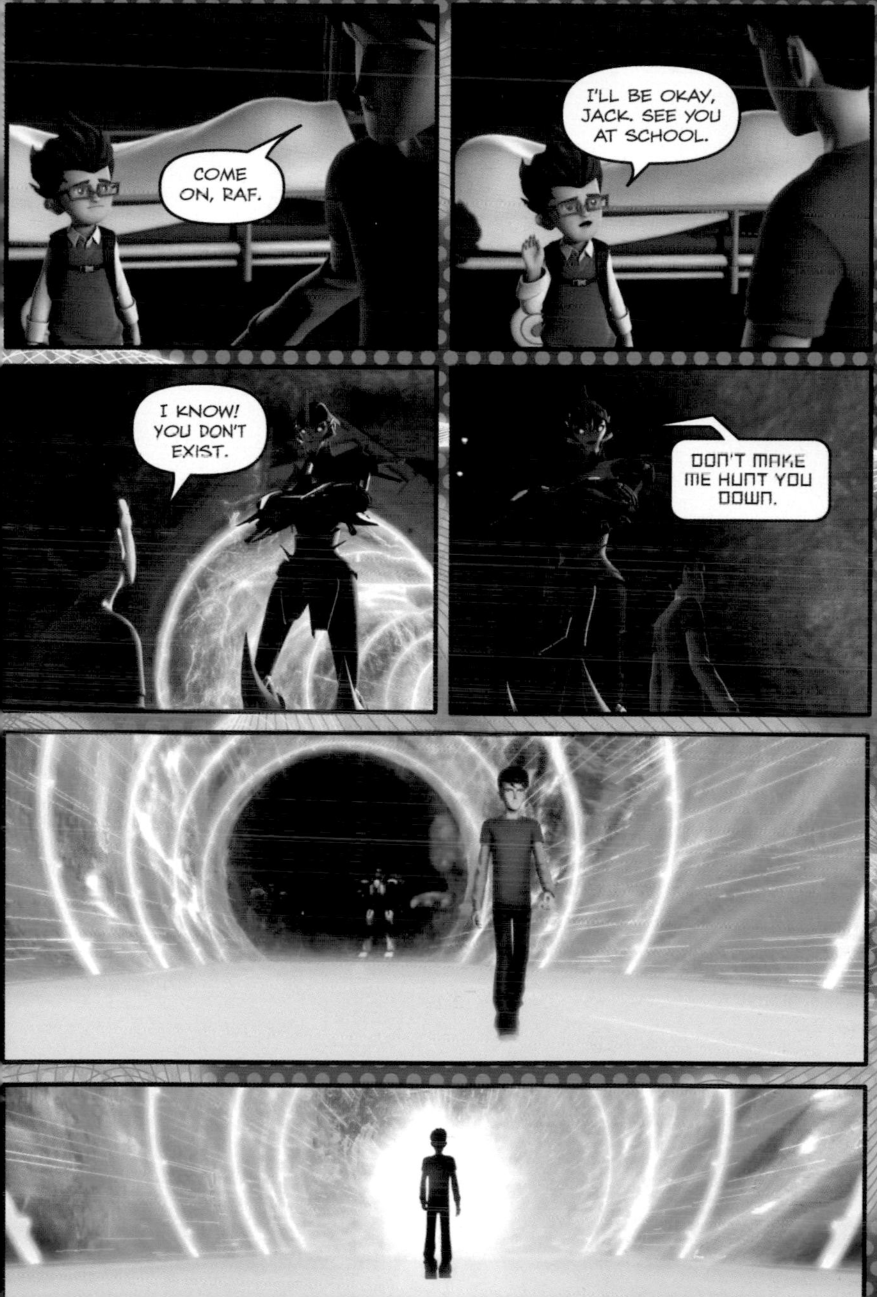
COME ON, RAF.
I'LL BE OKAY, JACK. SEE YOU AT SCHOOL.
I KNOW! YOU DON'T EXIST.
DON'T MAKE ME HUNT YOU DOWN.

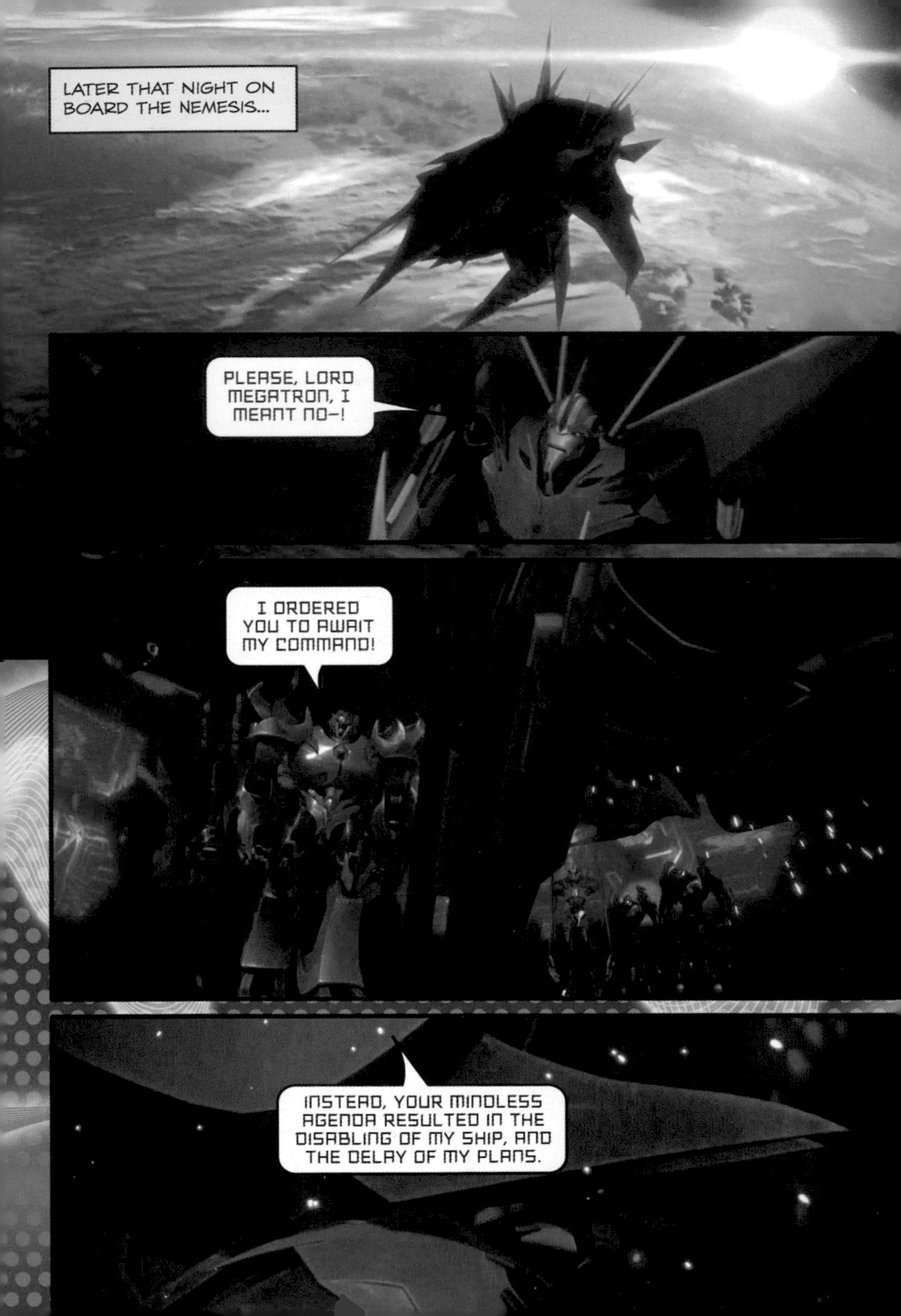
LATER THAT NIGHT ON BOARD THE NEMESIS...
PLEASE, LORD MEGATRON, I MEANT NO-!
I ORDERED YOU TO AWAIT MY COMMAND!
INSTEAD, YOUR MINDLESS AGENDA RESULTED IN THE DISABLING OF MY SHIP, AND THE DELAY OF MY PLANS.

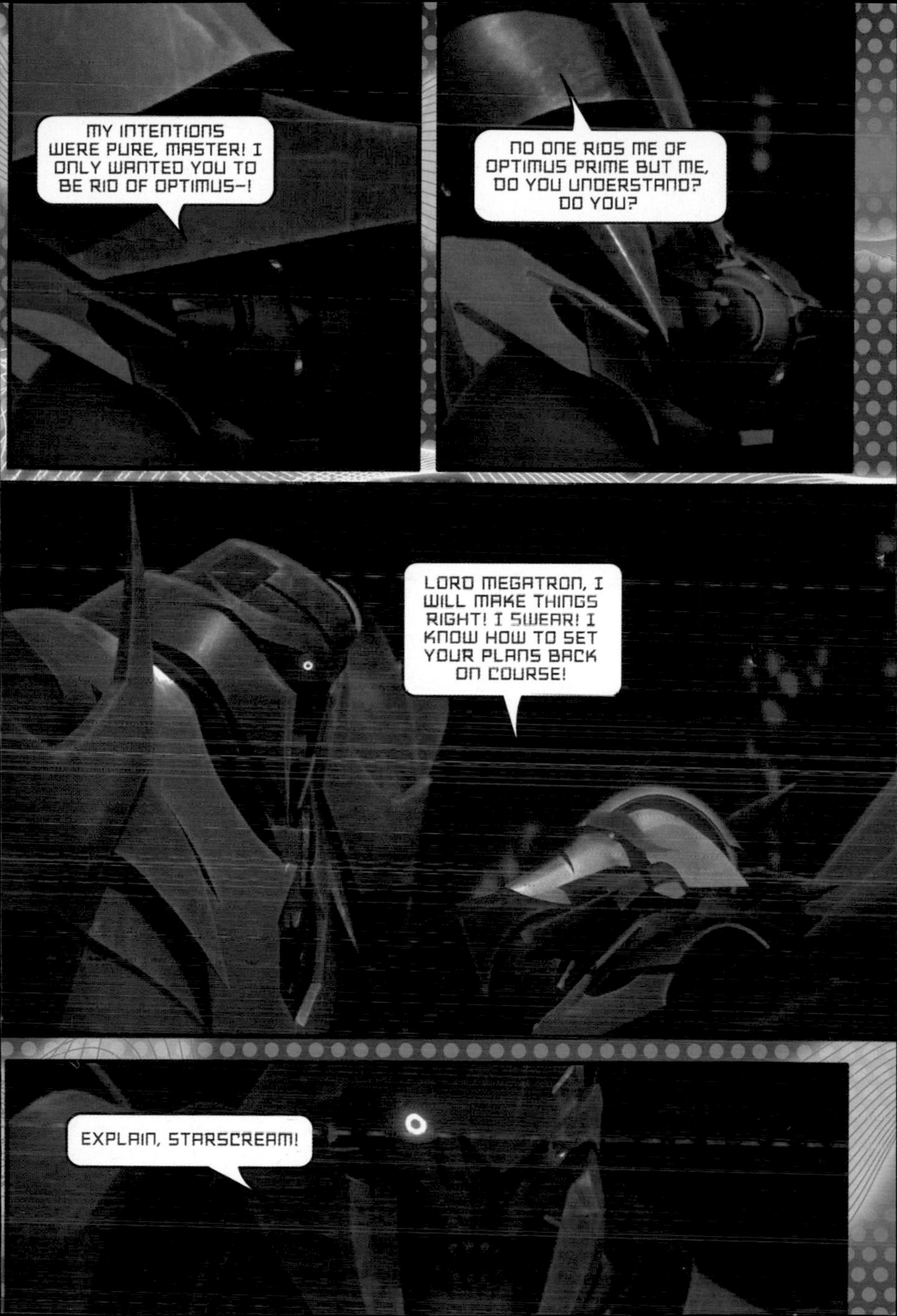
MY INTENTIONS WERE PURE, MASTER! I ONLY WANTED YOU TO BE RID OF OPTIMUS–!
NO ONE RIDS ME OF OPTIMUS PRIME BUT ME, DO YOU UNDERSTAND? DO YOU?
LORD MEGATRON, I WILL MAKE THINGS RIGHT! I SWEAR! I KNOW HOW TO SET YOUR PLANS BACK ON COURSE!
EXPLAIN, STARSCREAM!

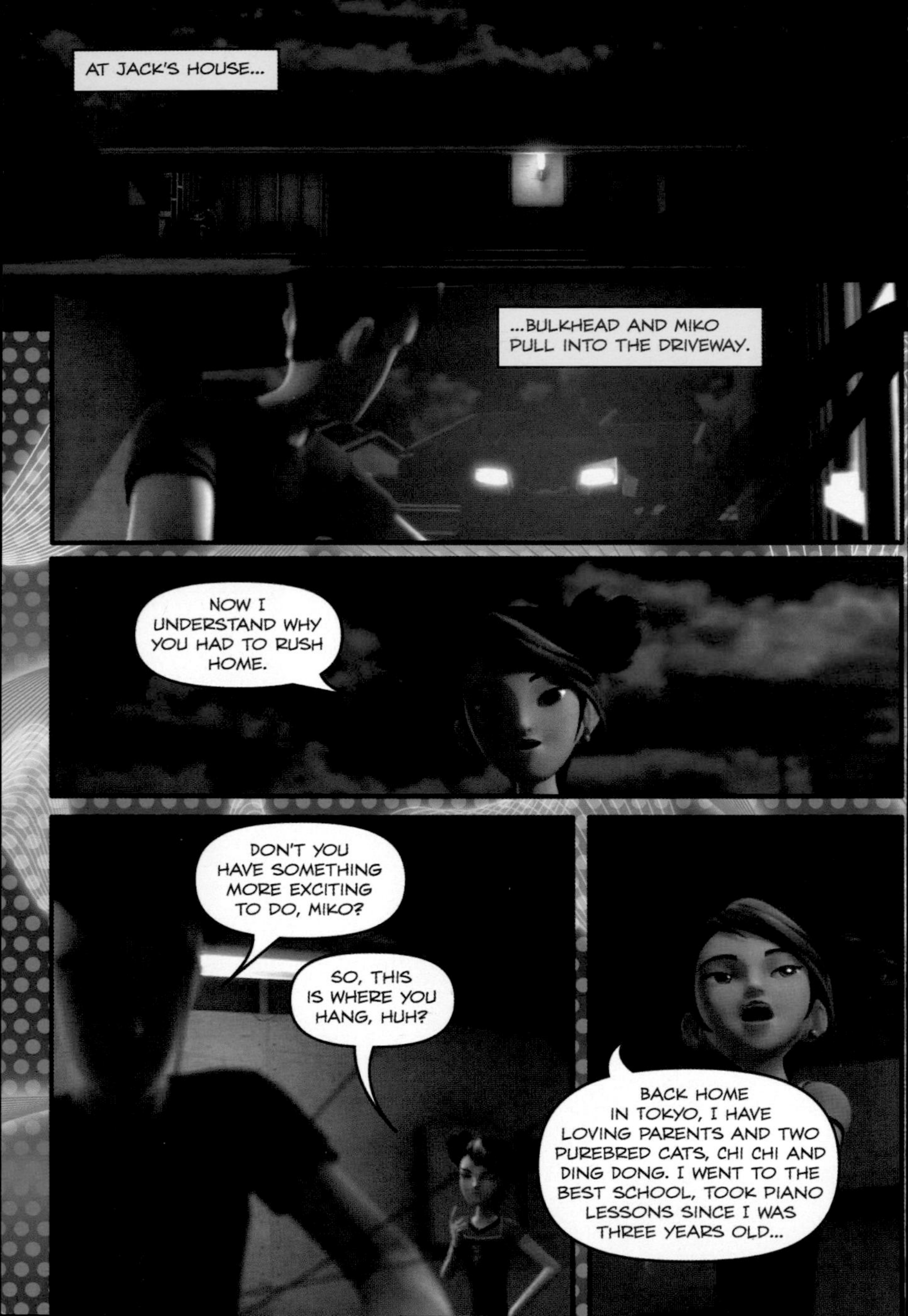

AT JACK'S HOUSE...
...BULKHEAD AND MIKO PULL INTO THE DRIVEWAY.
NOW I UNDERSTAND WHY YOU HAD TO RUSH HOME.
DON'T YOU HAVE SOMETHING MORE EXCITING TO DO, MIKO?
SO, THIS IS WHERE YOU HANG, HUH?
BACK HOME IN TOKYO, I HAVE LOVING PARENTS AND TWO PUREBRED CATS, CHI CHI AND DING DONG. I WENT TO THE BEST SCHOOL, TOOK PIANO LESSONS SINCE I WAS THREE YEARS OLD...

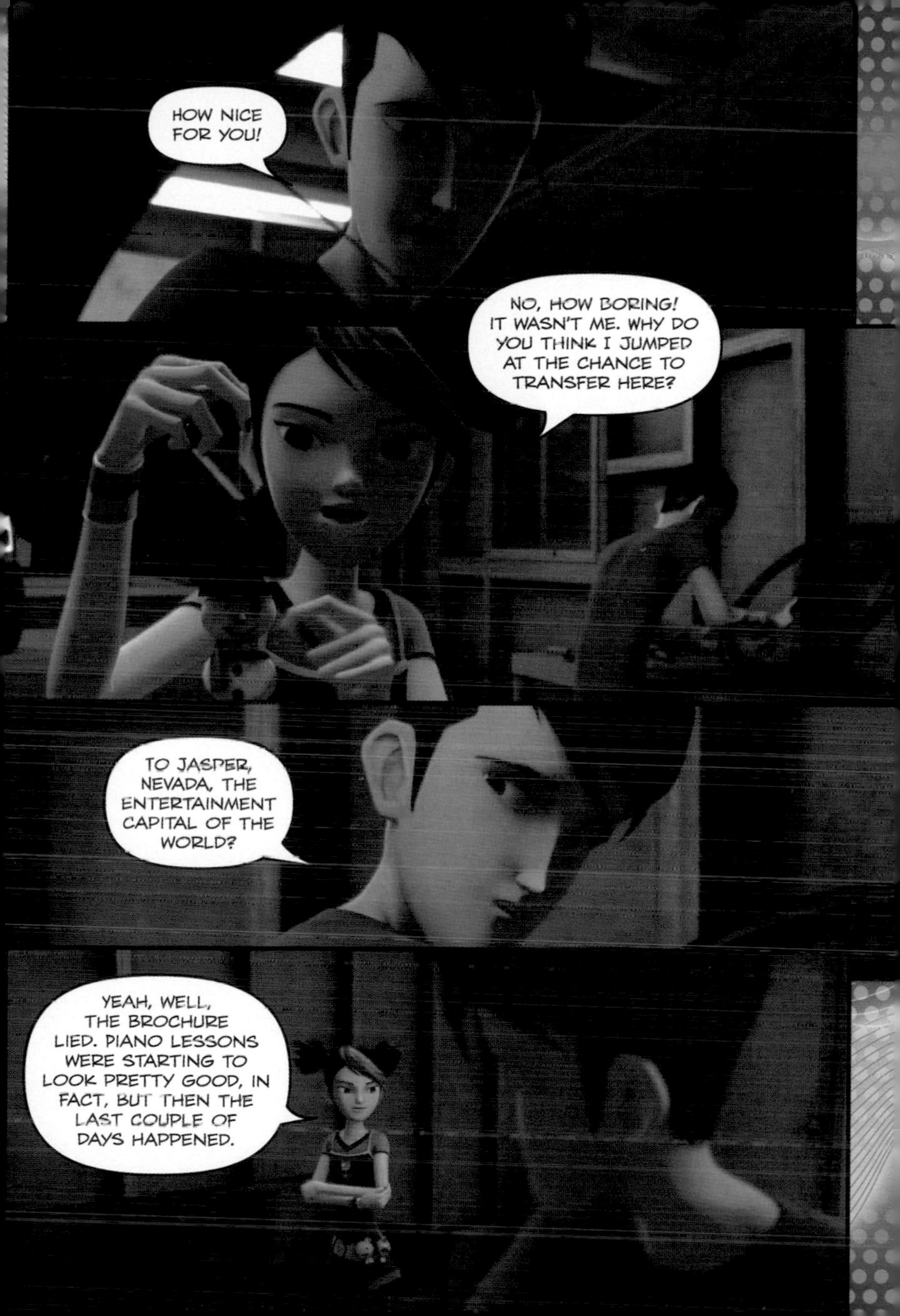
HOW NICE FOR YOU!
NO, HOW BORING! IT WASN'T ME. WHY DO YOU THINK I JUMPED AT THE CHANCE TO TRANSFER HERE?
TO JASPER, NEVADA, THE ENTERTAINMENT CAPITAL OF THE WORLD?
YEAH, WELL, THE BROCHURE LIED. PIANO LESSONS WERE STARTING TO LOOK PRETTY GOOD, IN FACT, BUT THEN THE LAST COUPLE OF DAYS HAPPENED.

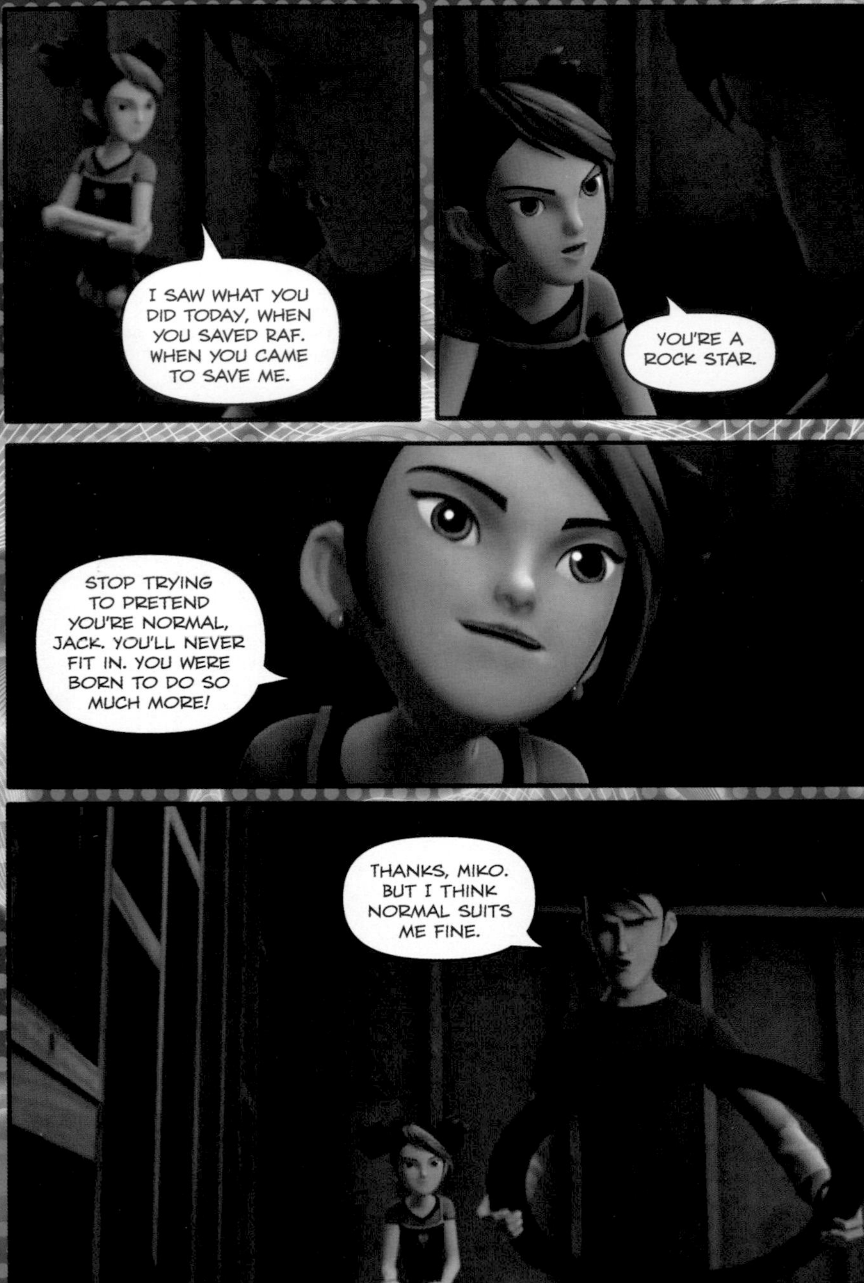
I SAW WHAT YOU DID TODAY, WHEN YOU SAVED RAF. WHEN YOU CAME TO SAVE ME.
YOU'RE A ROCK STAR.
STOP TRYING TO PRETEND YOU'RE NORMAL, JACK. YOU'LL NEVER FIT IN. YOU WERE BORN TO DO SO MUCH MORE!
THANKS, MIKO. BUT I THINK NORMAL SUITS ME FINE.

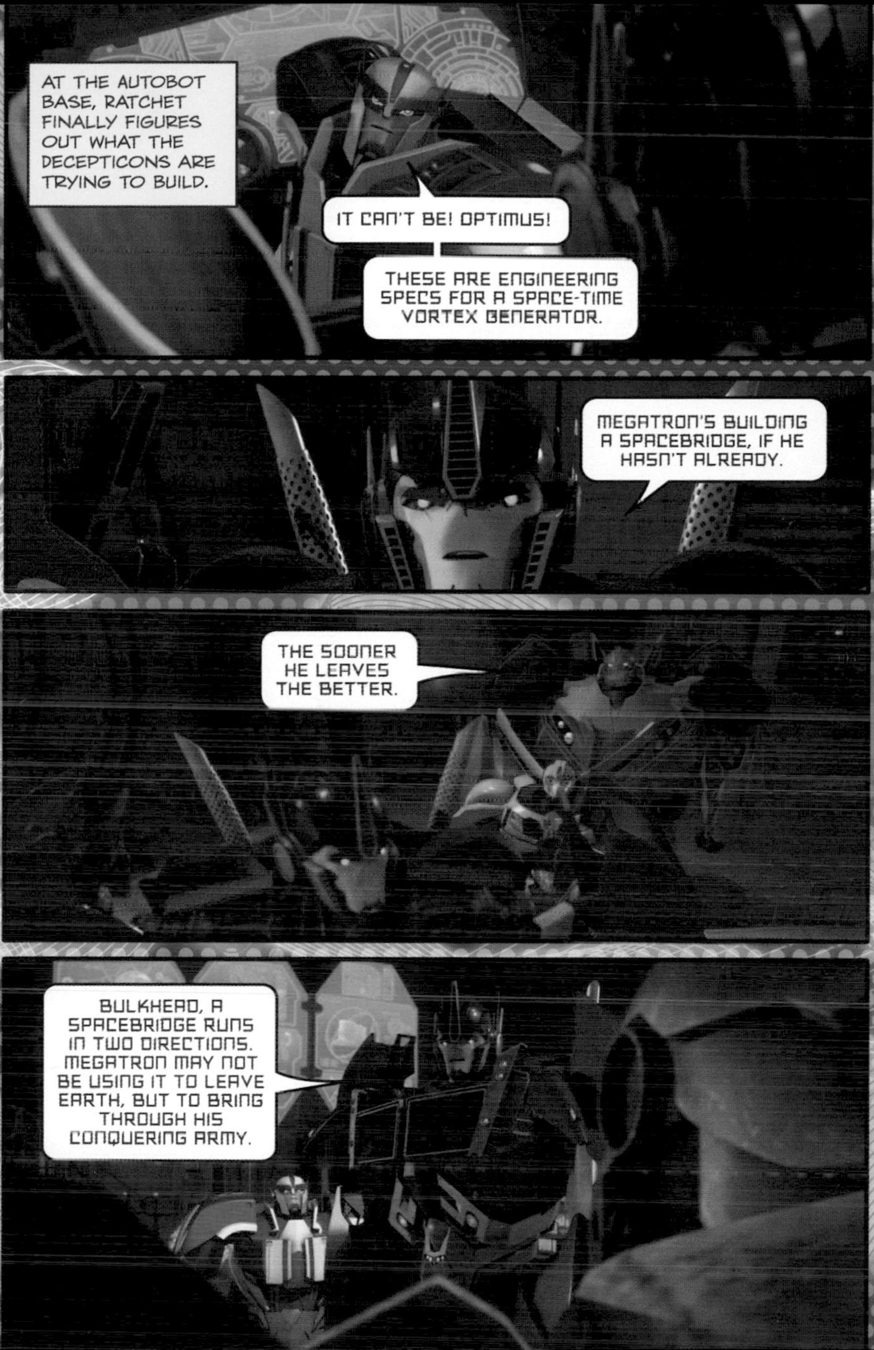
AT THE AUTOBOT BASE, RATCHET FINALLY FIGURES OUT WHAT THE DECEPTICONS ARE TRYING TO BUILD.
IT CAN'T BE! OPTIMUS!
THESE ARE ENGINEERING SPECS FOR A SPACE-TIME VORTEX GENERATOR.
MEGATRON'S BUILDING A SPACEBRIDGE, IF HE HASN'T ALREADY.
THE SOONER HE LEAVES THE BETTER.
BULKHEAD, A SPACEBRIDGE RUNS IN TWO DIRECTIONS. MEGATRON MAY NOT BE USING IT TO LEAVE EARTH, BUT TO BRING THROUGH HIS CONQUERING ARMY.

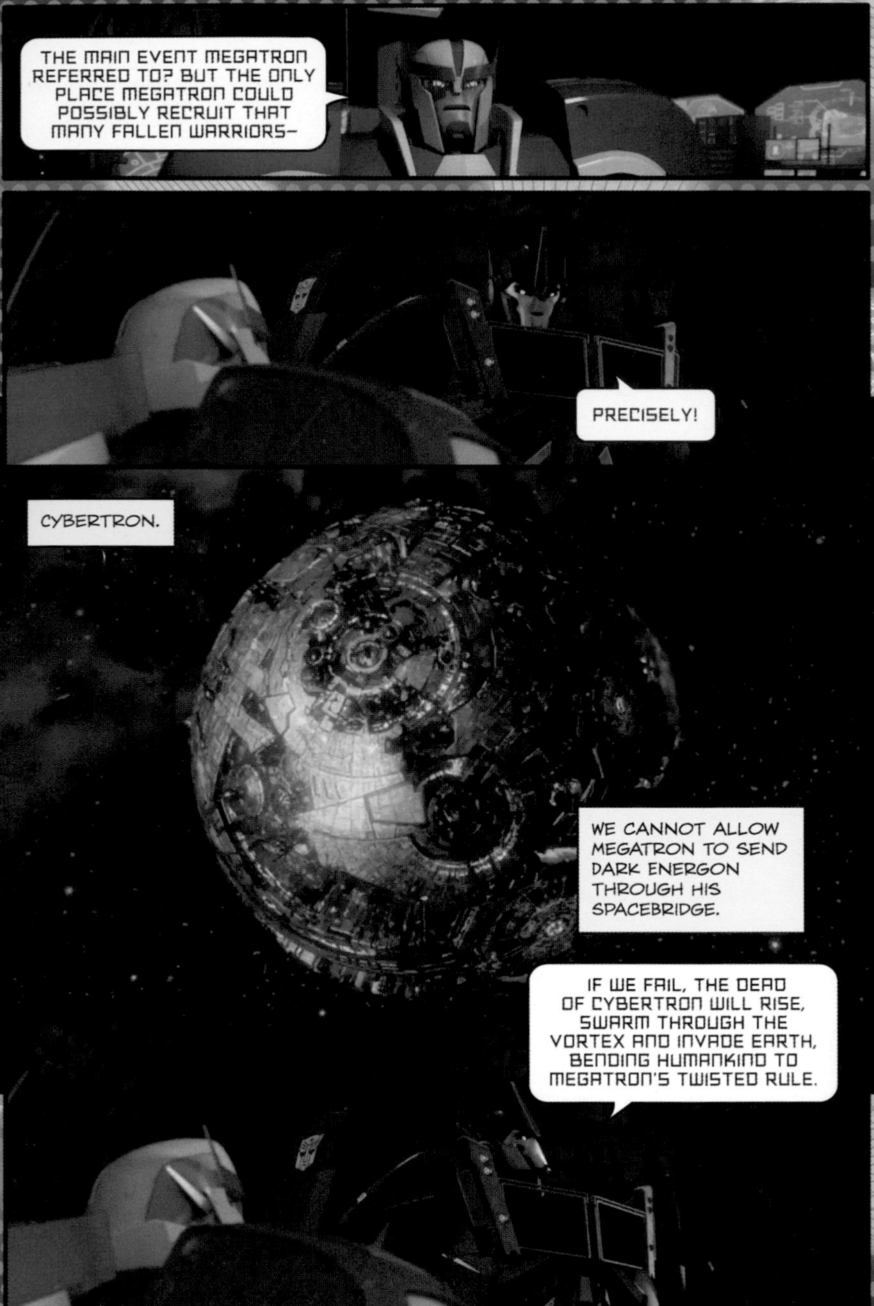
THE MAIN EVENT MEGATRON REFERRED TO? BUT THE ONLY PLACE MEGATRON COULD POSSIBLY RECRUIT THAT MANY FALLEN WARRIORS–
PRECISELY!
CYBERTRON.
WE CANNOT ALLOW MEGATRON TO SEND DARK ENERGON THROUGH HIS SPACEBRIDGE.
IF WE FAIL, THE DEAD OF CYBERTRON WILL RISE, SWARM THROUGH THE VORTEX AND INVADE EARTH, BENDING HUMANKIND TO MEGATRON'S TWISTED RULE.

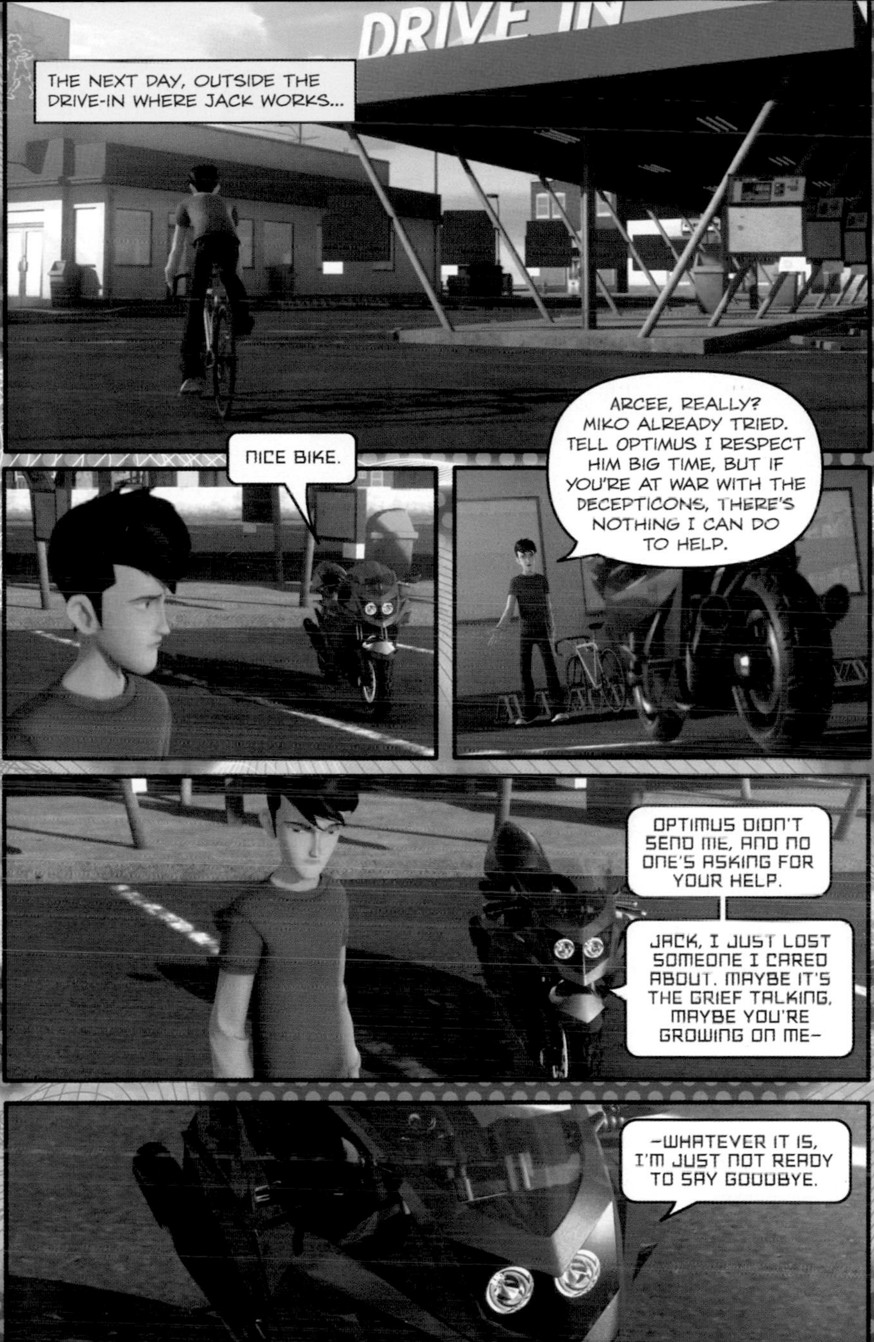
THE NEXT DAY, OUTSIDE THE DRIVE-IN WHERE JACK WORKS...
DRIVE IN
NICE BIKE.
ARCEE, REALLY? MIKO ALREADY TRIED. TELL OPTIMUS I RESPECT HIM BIG TIME, BUT IF YOU'RE AT WAR WITH THE DECEPTICONS, THERE'S NOTHING I CAN DO TO HELP.
OPTIMUS DIDN'T SEND ME, AND NO ONE'S ASKING FOR YOUR HELP.
JACK, I JUST LOST SOMEONE I CARED ABOUT. MAYBE IT'S THE GRIEF TALKING, MAYBE YOU'RE GROWING ON ME–
–WHATEVER IT IS, I'M JUST NOT READY TO SAY GOODBYE.

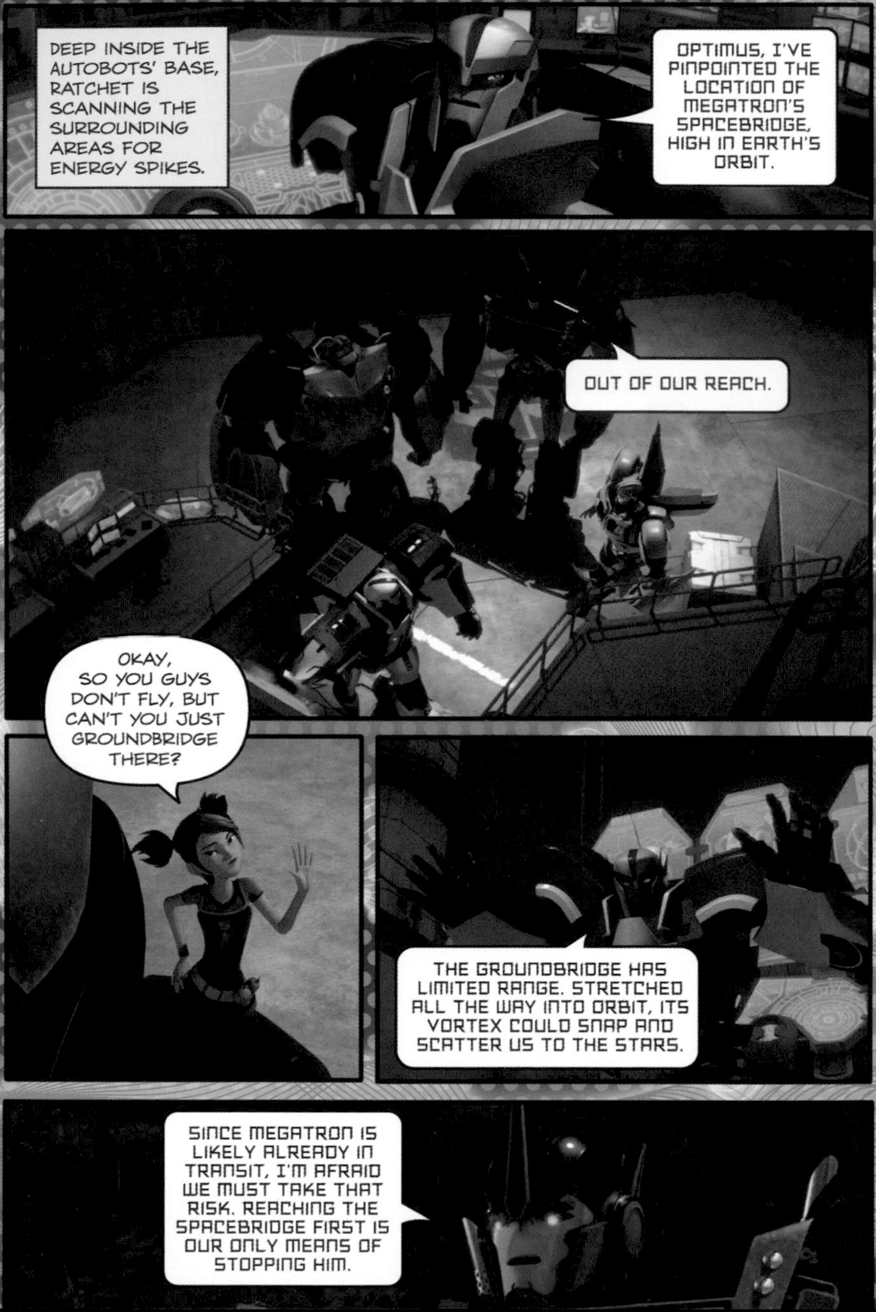
DEEP INSIDE THE AUTOBOTS' BASE, RATCHET IS SCANNING THE SURROUNDING AREAS FOR ENERGY SPIKES.
OPTIMUS, I'VE PINPOINTED THE LOCATION OF MEGATRON'S SPACEBRIDGE, HIGH IN EARTH'S ORBIT.
OUT OF OUR REACH.
OKAY, SO YOU GUYS DON'T FLY, BUT CAN'T YOU JUST GROUNDBRIDGE THERE?
THE GROUNDBRIDGE HAS LIMITED RANGE. STRETCHED ALL THE WAY INTO ORBIT, ITS VORTEX COULD SNAP AND SCATTER US TO THE STARS.
SINCE MEGATRON IS LIKELY ALREADY IN TRANSIT, I'M AFRAID WE MUST TAKE THAT RISK. REACHING THE SPACEBRIDGE FIRST IS OUR ONLY MEANS OF STOPPING HIM.

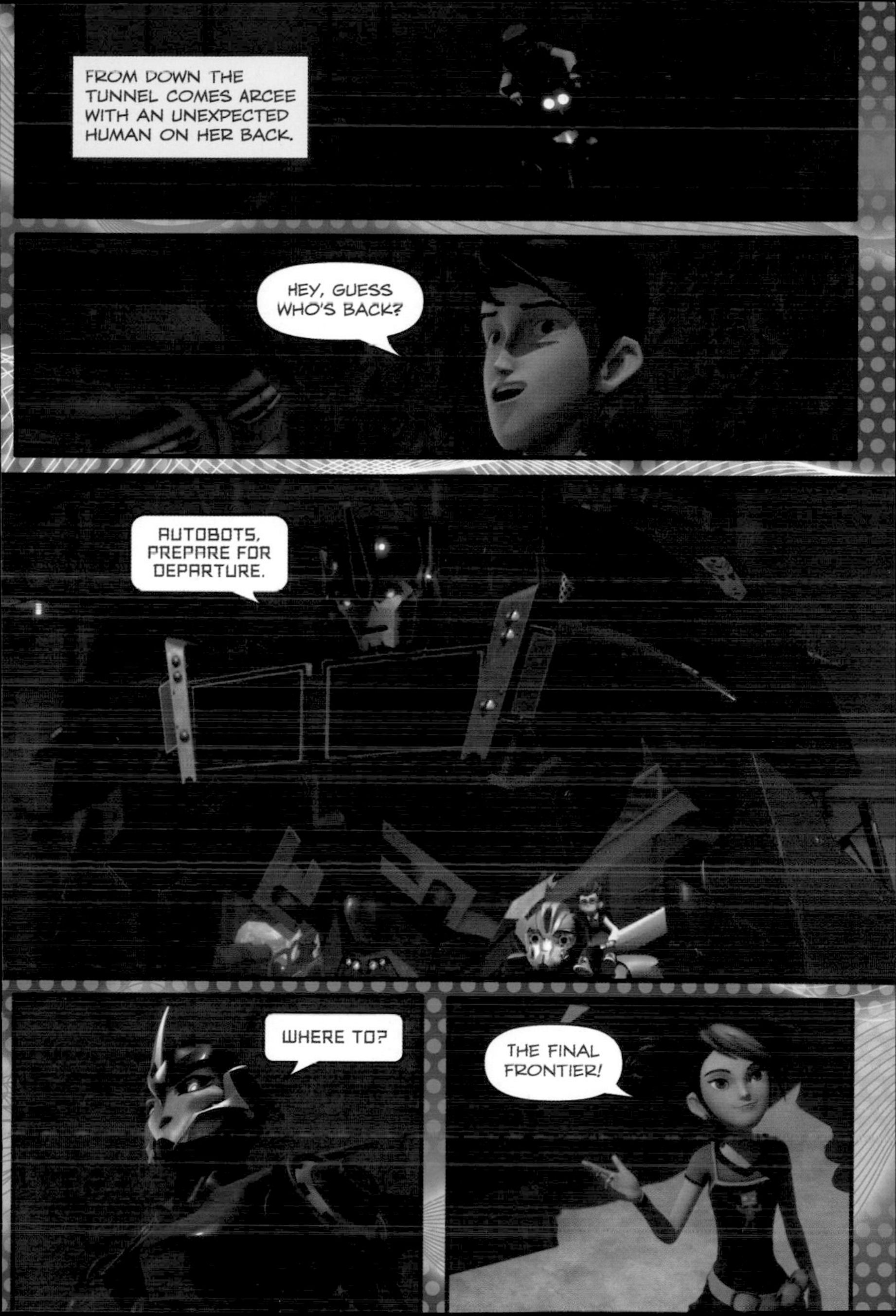
FROM DOWN THE TUNNEL COMES ARCEE WITH AN UNEXPECTED HUMAN ON HER BACK.
HEY, GUESS WHO'S BACK?
AUTOBOTS, PREPARE FOR DEPARTURE.
WHERE TO?
THE FINAL FRONTIER!

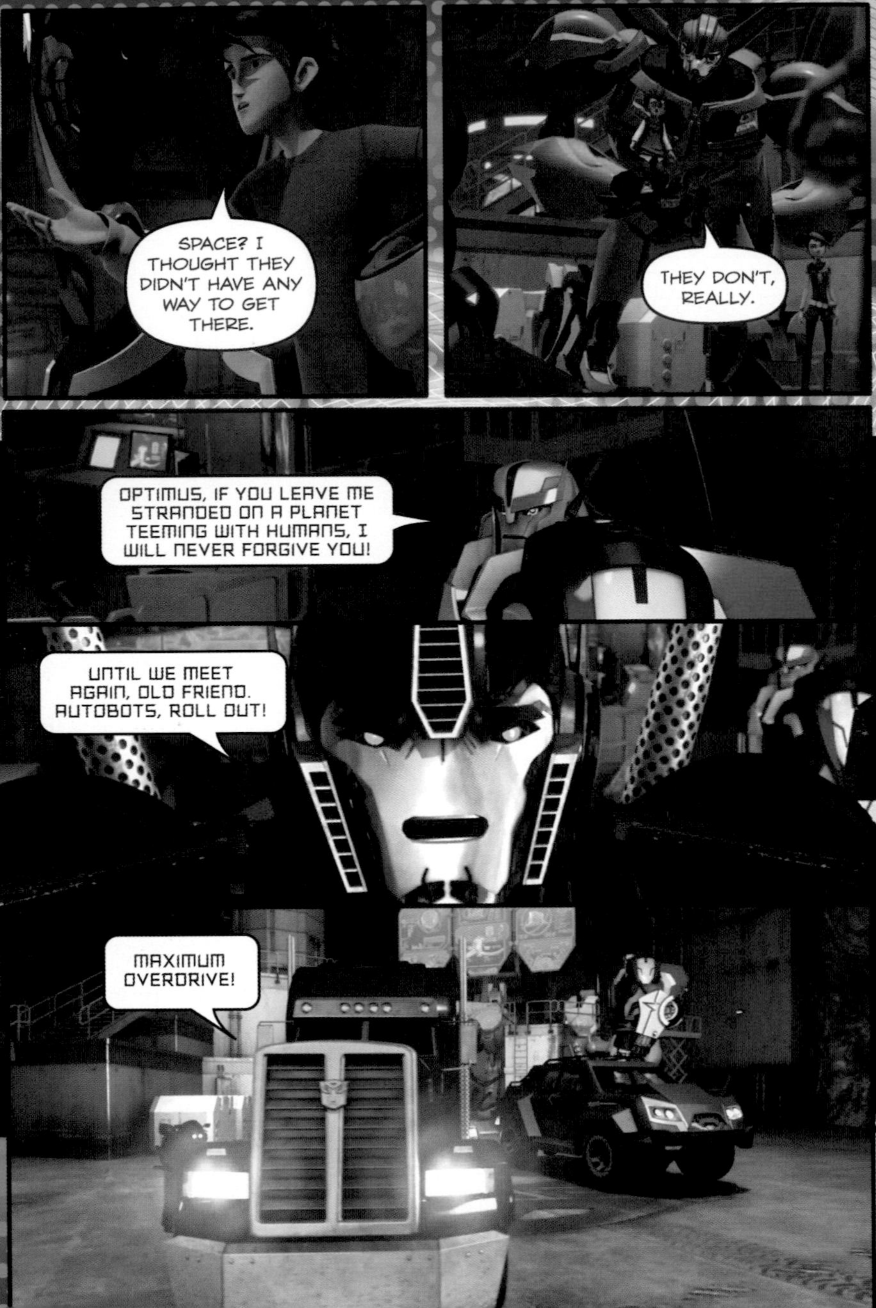
SPACE? I THOUGHT THEY DIDN'T HAVE ANY WAY TO GET THERE.
THEY DON'T, REALLY.
OPTIMUS, IF YOU LEAVE ME STRANDED ON A PLANET TEEMING WITH HUMANS, I WILL NEVER FORGIVE YOU!
UNTIL WE MEET AGAIN, OLD FRIEND. AUTOBOTS, ROLL OUT!
MAXIMUM OVERDRIVE!

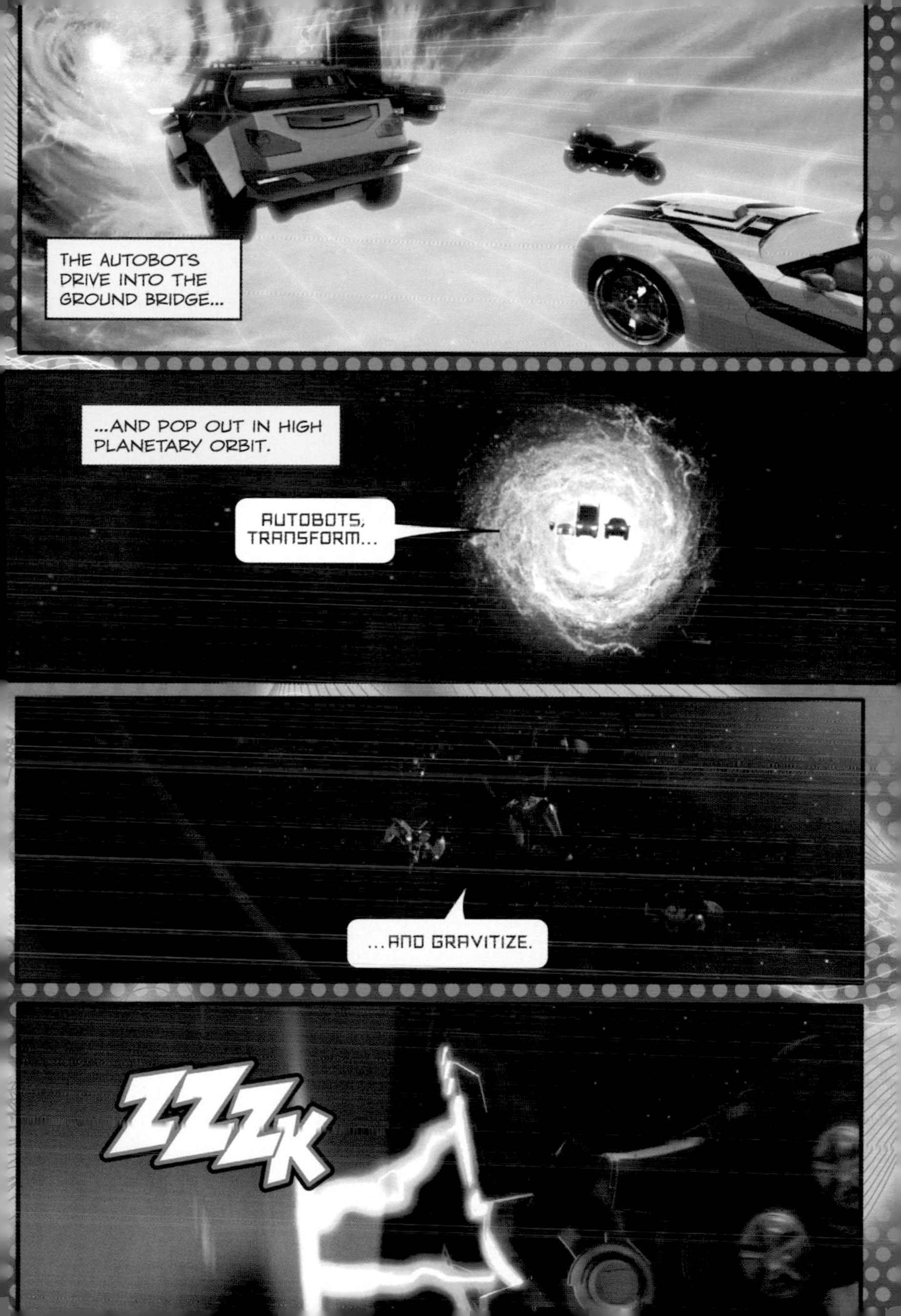
THE AUTOBOTS DRIVE INTO THE GROUND BRIDGE...
...AND POP OUT IN HIGH PLANETARY ORBIT.
AUTOBOTS, TRANSFORM...
...AND GRAVITIZE.
ZZZK

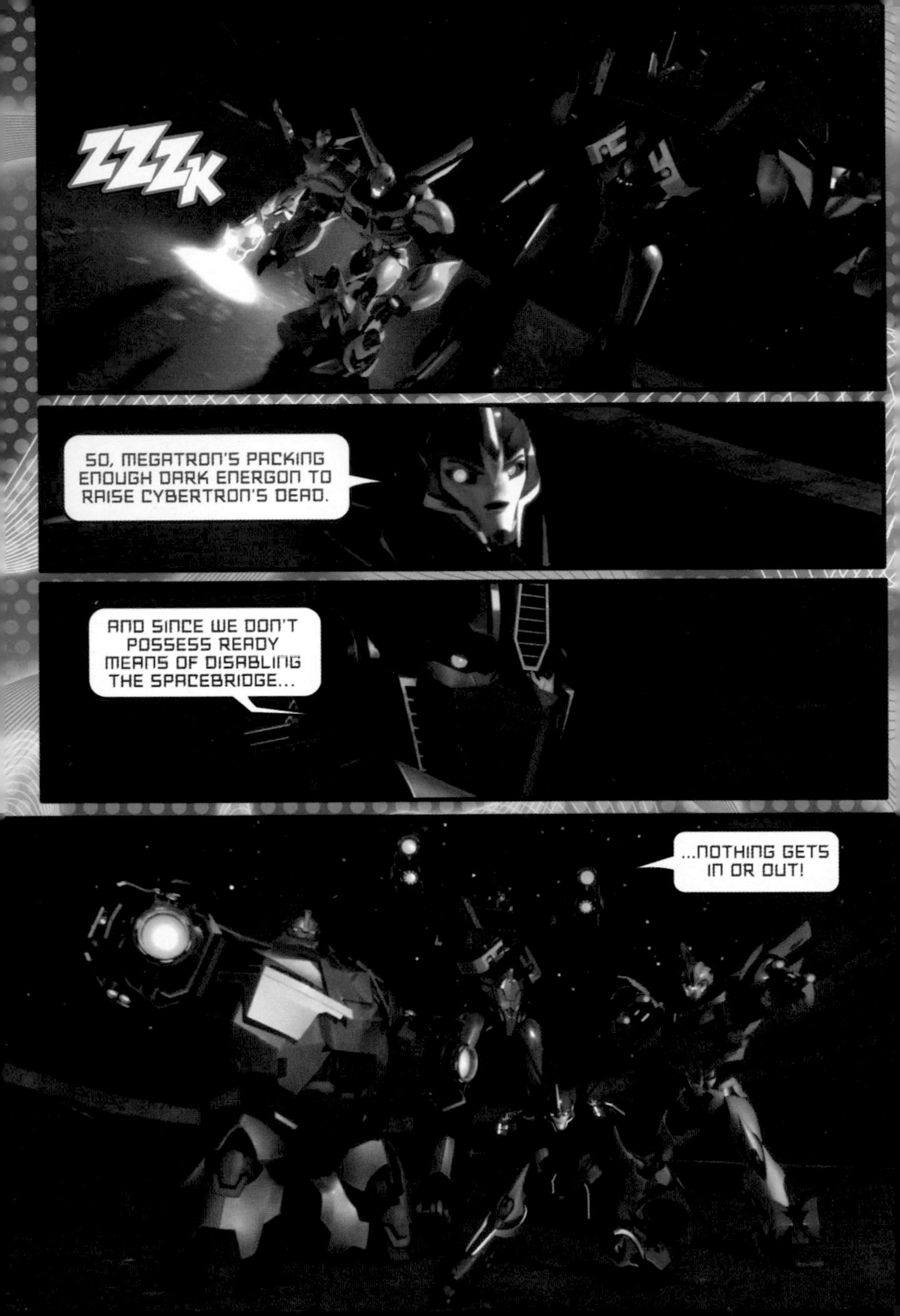
ZZZK
SO, MEGATRON'S PACKING ENOUGH DARK ENERGON TO RAISE CYBERTRON'S DEAD.
AND SINCE WE DON'T POSSESS READY MEANS OF DISABLING THE SPACEBRIDGE...
...NOTHING GETS IN OR OUT!

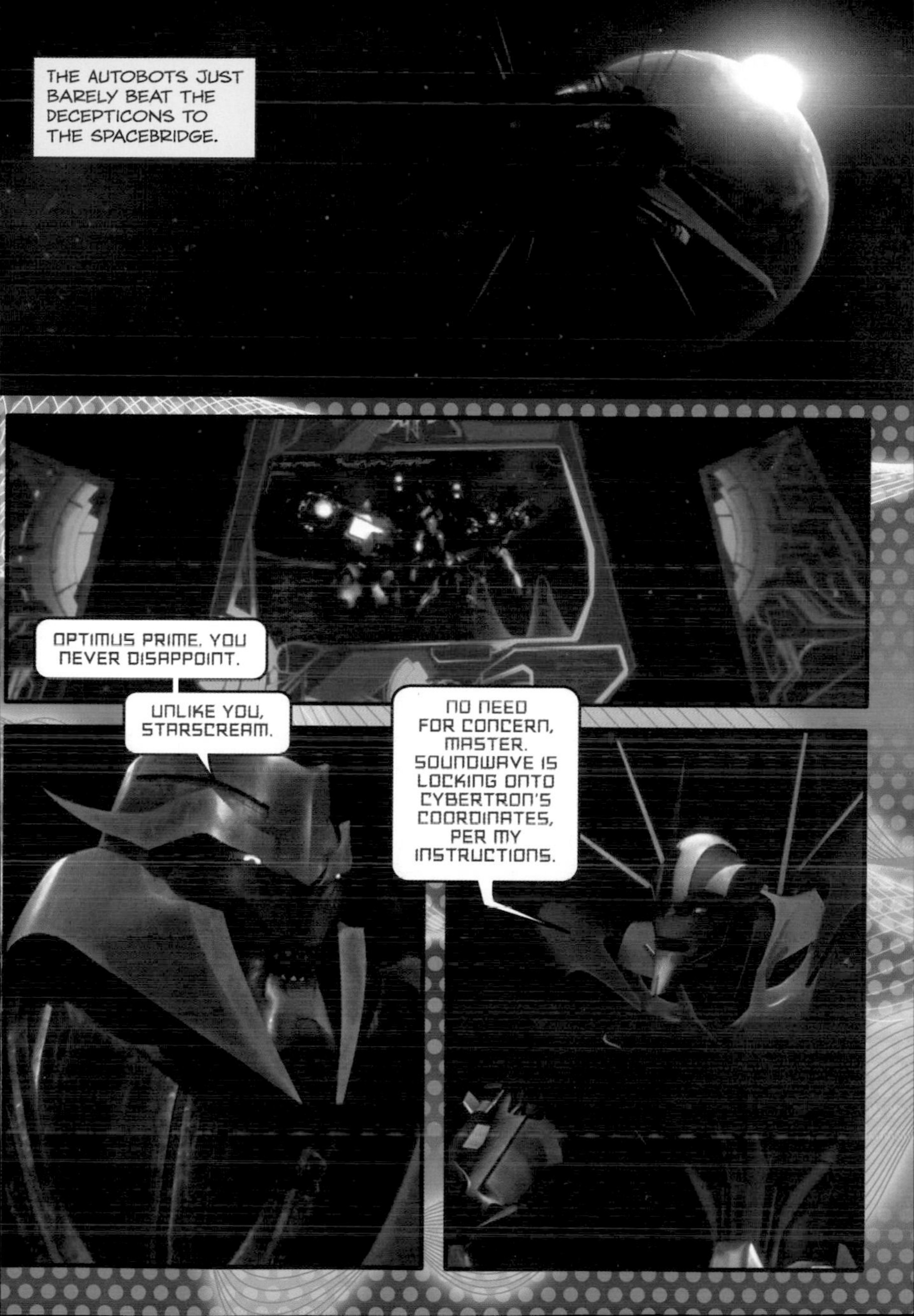
THE AUTOBOTS JUST BARELY BEAT THE DECEPTICONS TO THE SPACEBRIDGE.
OPTIMUS PRIME. YOU NEVER DISAPPOINT.
UNLIKE YOU, STARSCREAM.
NO NEED FOR CONCERN, MASTER. SOUNDWAVE IS LOCKING ONTO CYBERTRON'S COORDINATES, PER MY INSTRUCTIONS.

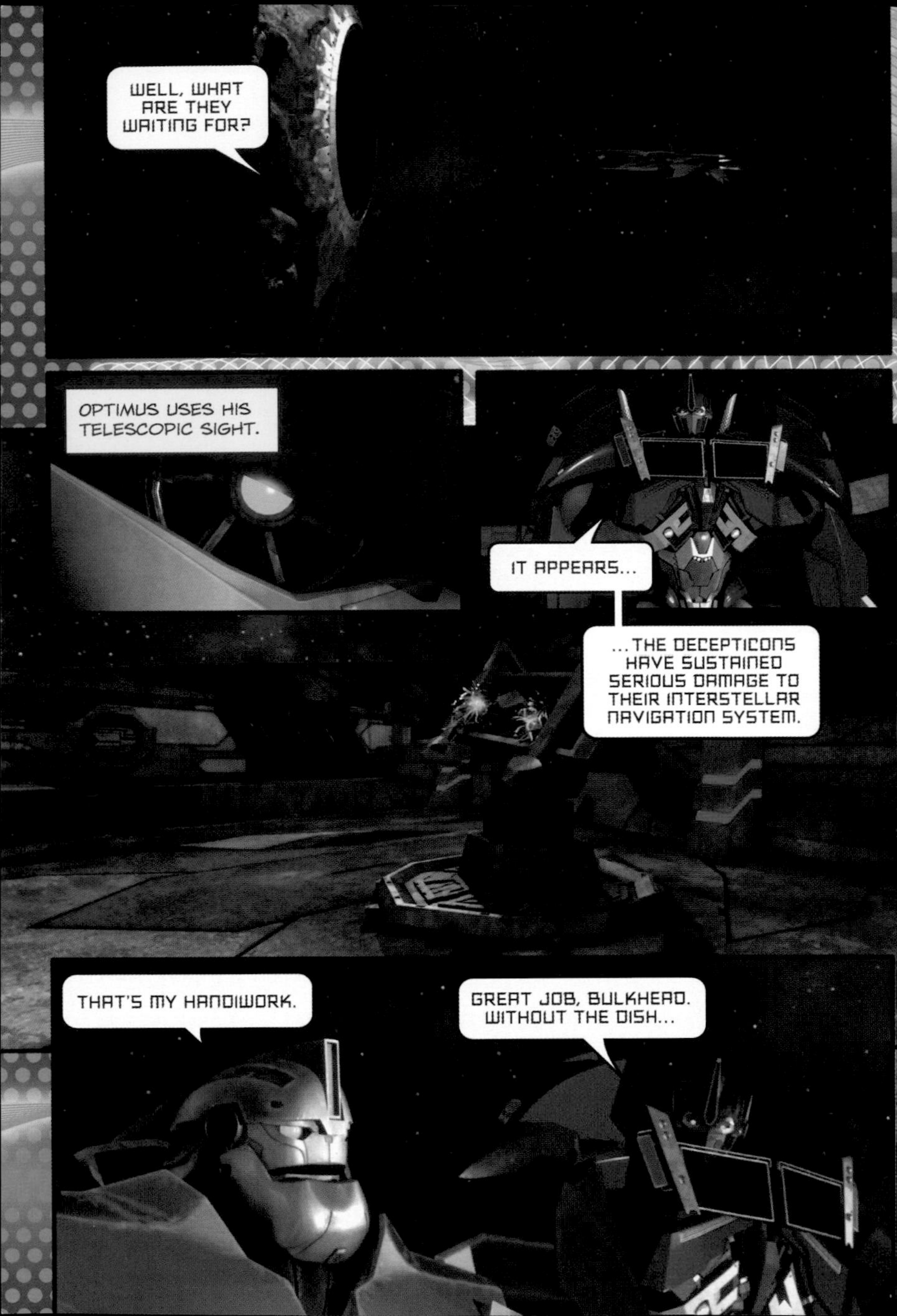
WELL, WHAT ARE THEY WAITING FOR?
OPTIMUS USES HIS TELESCOPIC SIGHT.
IT APPEARS...
...THE DECEPTICONS HAVE SUSTAINED SERIOUS DAMAGE TO THEIR INTERSTELLAR NAVIGATION SYSTEM.
THAT'S MY HANDIWORK.
GREAT JOB, BULKHEAD. WITHOUT THE DISH...

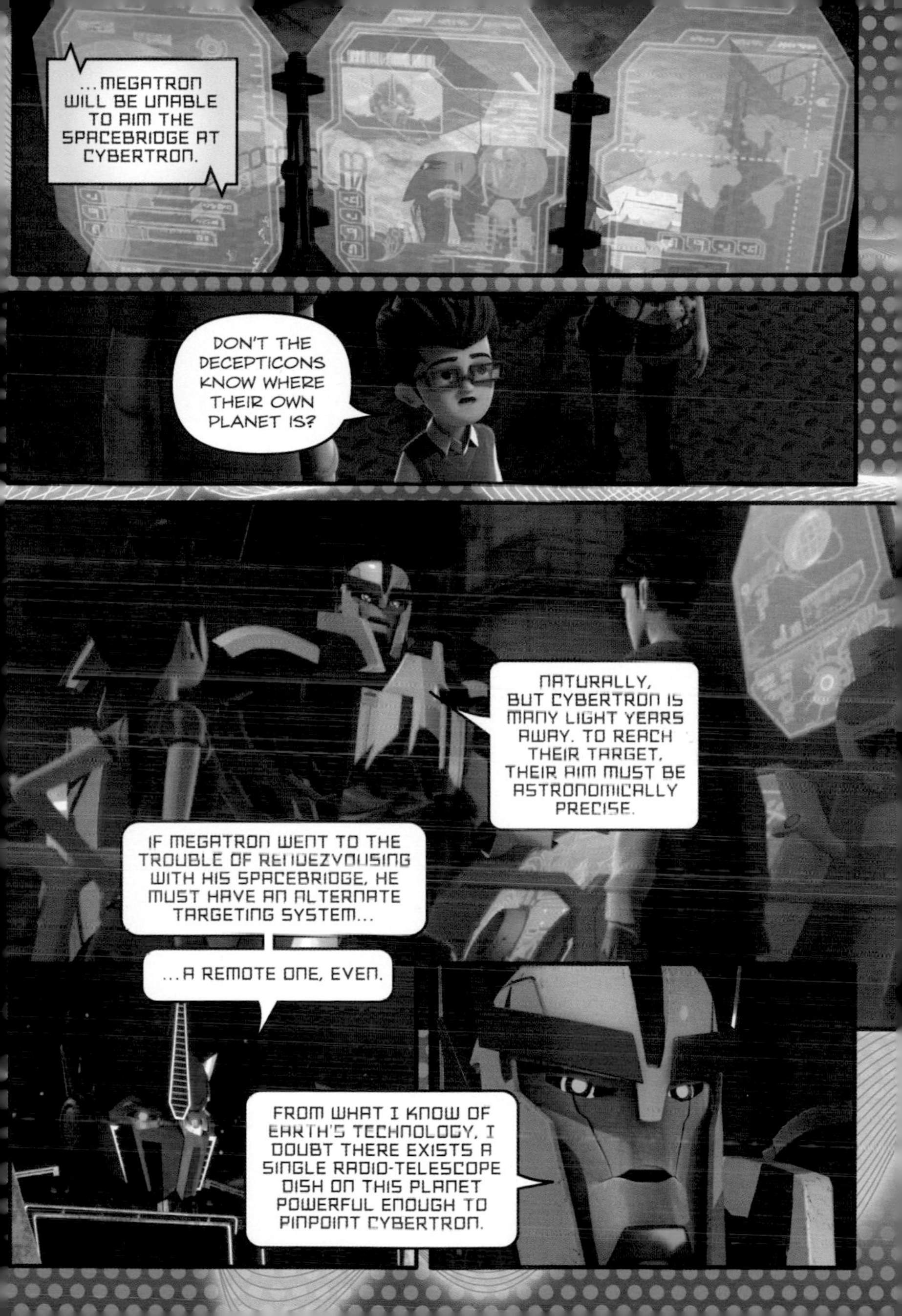

...MEGATRON WILL BE UNABLE TO AIM THE SPACEBRIDGE AT CYBERTRON.
DON'T THE DECEPTICONS KNOW WHERE THEIR OWN PLANET IS?
NATURALLY, BUT CYBERTRON IS MANY LIGHT YEARS AWAY. TO REACH THEIR TARGET, THEIR AIM MUST BE ASTRONOMICALLY PRECISE.
IF MEGATRON WENT TO THE TROUBLE OF RENDEZVOUSING WITH HIS SPACEBRIDGE, HE MUST HAVE AN ALTERNATE TARGETING SYSTEM...
...A REMOTE ONE, EVEN.
FROM WHAT I KNOW OF EARTH'S TECHNOLOGY, I DOUBT THERE EXISTS A SINGLE RADIO-TELESCOPE DISH ON THIS PLANET POWERFUL ENOUGH TO PINPOINT CYBERTRON.

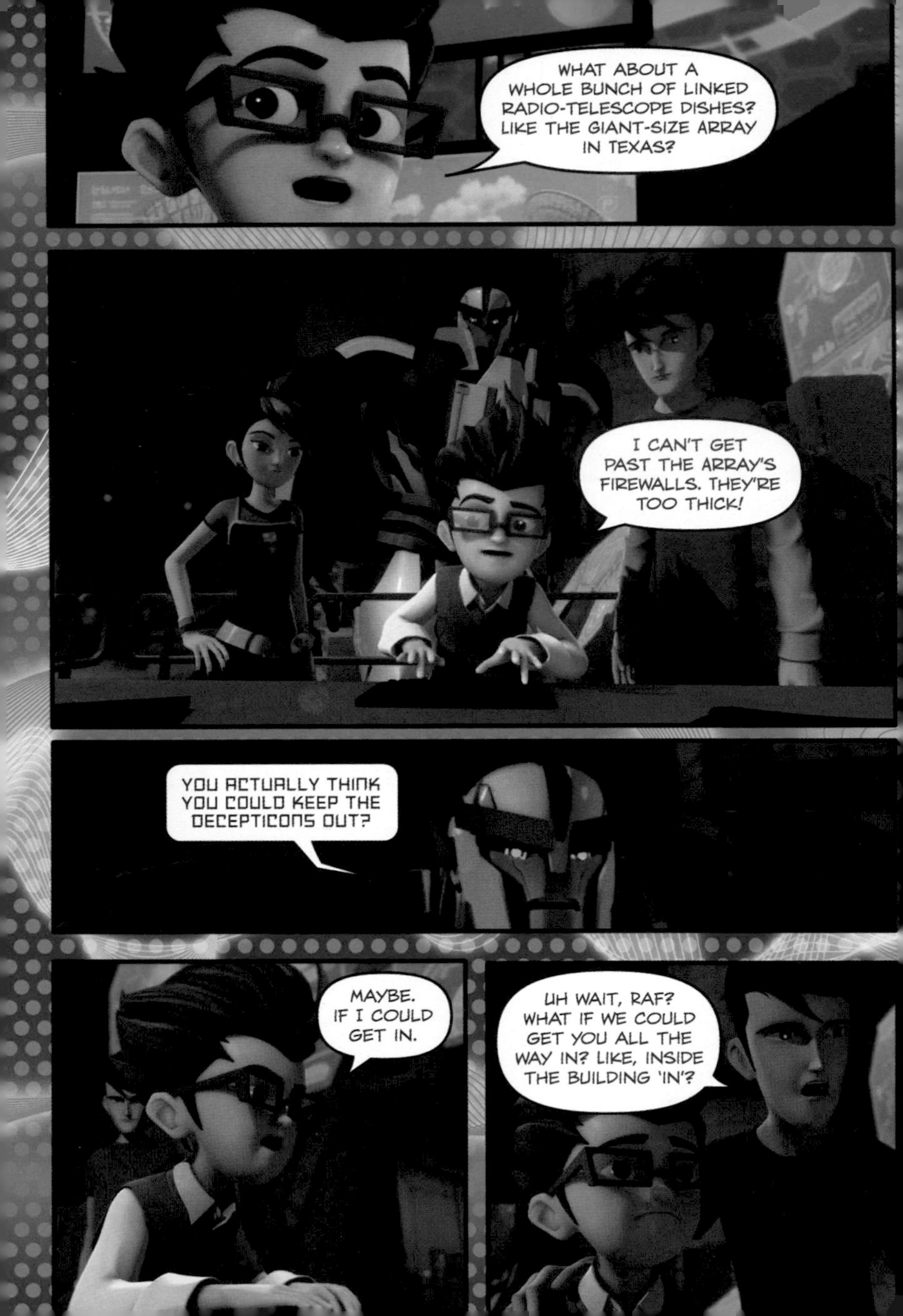
WHAT ABOUT A WHOLE BUNCH OF LINKED RADIO-TELESCOPE DISHES? LIKE THE GIANT-SIZE ARRAY IN TEXAS?
I CAN'T GET PAST THE ARRAY'S FIREWALLS. THEY'RE TOO THICK!
YOU ACTUALLY THINK YOU COULD KEEP THE DECEPTICONS OUT?
MAYBE. IF I COULD GET IN.
UH WAIT, RAF? WHAT IF WE COULD GET YOU ALL THE WAY IN? LIKE, INSIDE THE BUILDING 'IN'?

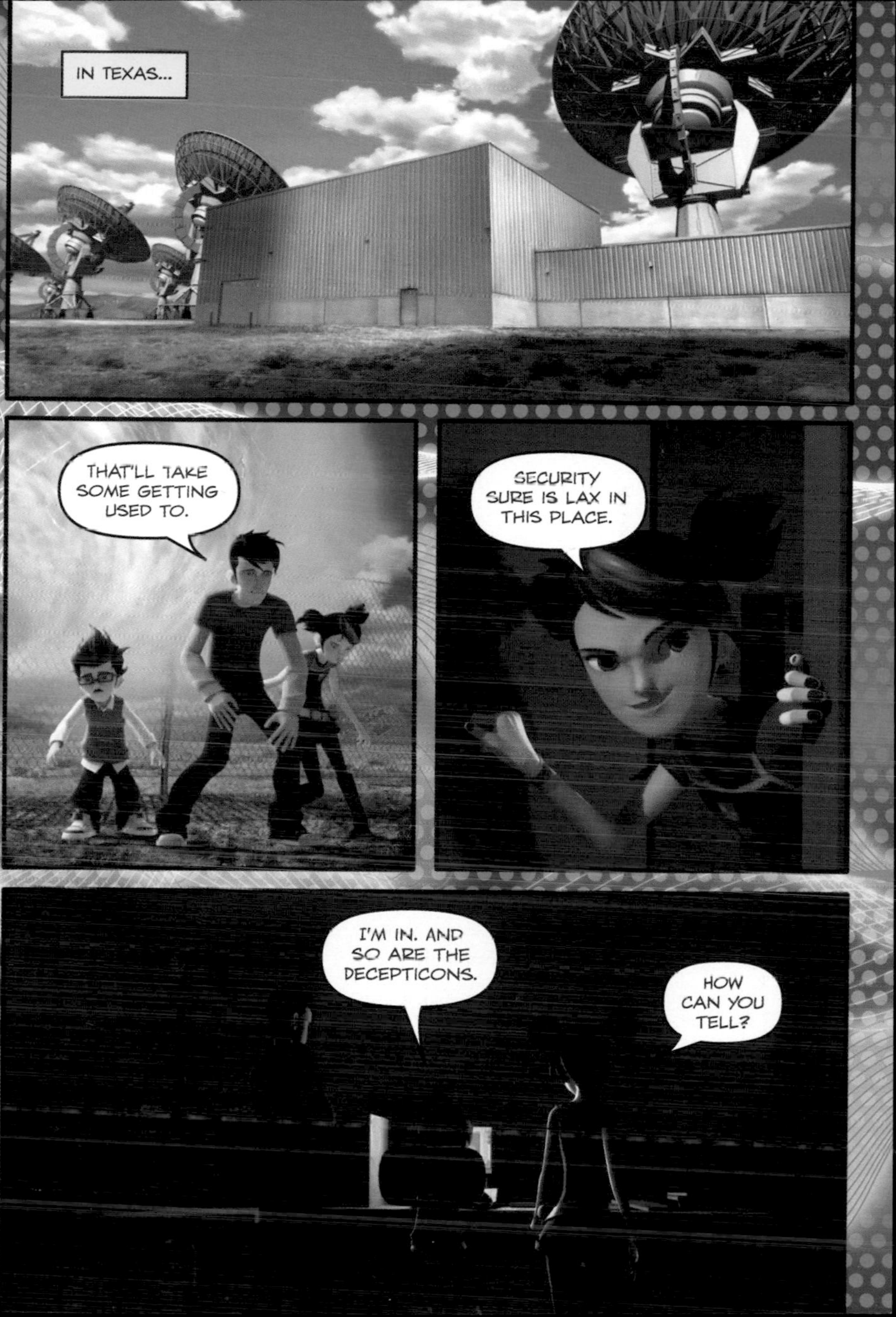
IN TEXAS...
THAT'LL TAKE SOME GETTING USED TO.
SECURITY SURE IS LAX IN THIS PLACE.
I'M IN. AND SO ARE THE DECEPTICONS.
HOW CAN YOU TELL?

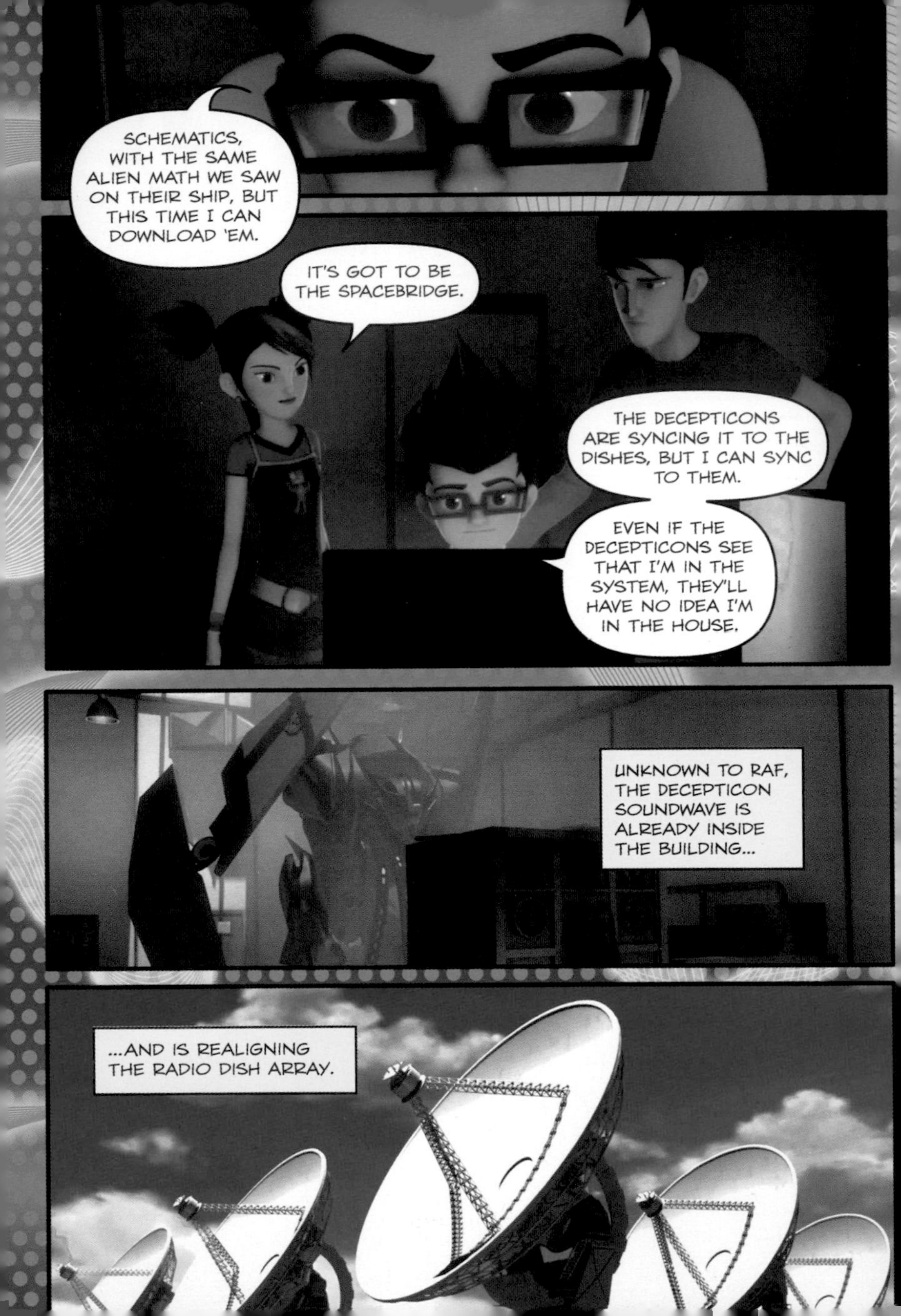
SCHEMATICS, WITH THE SAME ALIEN MATH WE SAW ON THEIR SHIP, BUT THIS TIME I CAN DOWNLOAD 'EM.
IT'S GOT TO BE THE SPACEBRIDGE.
THE DECEPTICONS ARE SYNCING IT TO THE DISHES, BUT I CAN SYNC TO THEM.
EVEN IF THE DECEPTICONS SEE THAT I'M IN THE SYSTEM, THEY'LL HAVE NO IDEA I'M IN THE HOUSE.
UNKNOWN TO RAF, THE DECEPTICON SOUNDWAVE IS ALREADY INSIDE THE BUILDING...
...AND IS REALIGNING THE RADIO DISH ARRAY.

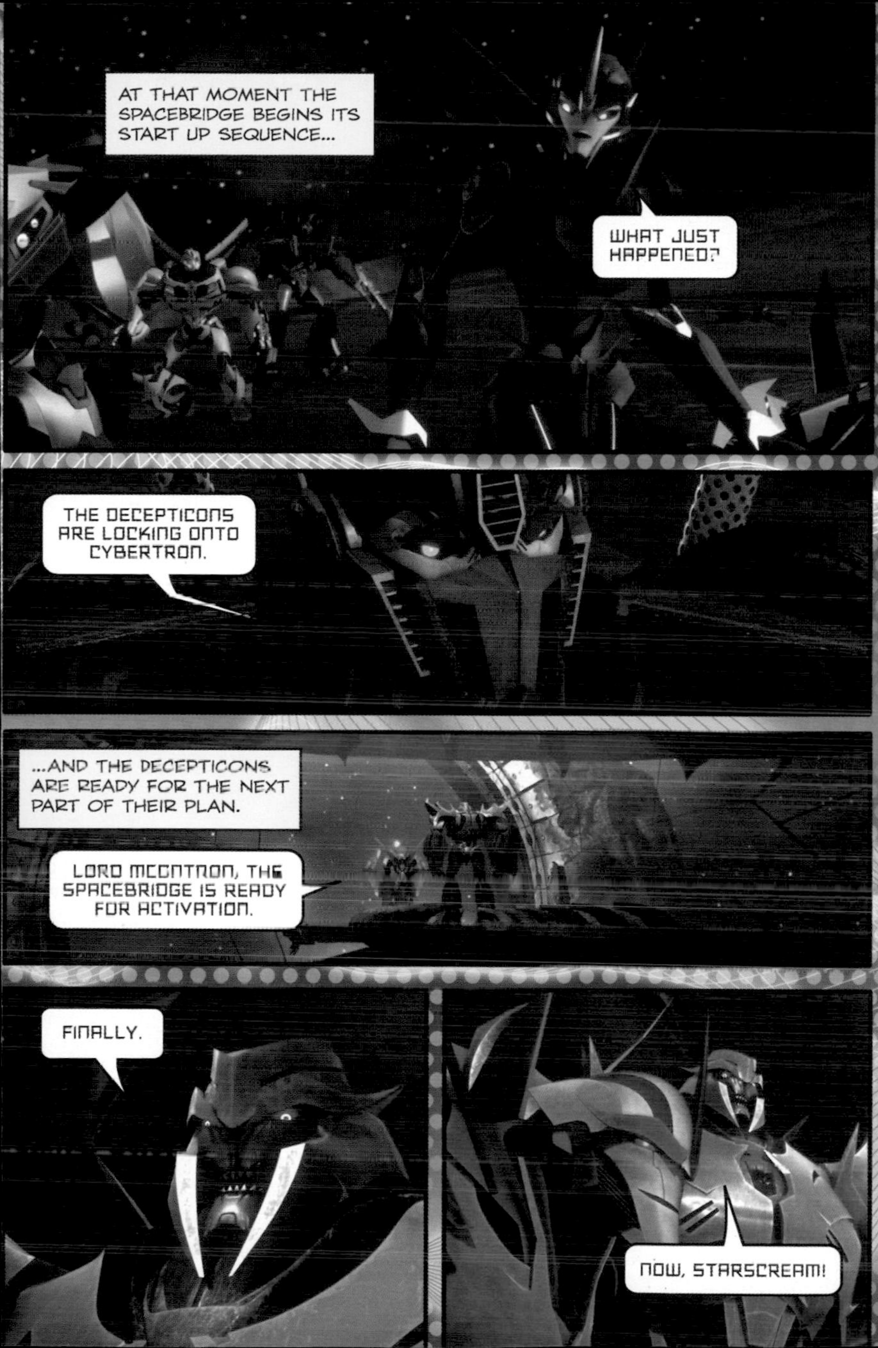

AT THAT MOMENT THE SPACEBRIDGE BEGINS ITS START UP SEQUENCE...
WHAT JUST HAPPENED?
THE DECEPTICONS ARE LOCKING ONTO CYBERTRON.
...AND THE DECEPTICONS ARE READY FOR THE NEXT PART OF THEIR PLAN.
LORD MEGATRON, THE SPACEBRIDGE IS READY FOR ACTIVATION.
FINALLY.
NOW, STARSCREAM!

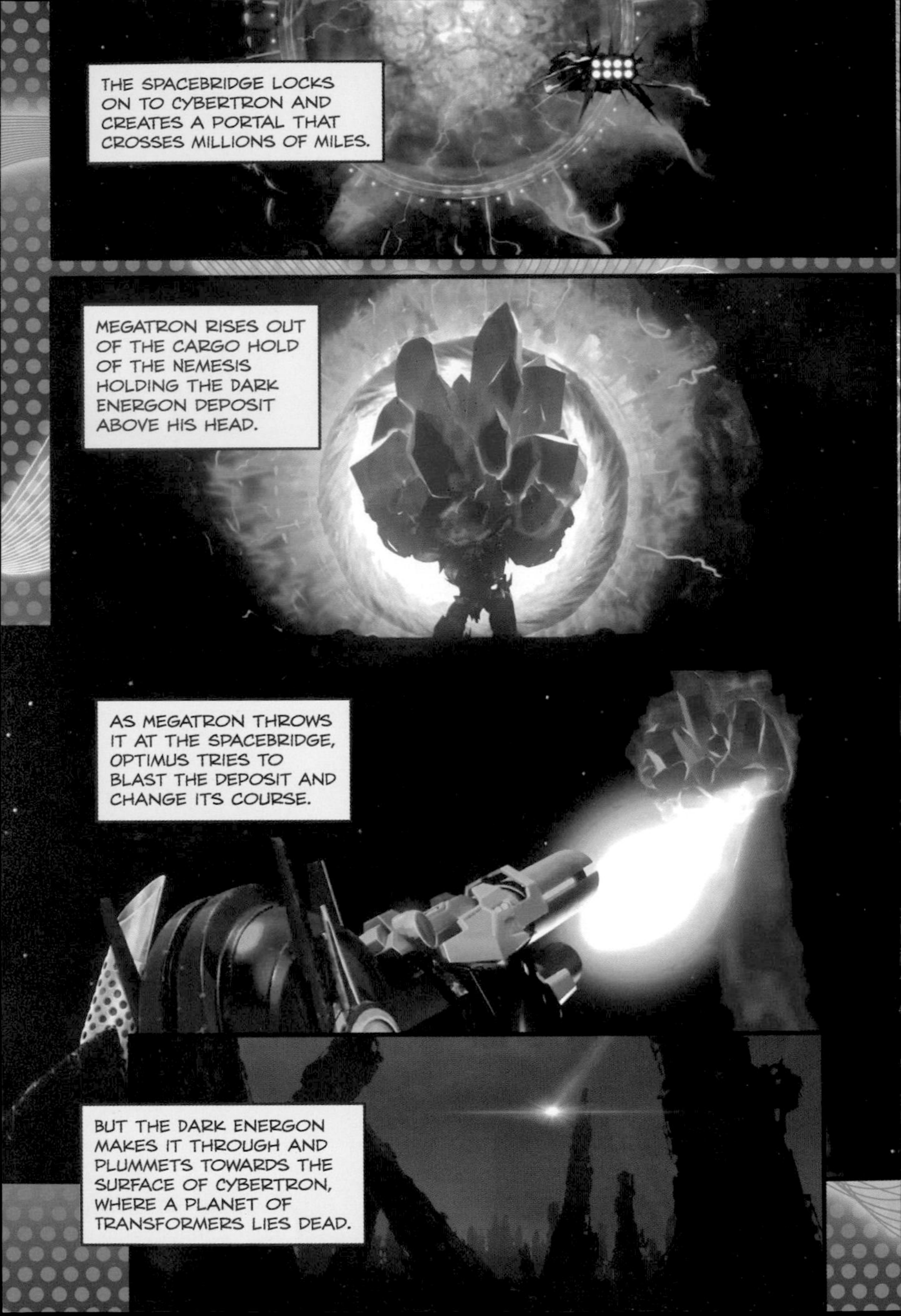
THE SPACEBRIDGE LOCKS ON TO CYBERTRON AND CREATES A PORTAL THAT CROSSES MILLIONS OF MILES.
MEGATRON RISES OUT OF THE CARGO HOLD OF THE NEMESIS HOLDING THE DARK ENERGON DEPOSIT ABOVE HIS HEAD.
AS MEGATRON THROWS IT AT THE SPACEBRIDGE, OPTIMUS TRIES TO BLAST THE DEPOSIT AND CHANGE ITS COURSE.
BUT THE DARK ENERGON MAKES IT THROUGH AND PLUMMETS TOWARDS THE SURFACE OF CYBERTRON, WHERE A PLANET OF TRANSFORMERS LIES DEAD.

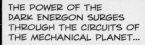
THE POWER OF THE
DARK ENERGON SURGES
THROUGH THE CIRCUITS OF
THE MECHANICAL PLANET...

...AND THE
DEAD COME
BACK TO LIFE.

HRISE, MY LEGION!

ARISE!

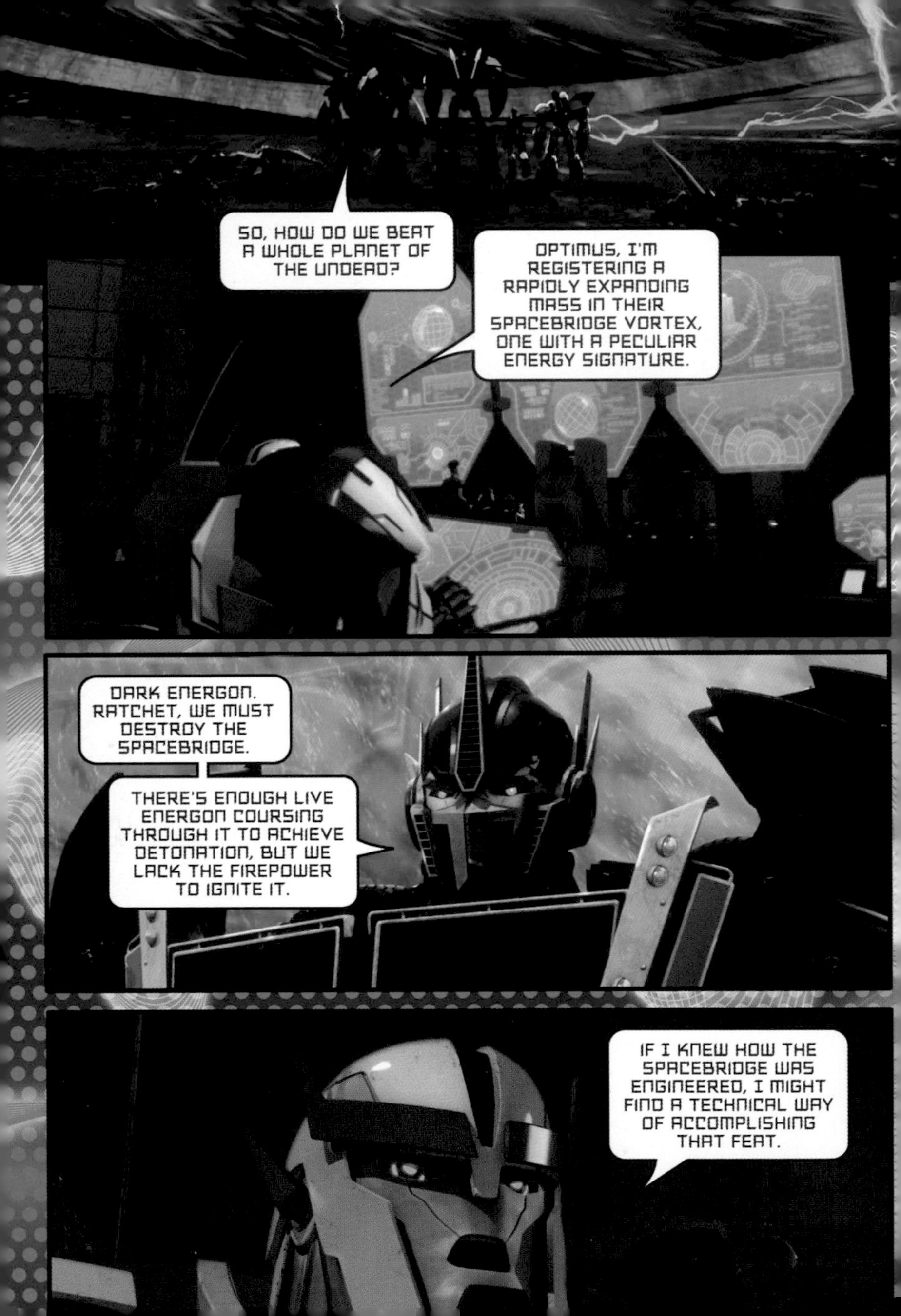
SO, HOW DO WE BEAT A WHOLE PLANET OF THE UNDEAD?
OPTIMUS, I'M REGISTERING A RAPIDLY EXPANDING MASS IN THEIR SPACEBRIDGE VORTEX, ONE WITH A PECULIAR ENERGY SIGNATURE.
DARK ENERGON. RATCHET, WE MUST DESTROY THE SPACEBRIDGE.
THERE'S ENOUGH LIVE ENERGON COURSING THROUGH IT TO ACHIEVE DETONATION, BUT WE LACK THE FIREPOWER TO IGNITE IT.
IF I KNEW HOW THE SPACEBRIDGE WAS ENGINEERED, I MIGHT FIND A TECHNICAL WAY OF ACCOMPLISHING THAT FEAT.

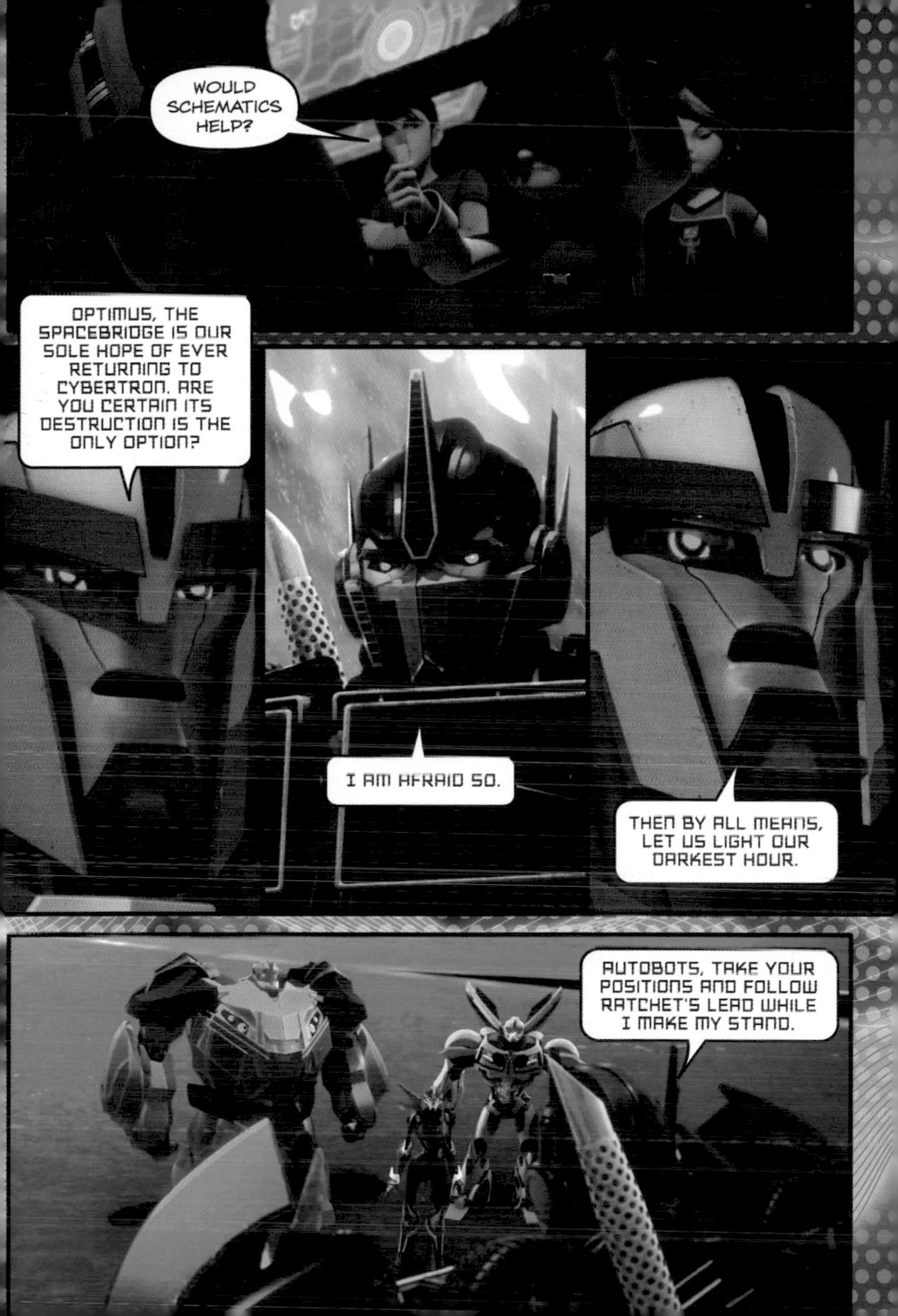
WOULD SCHEMATICS HELP?
OPTIMUS, THE SPACEBRIDGE IS OUR SOLE HOPE OF EVER RETURNING TO CYBERTRON. ARE YOU CERTAIN ITS DESTRUCTION IS THE ONLY OPTION?
I AM AFRAID SO.
THEN BY ALL MEANS, LET US LIGHT OUR DARKEST HOUR.
AUTOBOTS, TAKE YOUR POSITIONS AND FOLLOW RATCHET'S LEAD WHILE I MAKE MY STAND.

ENTICED BY HIS NEAR SUCCESS, MEGATRON FLIES OVER TO THE SPACEBRIDGE.

YOUR FELLOW AUTOBOTS ARE WISE, OPTIMUS. THEY KNOW WHEN TO RETREAT.

I HOLD NO ILLUSIONS ABOUT ENGAGING YOUR ARMY, MEGATRON. BUT I MIGHT DERAIL ITS OBJECTIVE BY REMOVING ITS HEAD!

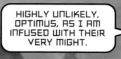

HIGHLY UNLIKELY, OPTIMUS, AS I AM INFUSED WITH THEIR VERY MIGHT.

ONE SHALL STAND, ONE SHALL FALL!

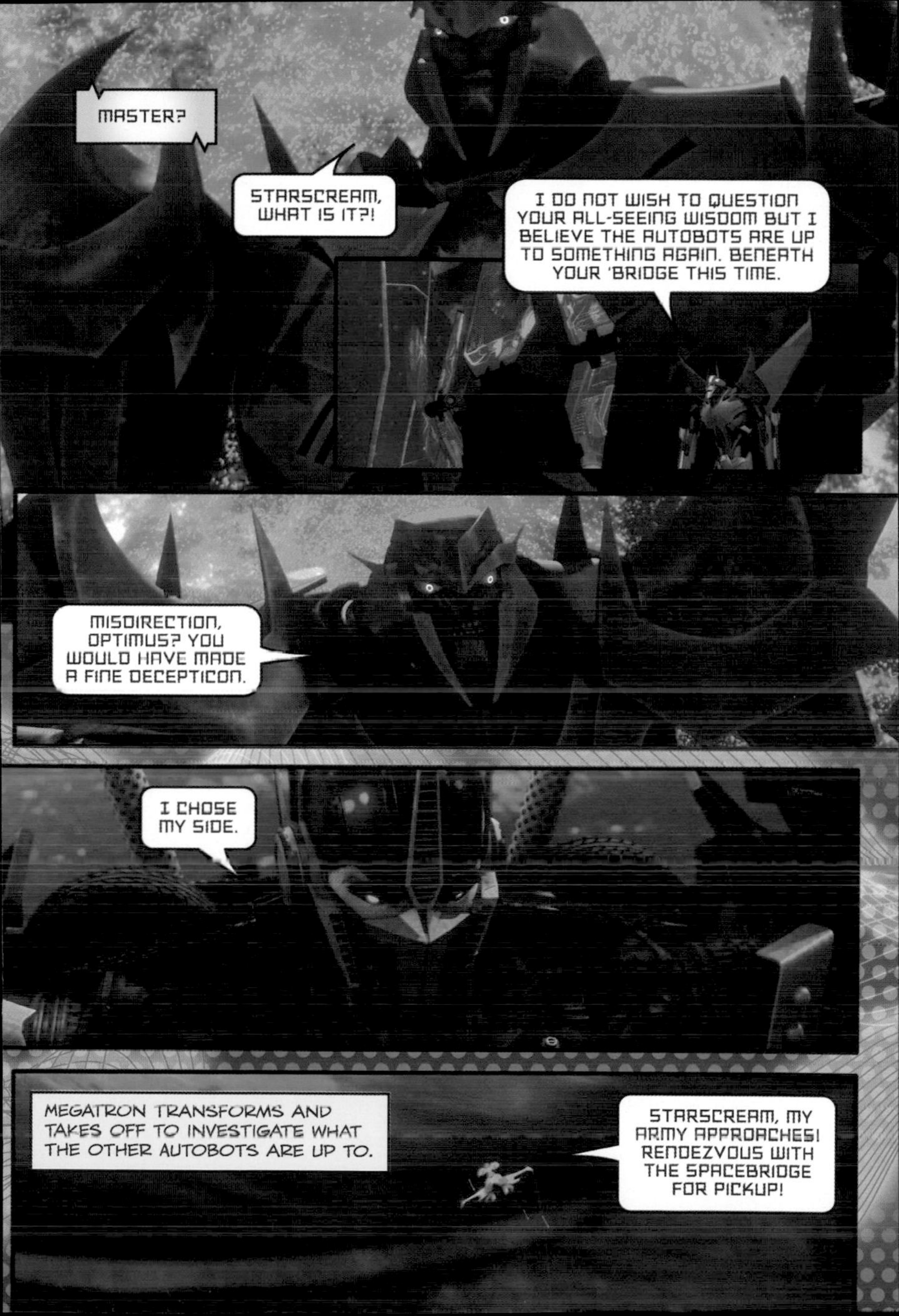
MASTER?
STARSCREAM, WHAT IS IT?!
I DO NOT WISH TO QUESTION YOUR ALL-SEEING WISDOM BUT I BELIEVE THE AUTOBOTS ARE UP TO SOMETHING AGAIN. BENEATH YOUR 'BRIDGE THIS TIME.
MISDIRECTION, OPTIMUS? YOU WOULD HAVE MADE A FINE DECEPTICON.
I CHOSE MY SIDE.
MEGATRON TRANSFORMS AND TAKES OFF TO INVESTIGATE WHAT THE OTHER AUTOBOTS ARE UP TO.
STARSCREAM, MY ARMY APPROACHES! RENDEZVOUS WITH THE SPACEBRIDGE FOR PICKUP!

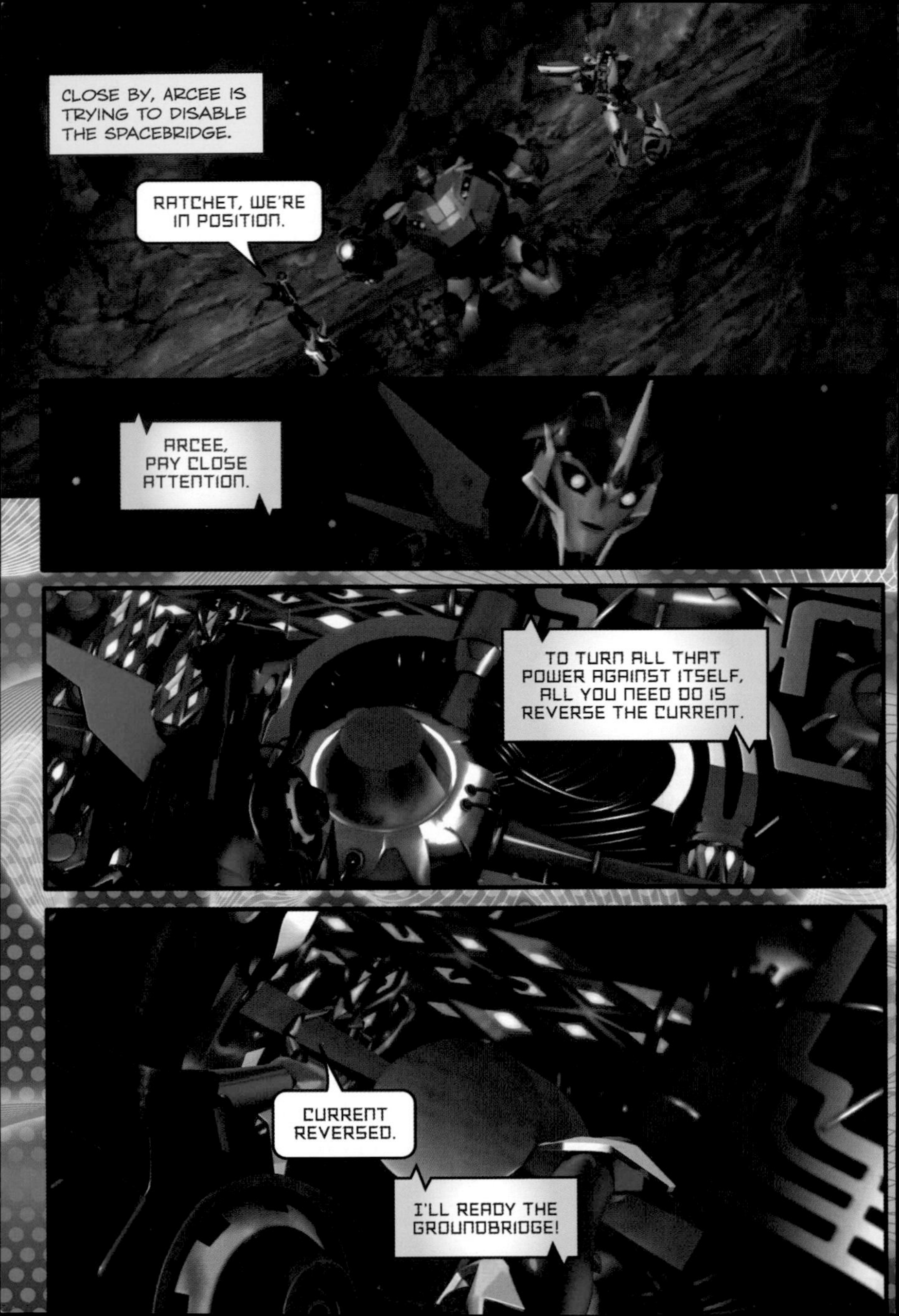
CLOSE BY, ARCEE IS TRYING TO DISABLE THE SPACEBRIDGE.
RATCHET, WE'RE IN POSITION.
ARCEE, PAY CLOSE ATTENTION.
TO TURN ALL THAT POWER AGAINST ITSELF, ALL YOU NEED DO IS REVERSE THE CURRENT.
CURRENT REVERSED.
I'LL READY THE GROUNDBRIDGE!

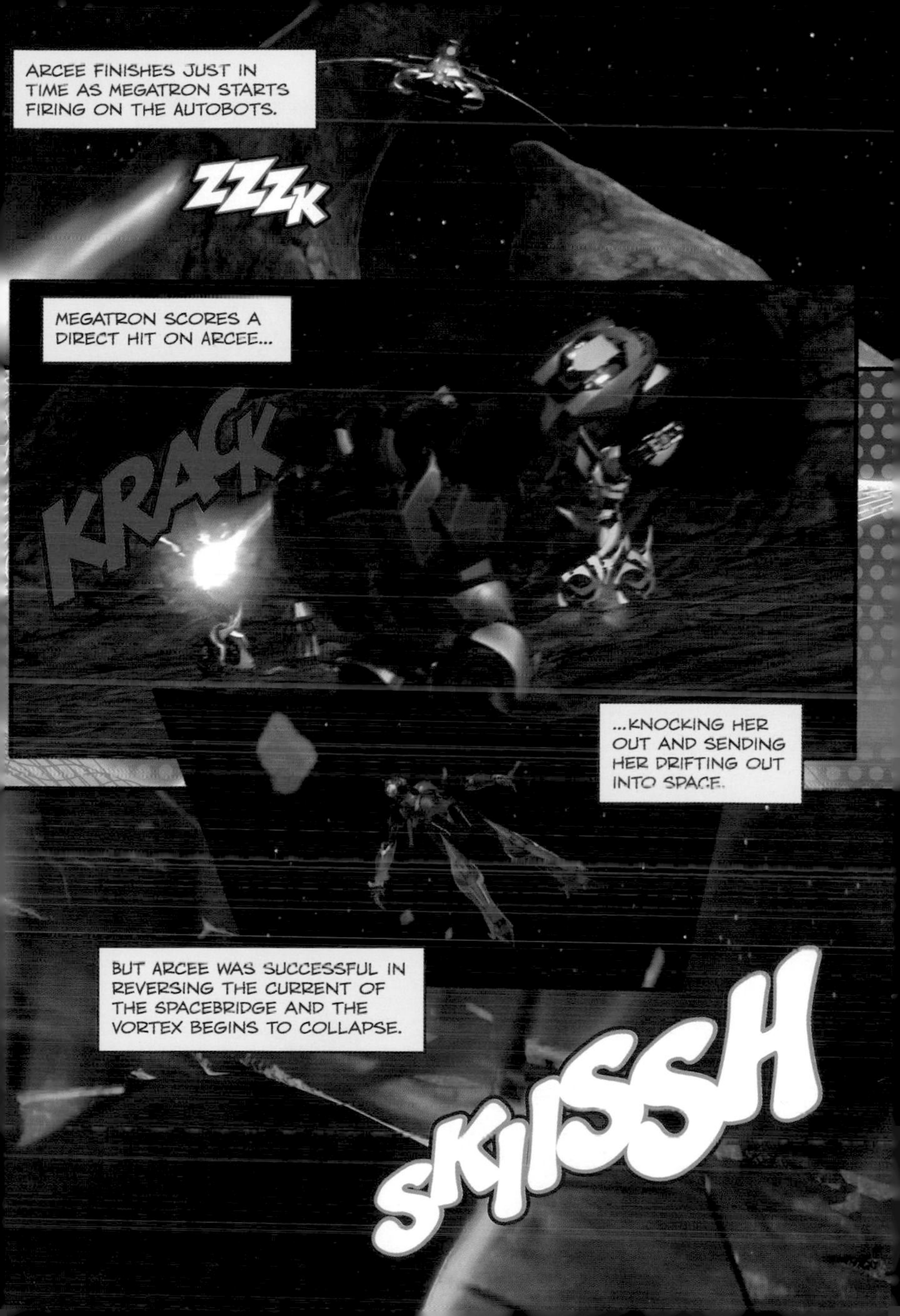
ARCEE FINISHES JUST IN TIME AS MEGATRON STARTS FIRING ON THE AUTOBOTS.
ZZZK
MEGATRON SCORES A DIRECT HIT ON ARCEE...
KRACK
...KNOCKING HER OUT AND SENDING HER DRIFTING OUT INTO SPACE.
BUT ARCEE WAS SUCCESSFUL IN REVERSING THE CURRENT OF THE SPACEBRIDGE AND THE VORTEX BEGINS TO COLLAPSE.
SKISSSH

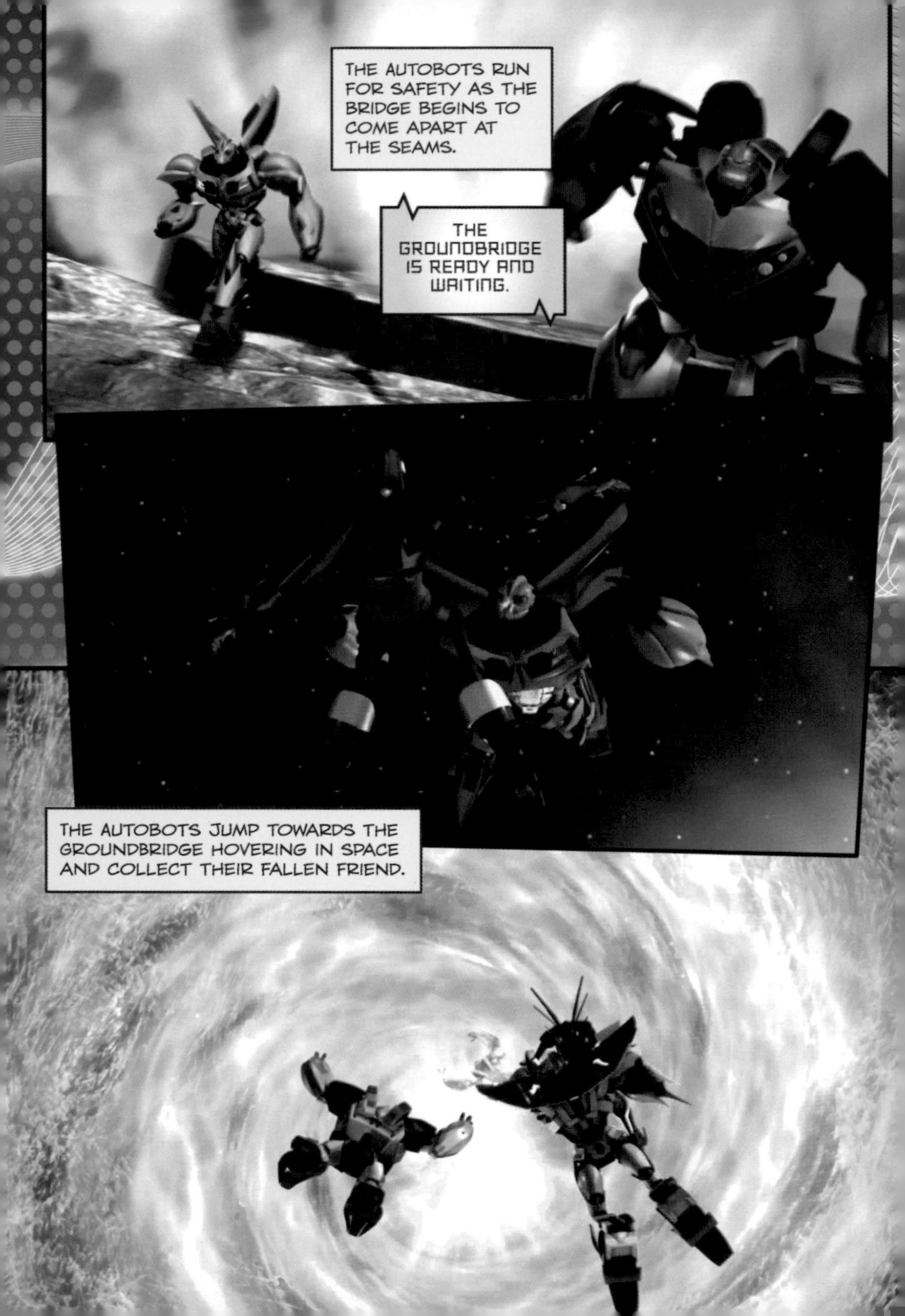
THE AUTOBOTS RUN FOR SAFETY AS THE BRIDGE BEGINS TO COME APART AT THE SEAMS.
THE GROUNDBRIDGE IS READY AND WAITING.
THE AUTOBOTS JUMP TOWARDS THE GROUNDBRIDGE HOVERING IN SPACE AND COLLECT THEIR FALLEN FRIEND.

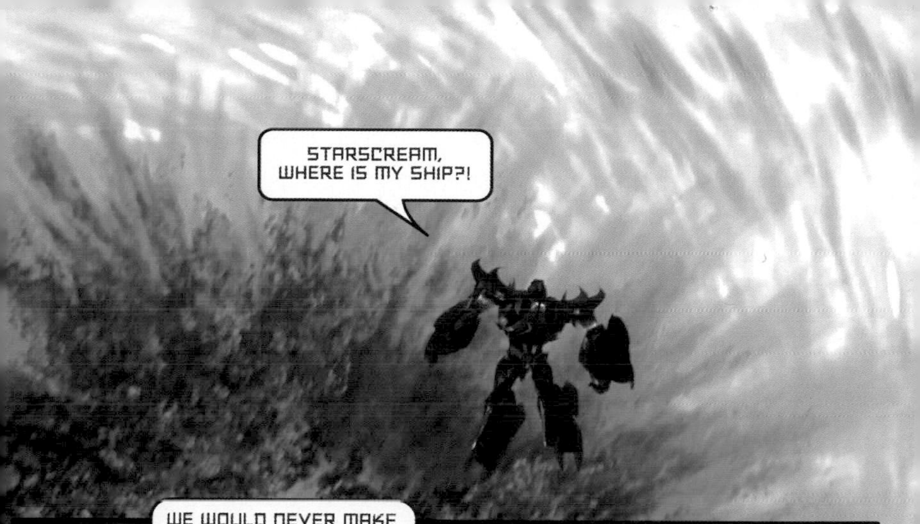
STARSCREAM, WHERE IS MY SHIP?!

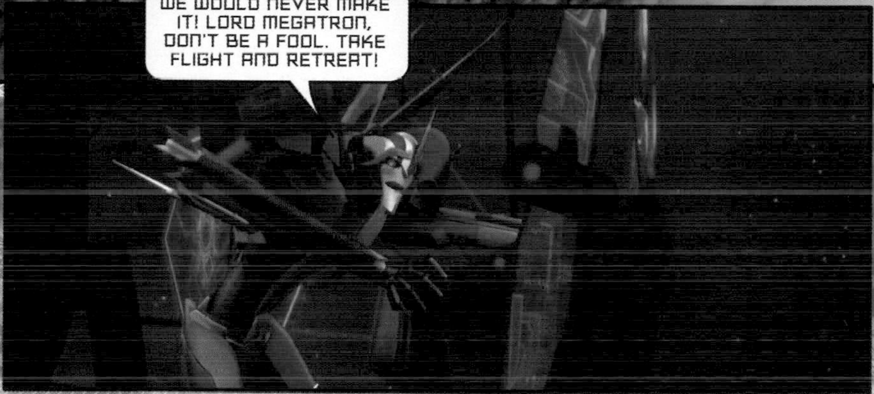
WE WOULD NEVER MAKE IT! LORD MEGATRON, DON'T BE A FOOL. TAKE FLIGHT AND RETREAT!

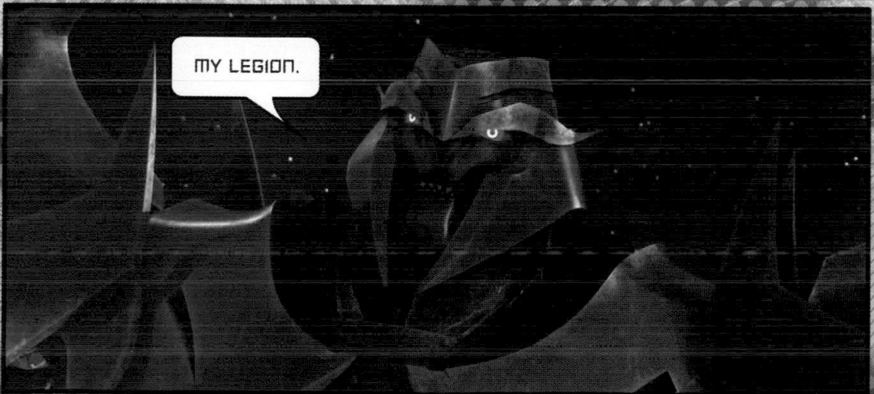
MY LEGION.

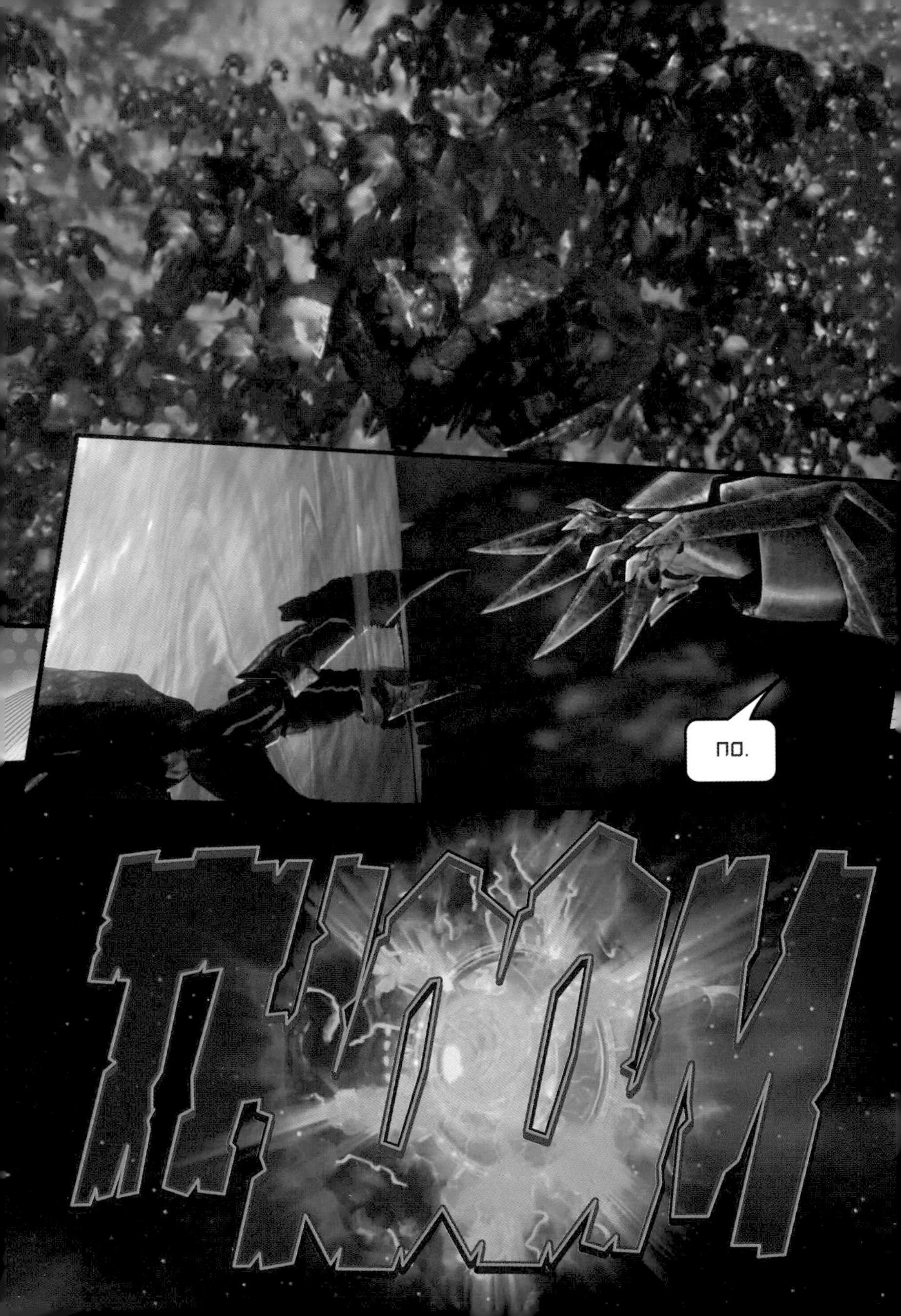
NO.
THOOM

DIRECTLY AFTER THE DESTRUCTION OF THE SPACEBRIDGE, STARSCREAM ADDRESSES THE REMAINING DECEPTICONS.

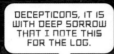

DECEPTICONS, IT IS WITH DEEP SORROW THAT I NOTE THIS FOR THE LOG.

MEGATRON'S SPARK HAS BEEN EXTINGUISHED.

ALL HAIL STARSCREAM.

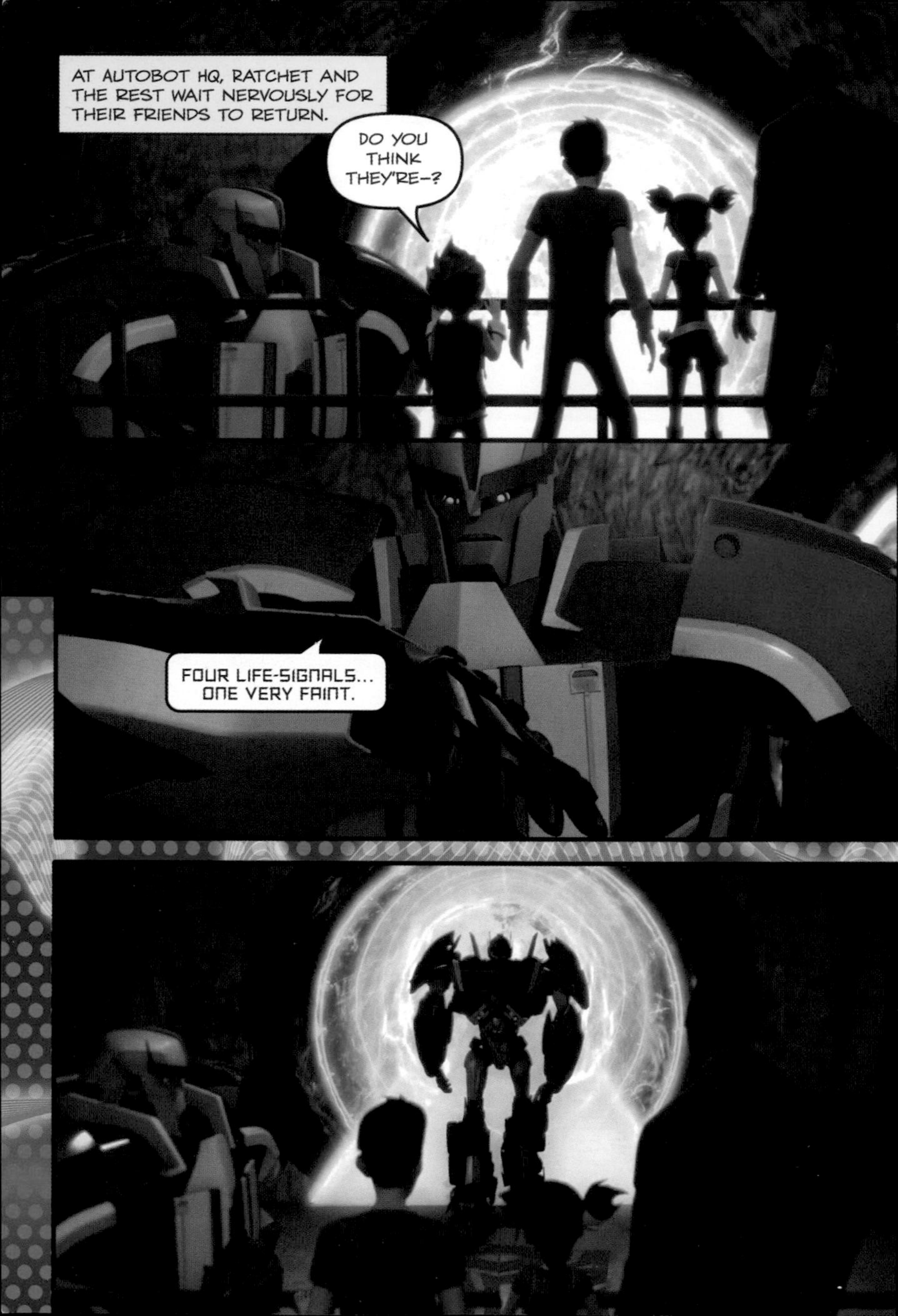
AT AUTOBOT HQ, RATCHET AND THE REST WAIT NERVOUSLY FOR THEIR FRIENDS TO RETURN.
DO YOU THINK THEY'RE–?
FOUR LIFE-SIGNALS... ONE VERY FAINT.

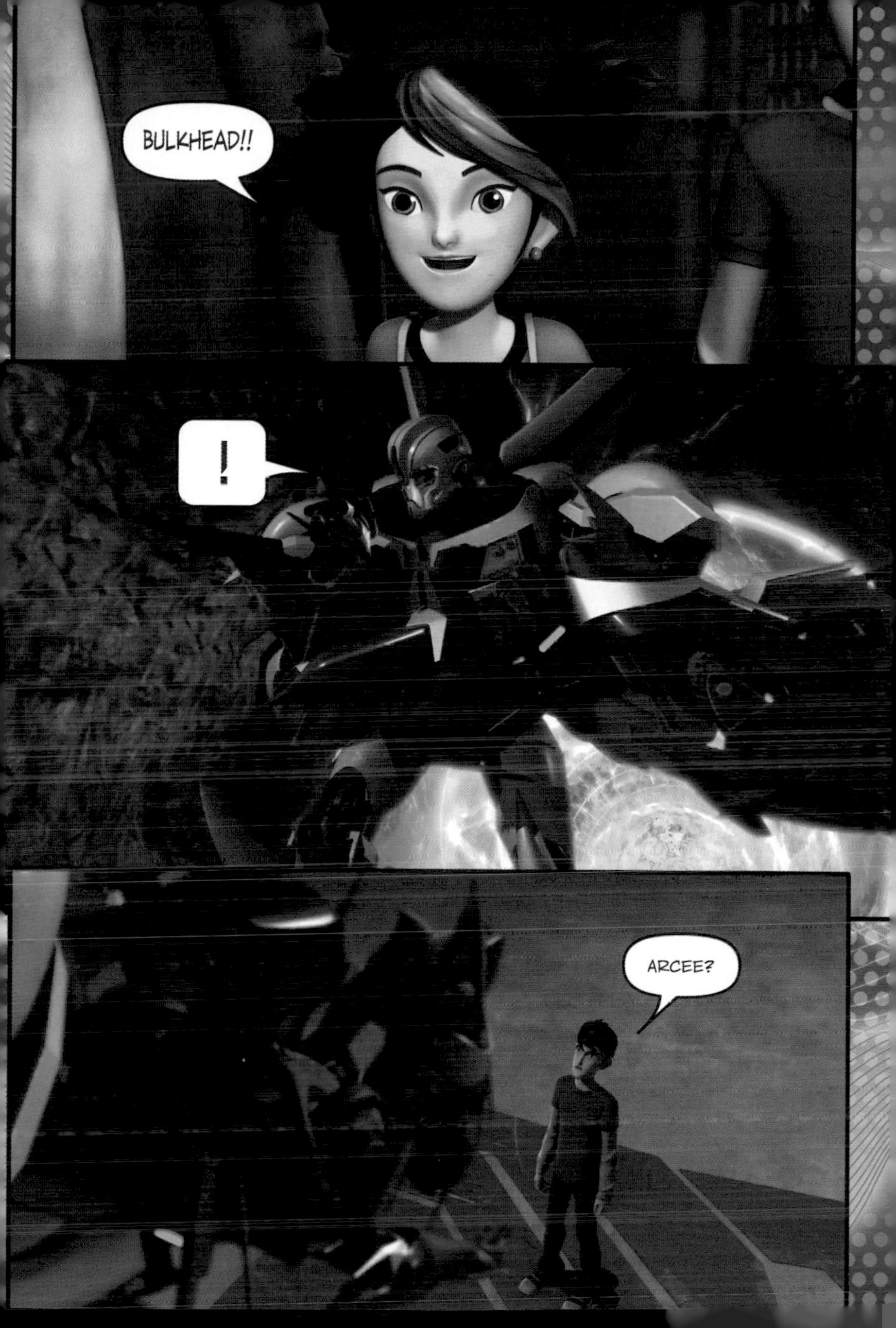
BULKHEAD!!
!
ARCEE?

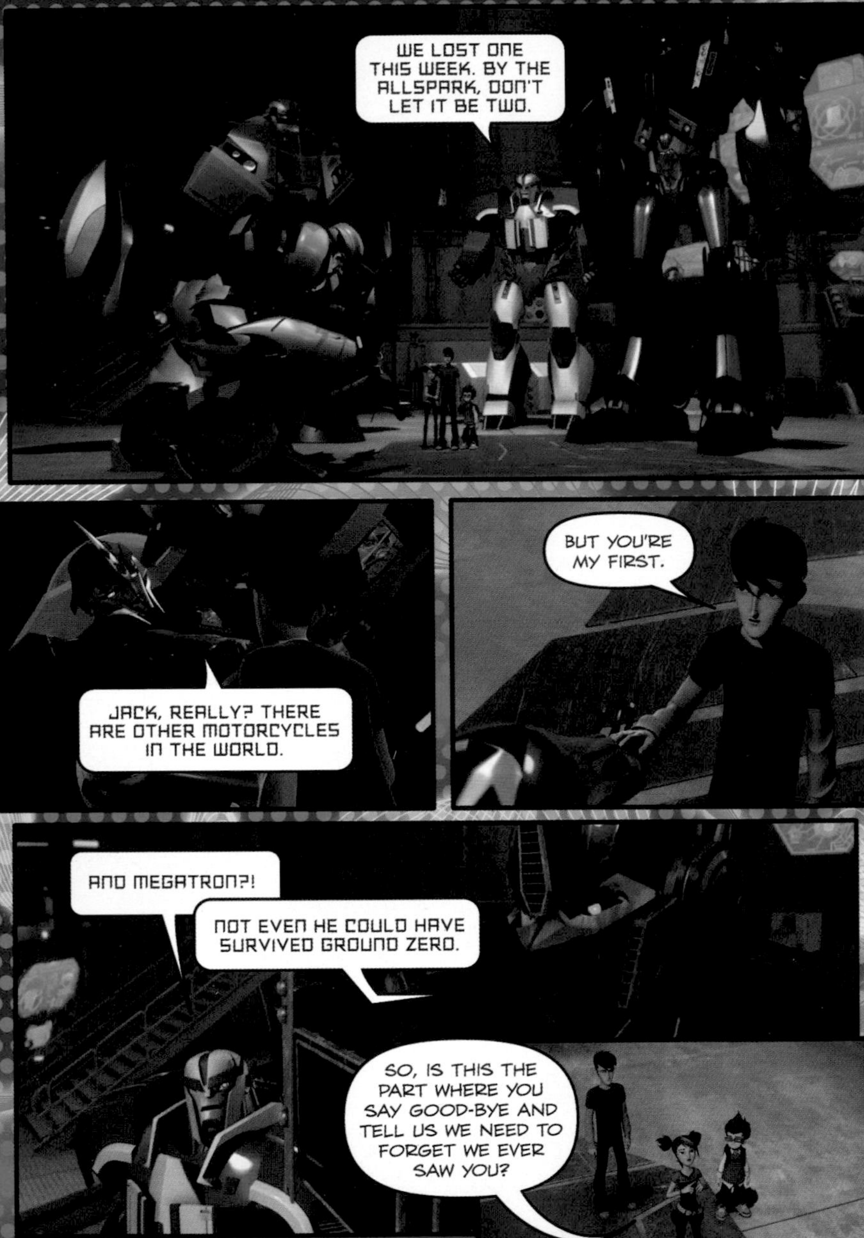
WE LOST ONE THIS WEEK. BY THE ALLSPARK, DON'T LET IT BE TWO.
JACK, REALLY? THERE ARE OTHER MOTORCYCLES IN THE WORLD.
BUT YOU'RE MY FIRST.
AND MEGATRON?!
NOT EVEN HE COULD HAVE SURVIVED GROUND ZERO.
SO, IS THIS THE PART WHERE YOU SAY GOOD-BYE AND TELL US WE NEED TO FORGET WE EVER SAW YOU?

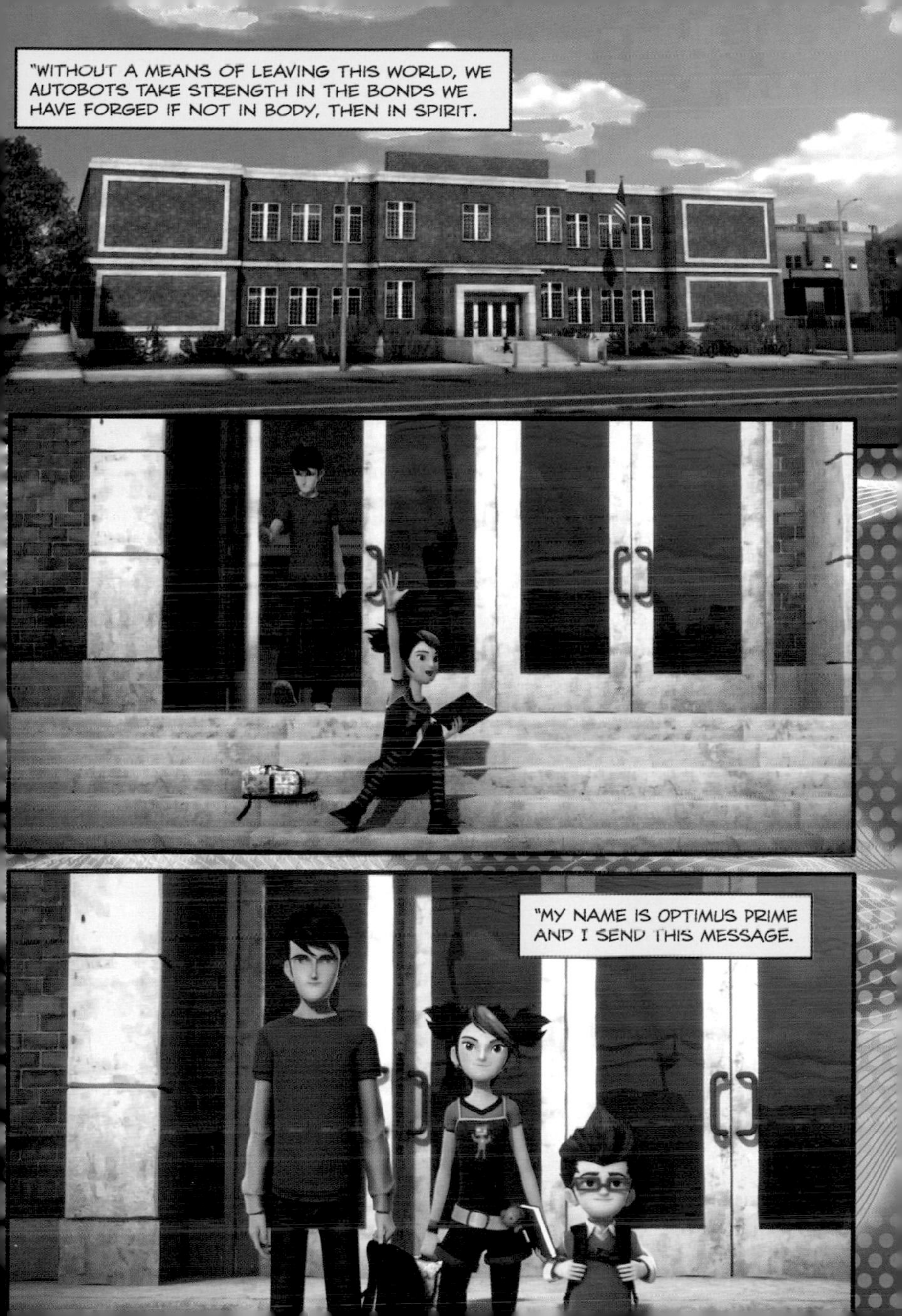
"WITHOUT A MEANS OF LEAVING THIS WORLD, WE AUTOBOTS TAKE STRENGTH IN THE BONDS WE HAVE FORGED IF NOT IN BODY, THEN IN SPIRIT.
"MY NAME IS OPTIMUS PRIME AND I SEND THIS MESSAGE.

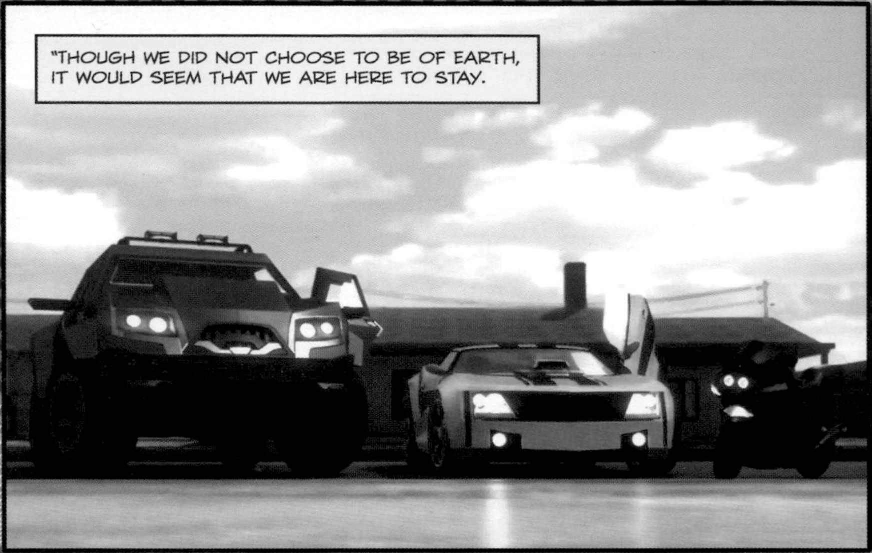
"THOUGH WE DID NOT CHOOSE TO BE OF EARTH, IT WOULD SEEM THAT WE ARE HERE TO STAY.

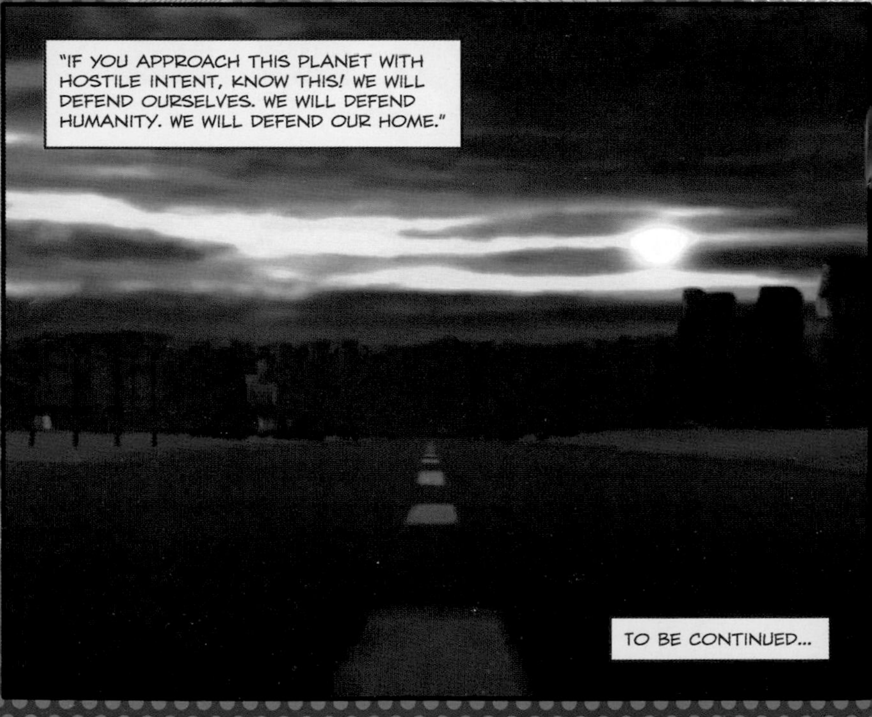
"IF YOU APPROACH THIS PLANET WITH HOSTILE INTENT, KNOW THIS! WE WILL DEFEND OURSELVES. WE WILL DEFEND HUMANITY. WE WILL DEFEND OUR HOME."
TO BE CONTINUED...